I0803141

IMAGES
of America

LINCOLNSHIRE

Village of Lincolnshire

Mayor: FRED BALZER

Trustees: ALEX STEINFORTH • ROBERT W. LINDGREN • MILES L. ABEL • CLYDE W. NELSON • JEROME WESTERFIELD • REECE WENGENROTH

Clerk-Collector: JEAN LINDGREN • Treasurer: WILLIAM RIEDLE • Attorney: NEWELL N. JENKINS

The original letterhead from the official correspondence of the newly formed village of Lincolnshire conveys a sense of classic elegance and stately presence in the script. The names of some of the "founding fathers" of the village are also listed. (Courtesy of the Village of Lincolnshire.)

ON THE COVER: Children enjoyed a much slower pace of life during the mid-1920s, when this photograph was taken. The Gilman family pauses to enjoy a moment's respite near a classic snack spot that offered such indulgences as Cracker Jack and soda pop. This stand was located on the southwest corner of Milwaukee Avenue and the original Route 22, now renamed Olde Half Day Road. (Courtesy of Vernon Township.)

IMAGES
of America

LINCOLNSHIRE

Lisa Marie Smith

ARCADIA
PUBLISHING

ISBN 978-0-7385-9196-4

Published by Arcadia Publishing
Charleston, South Carolina

Printed in the United States of America

Library of Congress Control Number: 2012931296

For all general information, please contact Arcadia Publishing:
Telephone 843-853-2070
Fax 843-853-0044
E-mail sales@arcadiapublishing.com
For customer service and orders:
Toll-Free 1-888-313-2665

Visit us on the Internet at www.arcadiapublishing.com

This book is dedicated to my loving husband, Paul, my brother Bob, and my late mom, Delphine. You are missed more than you know.

Contents

Acknowledgments

I would like to acknowledge some of the very important people without whom this book would never have come to pass. First, I would like to thank my coworkers at the Vernon Area Public Library, who have been invaluable sources of assistance and support. I truly appreciate the cooperation I have received from both the Village of Lincolnshire and Vernon Township, especially from Leslie Ulibarri, Mayor Brett Blomberg, supervisor William Peterson, and clerk Barbara Barnabee. Thanks also to Bob Griep and the good folks from the Washburn Congregational Church, who have not only embraced the project, but have made me feel like a part of their congregation. I would like to thank the ever-gracious Mary Sue Didier for taking me into her home and sharing her life, her family, and a bowl of soup with me. The entire Keough family has made me feel like one of their own. A huge thank-you goes out to the talents of Dave and Mary Iserman. I would like to also thank the following people who all contributed, whether it was in the form of moral support, a story, or an image: chief Fred Kruger and Lt. Ray Amidei from the Lincolnshire-Riverwoods Fire Department; my friends at District 103; the library at Stevenson High School; Alice Moody; Patty Monaghen; Barbara Gilman; Loretta Foss; Vicki Dellinger; Megan Lisafeld; and Chris Acampora. Thanks go out to my editor, Jeff Reutsche, for your understanding, support, and faith in me from the beginning. My undying love and gratitude go out to my husband, Paul, who has not only supported me, but also made sure that I eat, sleep, and breathe during this project. Without you, I would probably be emaciated and still asleep on top of my laptop. Finally, thanks to my dear friend and chief computer go-to person, Mary Wachenheim, without whom I'd still be staring at my scanner.

The photographs in this volume appear courtesy of the Vernon Area Public Library, unless otherwise noted.

INTRODUCTION

It is easy to be caught up in the beauty of nature on a stroll down the tree-lined streets of Lincolnshire. The peacefulness of small town America is evident all around; however, there is much more here than meets the eye. The quiet subdivisions and well-manicured parks only tell a small part of the story. Peeling back the layers of unseen history in this tranquil suburban hamlet will reveal that this historic place is the epicenter of bustling metropolitan northern Illinois, the place where it all began.

Glaciers formed the area tens of thousands of years ago, and the resulting landscape is full of rivers and lakes that were carved from limestone bedrock. The largest lake in the area, Lake Michigan, lies to the east, and the largest river, the Des Plaines River, flows from north to south nearby. This verdant area from the lakeshore to the nearby river is full of sugar maples, oak, and beech, which acted like a natural fire block and protected against the frequent prairie fires that swept eastward across the miles of flat terrain to the west.

In the later half of the 18th century, the Potawatomi were the primary group of Native Americans to call this area of beauty and plentiful game their own. French trader Louis Joliet and missionary Jacques Marquette are notable for having travelled northward to Wisconsin using the river as a transportation route, but did not remain in the area. The State of Illinois, founded in 1818, was settled from the bottom up, from south to the north. Fort Dearborn was built, and the City of Chicago was founded in 1832, which quickly grew because of its key location at the base of Lake Michigan.

The United States and representatives from the Chippewa, Ottawa, and Potawatomi Nations signed the Treaty of Chicago in September 1833. Five million acres were thereby purchased by the United States, with the details stipulating that the Native Americans must vacate the land by 1835 and resettle west of the Mississippi River. With the newly acquired land emptied, settlers could move in and stake property claims. It cleared the way for hardy settlers to move into lands that were previously occupied. Even before the treaty was enacted, an adventurous soul came north from Chicago looking for virgin land on which to settle.

As a veteran of the War of 1812, Daniel Wright was a capable and resourceful man. He had traveled to Illinois from Vermont via way of Ohio, where he had brought his family to live after the conflict. Having been raised in Vermont, his independent spirit and self-sufficiency had already taken him west once, and now it brought him for a second and final adventure. He decided on a place near the Des Plaines River about 35 miles north of his nearest neighbors at Fort Dearborn. He made friends with the local Potawatomi and their leader, Chief Aptakisic, who was also known as Halfda, which translates to "sun at the meridian." Aptakisic was said to be able to do a whole days work in just half a day. Their village was immediately northwest of Wright's cabin, running from the current Aptakisic Road to Route 22 along Milwaukee Avenue. Wright and the tribe got along so well that they helped him build his cabin before that first winter arrived. Wright sent for his family to join him, but just days after his wife, Ruth, and children arrived from Ohio, both Ruth and their young son Daniel died.

The tribe started leaving the area after other non-native settlers began to trickle in. Soon, Hiram Kennicott built the first gristmill south of Wright's property on the Des Plaines River. The area of Vernon was growing. In 1836, the first school was in session with Laura B. Sprague as teacher, and Seth Washburn was named first postmaster. It wasn't long before the area's first marriage took place between Wright's daughter Caroline and another newcomer, William Whigham. The ceremony was performed by Hiram Kennicott, justice of the peace.

The area had several important trails and was the sight of a council tree, a place where meetings were held. With a circumference of five feet, the tree was actually three trees intertwined, and was thought to be hundreds of years old. Found at a main intersection of trails, it was said to be a significant spot for the Potawatomi. The tree was purported to be located near Oxford Drive and Route 22 in Lincolnshire, but was inadvertently removed in 1956 during the area's development. Milwaukee Avenue was already in existence as an important path and was quickly widened to become a stagecoach route leading from Chicago to Milwaukee. The town of Half Day was an important stopover, and businesses grew up around the travelers. The town was named Halfda in honor of the former chief of the Potawatomi, who was said to be a gifted orator. Somehow, the name changed into Half Day because of either a mapmaker's or post office mistake. Many people over the years have mistakenly thought it was named because it was a half-day's journey from Chicago, leaving Chief Halfda to be forgotten. The town grew and was much larger than it is today with a town hall, several hotels, a general store, taverns, a school, church, doctor, blacksmith shops, and a pharmacy, among others.

When the railway was built nearby in 1886, transit moved from horse and buggy to iron horse. A new town was formed and built around the rail depot. One of its first residents, John Easton, wanted to name the town Easton after himself, but others did not agree. Someone came up with the name of Prairie View, because it was a "prairie with a view," and the name was agreed upon. People's lives were greatly affected by the advent of rail transportation. Most goods were now received by rail, and it became an important mode of transportation. The town grew up around the tracks and was in the midst of expansion when a fire devastated the area in 1920. Luckily, no lives were lost, but it took years to recover from the tragedy.

As transportation patterns shifted to the automobile from the railway, development did as well. Prairie View stagnated as Half Day was reinvigorated. A developer by the name of Roger Ladd discovered the beauty and accessibility of the area and decided to develop there. He placed his new development of single-family homes on large half-acre lots just minutes from the new Illinois Tollway, and Ladd's Lincolnshire was founded. The residents of Lincolnshire appreciated the natural beauty, and more people moved in as the secret was out. Incorporating into a village was the next natural step, and the Village of Lincolnshire was born. The small-town feel and local camaraderie remains as it was in the old days, and the spirit of the area lives on in the next generation.

One

Early Beginnings and Half Day

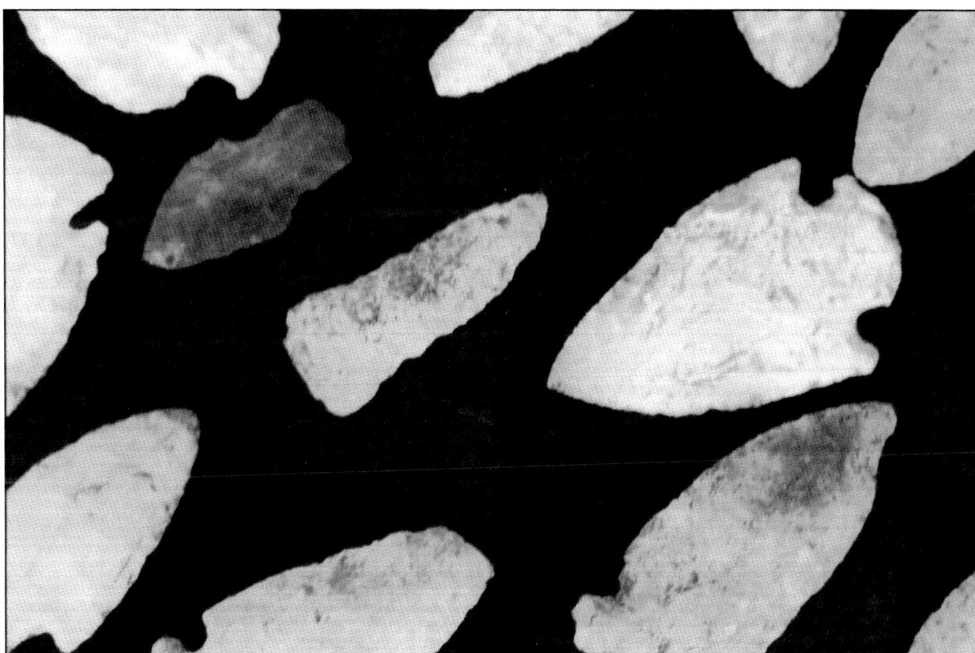

The land where the first settlers farmed yielded arrowheads, such as these pictured, for many years after the Potawatomi had relocated. Children would regularly discover them when they were playing, and many created collections. The artifacts were constant reminders to anyone who found them that they were not the first to come that way. (Courtesy of the author.)

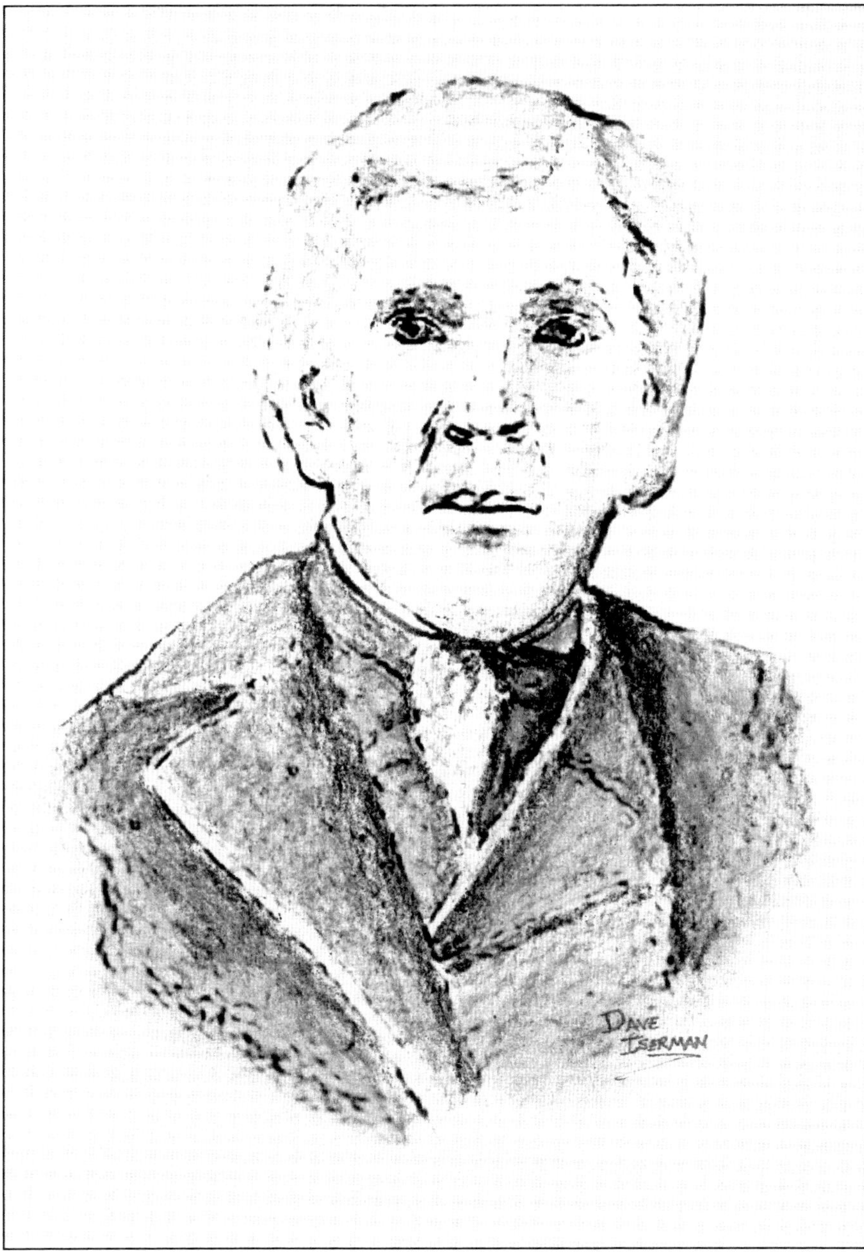

Daniel Wright has the distinction of being the first non-native to settle in the area. He arrived in what was to be known as Half Day in 1833. He befriended the local Potawatomi, who had villages in the area. Wright's cabin, which was located a mile and a half south of Lincolnshire on the banks of the Des Plaines River, the land is now a part of the Ryerson Forest Preserve. Once word was received, Wright's family came west from Licking County, Ohio, to join him. The arduous trip proved too much for his wife, Ruth, and young son Daniel, who became the first recorded fatalities in the county when they died shortly after their arrival. Wright's daughter Caroline, her husband, William Whigham, and their family lived in the Wright homestead for many years. Ultimately, it was Wright's grandson William Whigham Jr. who sold the land to Edward Ryerson. (Courtesy of Dave Iserman.)

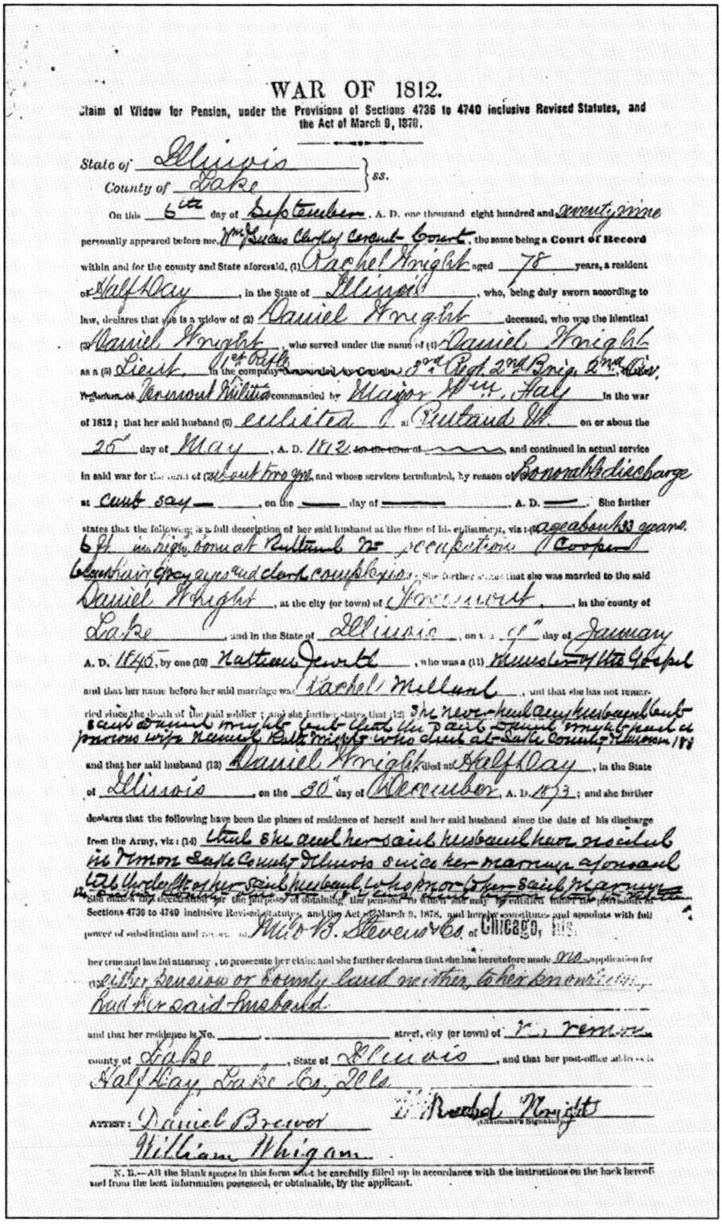

WAR OF 1812.

Claim of Widow for Pension, under the Provisions of Sections 4736 to 4740 inclusive Revised Statutes, and the Act of March 9, 1878.

State of Illinois
County of Lake } ss.

On this 6th day of September, A. D. one thousand eight hundred and seventy nine personally appeared before me, Wm Lucas Clerk of Circuit Court, the same being a Court of Record within and for the county and State aforesaid, (1) Rachel Wright aged 78 years, a resident of Half Day, in the State of Illinois, who, being duly sworn according to law, declares that she is a widow of (2) Daniel Wright deceased, who was the identical (3) Daniel Wright, who served under the name of (4) Daniel Wright as a (5) Lieut. 1st Rifle in the company 3rd Regt 2nd Brig 2nd Div. Vermont Militia commanded by Major Wm. Hal[illegible] in the war of 1812; that her said husband (6) enlisted at Rutland Vt. on or about the 25 day of May, A. D. 1812, [illegible] and continued in actual service in said war for the term of about two yrs. and whose services terminated, by reason of honorable discharge at [illegible], on the ___ day of ___, A. D. ___. She further states that the following is a full description of her said husband at the time of his enlistment, viz: age about 33 years 6 ft in height born at Rutland Vt occupation Cooper dark hair grey eyes and dark complexion. She further states that she was married to the said Daniel Wright, at the city (or town) of Vernon, in the county of Lake and in the State of Illinois, on the 9th day of January, A. D. 1845, by one (10) Matthew Jewett, who was a (11) Minister of the Gospel and that her name before her said marriage was Rachel Millard, and that she has not remarried since the death of the said soldier; and she further states that (12) she never had any husband but said Daniel Wright but that the said Daniel Wright had a previous wife named Ruth Wright who died at Lake County Illinois 18[illegible] and that her said husband (13) Daniel Wright died at Half Day, in the State of Illinois, on the 30th day of December, A. D. 1873; and she further declares that the following have been the places of residence of herself and her said husband since the date of his discharge from the Army, viz: (14) that she and her said husband have resided in Vernon Lake County Illinois since her marriage aforesaid [illegible] She makes this declaration for the purpose of obtaining the pension to which she may be entitled under the provisions of Sections 4736 to 4740 inclusive Revised Statutes, and the Act of March 9, 1878, and hereby constitutes and appoints with full power of substitution and revocation, Milo B. Stevens & Co. of Chicago, Ills. her true and lawful attorney, to prosecute her claim; and she further declares that she has heretofore made no application for (15) either pension or bounty land neither to her knowledge [illegible] had her said husband.

and that her residence is No. ___ street, city (or town) of Vernon county of Lake, State of Illinois, and that her post-office address is Half Day, Lake Co, Ills.

ATTEST: Daniel Brewer
William Whigam

Rachel Wright
(Claimant's Signature.)

N. B.—All the blank spaces in this form must be carefully filled up in accordance with the instructions on the back hereof and from the best information possessed, or obtainable, by the applicant.

Daniel Wright was born in Rutland, Vermont, on June 6, 1778, during the Revolutionary War. His parents were Simeon Wright Jr. and Freelove (Martha) Foot. He enlisted to fight in the War of 1812 at the age of 33. The Wright family hailed from Vermont and had a history of military service. His grandfather Simeon Wright was an officer and fought in the War for Independence, and Daniel Wright's own father also served his country in both the Revolution and the War of 1812. Daniel moved with his wife, Ruth Todd, and family from Vermont to Croton, Ohio, where he lived for 20 years before coming to Illinois at the age of 55. The marriage produced seven children. Years after Ruth's death, Daniel remarried Rachel Millard in 1845. Pictured is a copy of Millard's application to receive widows' benefits for veterans of the War of 1812. It was submitted in 1879, a year after an act was passed to provide compensation. (Courtesy of Daniel Wright Middle School.)

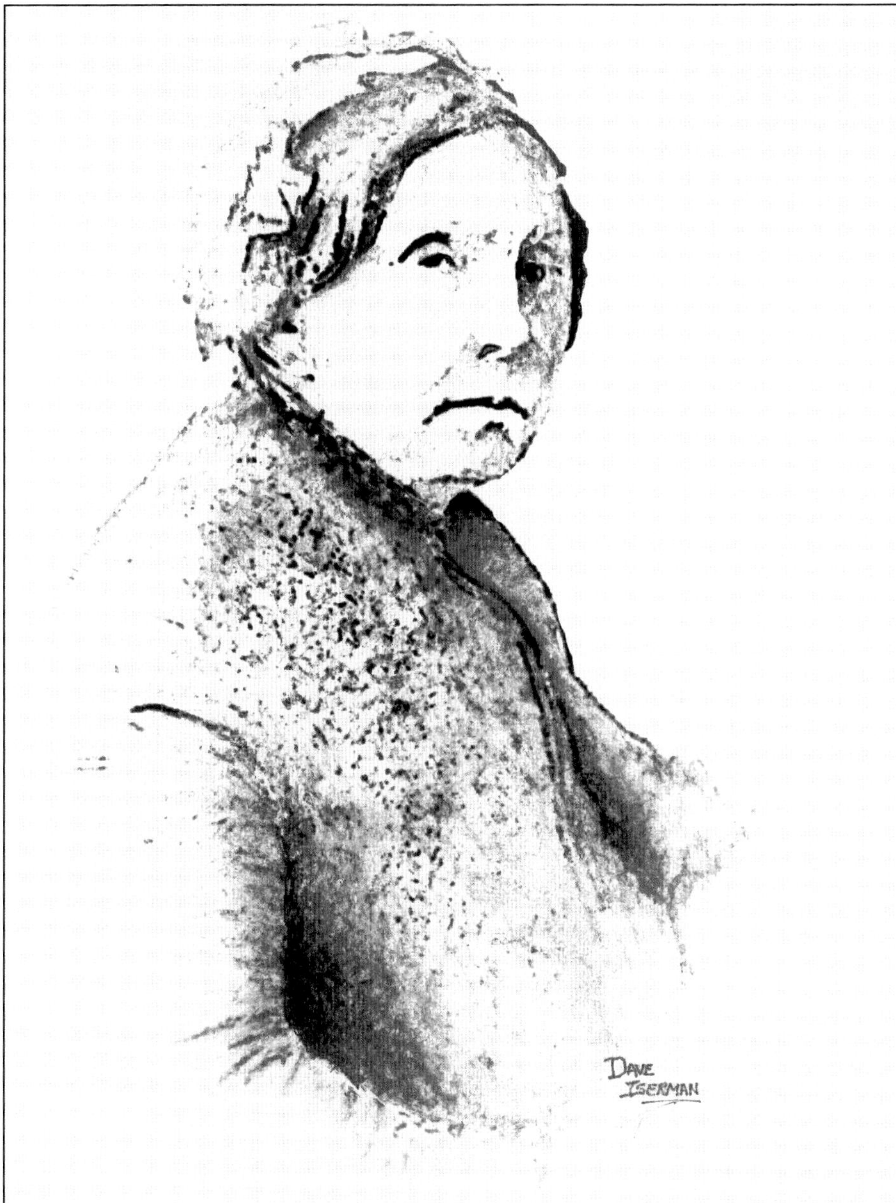

In 1836, Laura B. Sprague came to the area that would become known as Half Day with her parents and family. The Spragues came to Illinois from New York, where Laura had been educated as a teacher. It took them four weeks and two days to get to Illinois by wagon. After stopping in Chicago, the family settled on the banks of Indian Creek. Laura taught school in Zarley's Grove near Joliet for a short time in the summer, but returned to Half Day in the fall to become the first teacher in Lake County. She held school sessions in the Spragues' family home for 25 area children. Her compensation was $1.50 per week along with board. She met and married Edward Simons the next year, and since married women were not allowed to work outside the home, her brief career came to a close. She would soon move to Chicago and raise her own family. This illustration is based on the only known photograph of Laura B. Sprague, which was taken much later in her life. (Courtesy of Dave Iserman.)

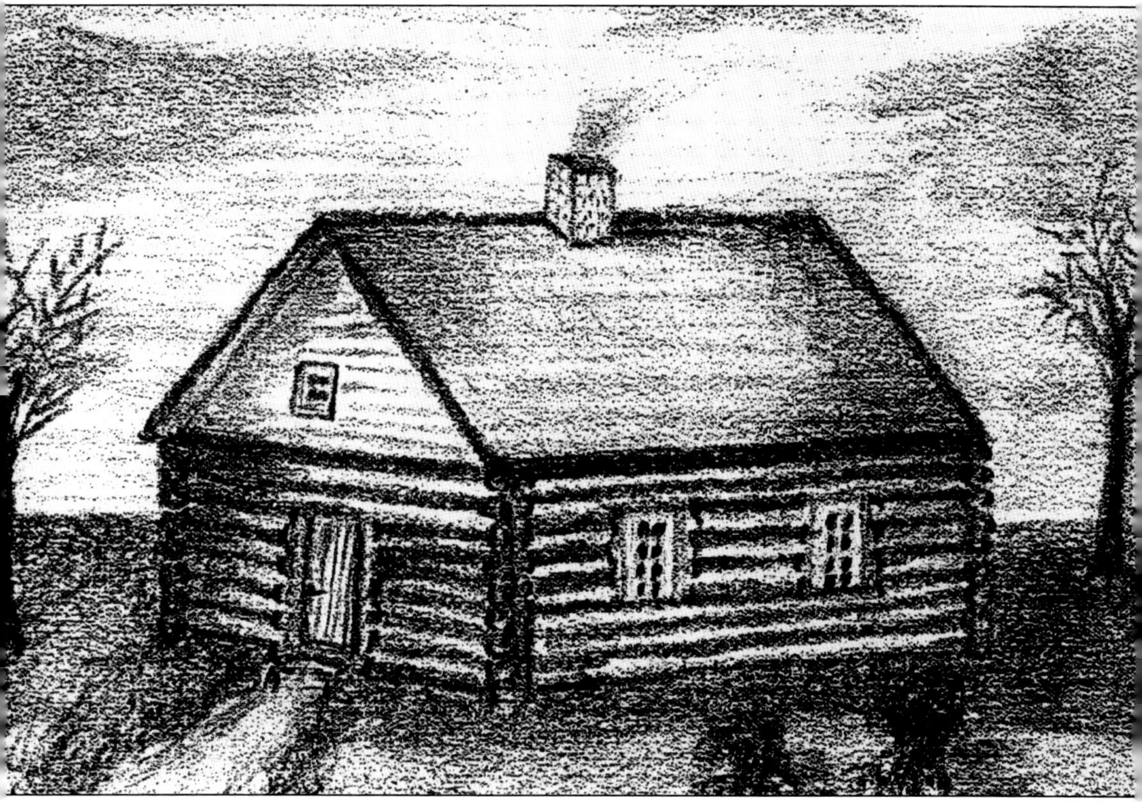

In this representation, it is possible to see a typical one-room schoolhouse used by early settlers. The log schoolhouse would have a puncheon floor, which was made from rough-hewn logs. The teacher would have many different students, who could all be different ages and levels. Every student sat in the same room while they were each getting individualized instruction. Discipline could be a problem in situations like this. Many students were unruly, and it was difficult, if not impossible, to keep order unless one had a stern hand. This drawing of the first known schoolhouse in Lake County was taken from one of the 1918 school histories of Vernon Township. In honor of the centennial of Illinois's statehood, every student in Lake County was given the same assignment—to write a history of his or her community. Many of these papers survive and can be found in local libraries or museums.

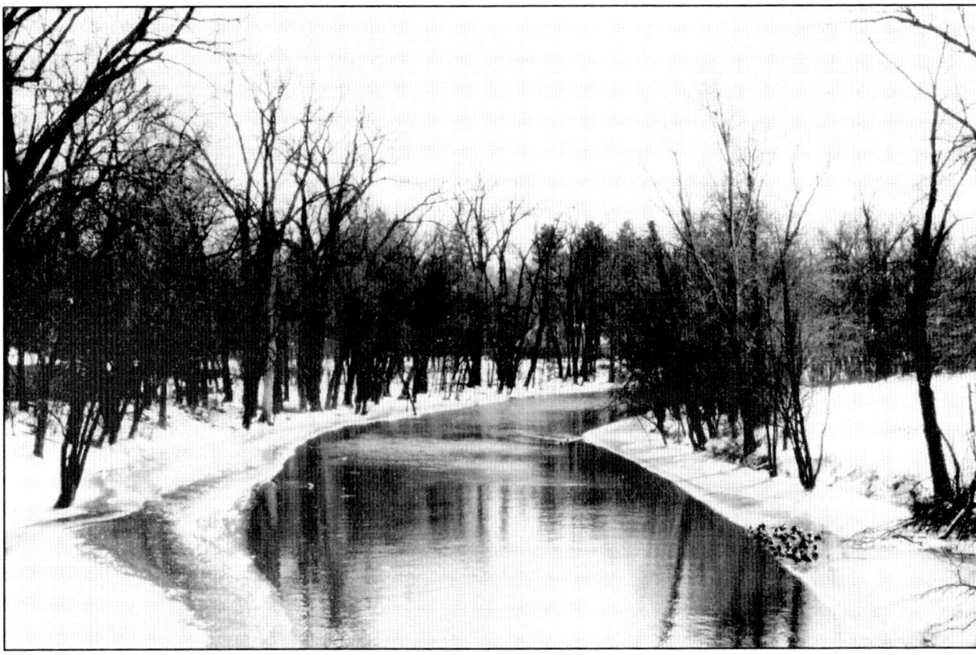

The ice on the Des Plaines River (above) could be up to one foot thick in places during the bitterly cold winters. Families, as well as saloons and restaurants, would cut their ice from the river and store it in a separate building called an icehouse. These well-insulated buildings were filled with sawdust, which kept the ice cold enough to prevent melting for months on end. People would attach blades to the runners on the bottom of their sleighs, which were pulled by horses, and drive them across the ice-covered river while cutting large swaths of ice. The advertisement below is for a typical type of sleigh that might have been used. (Above, courtesy of the Village of Lincolnshire; below, courtesy of Gertrude Moon.)

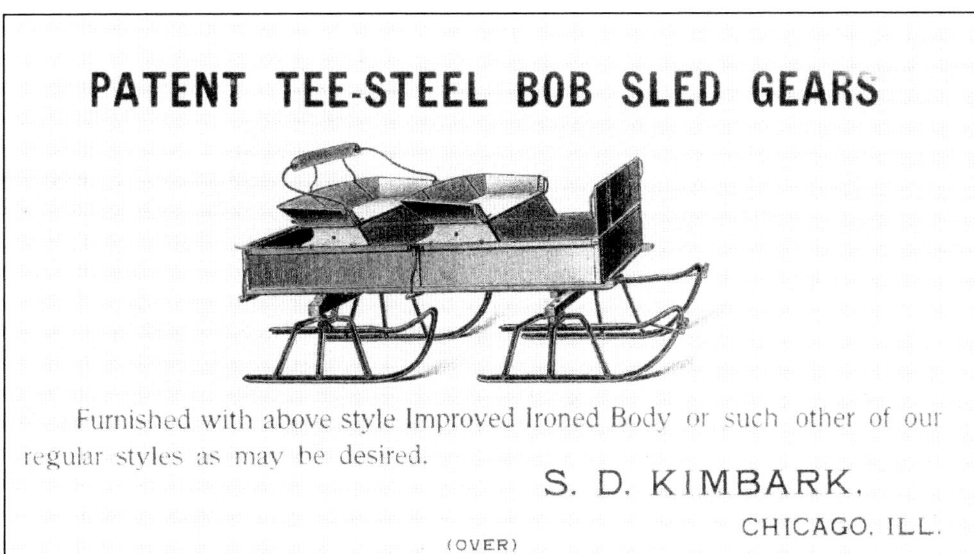

The land in Vernon Township wasn't surveyed or divided into sections by the US government until 1840. Prior to that time, people who settled on property squatted on it until it was officially up for sale. People had to make the trip to Chicago when the land was available and were required to make the purchase in person. It is interesting to note that one Chicago land speculator, Dr. John H. Foster, purchased hundreds of acres of land in Lake County at that time. Both this 1907 map of Half Day and the 1936 one of Prairie View show the towns at a later time but are similar in style to those very first maps' names and property lines.

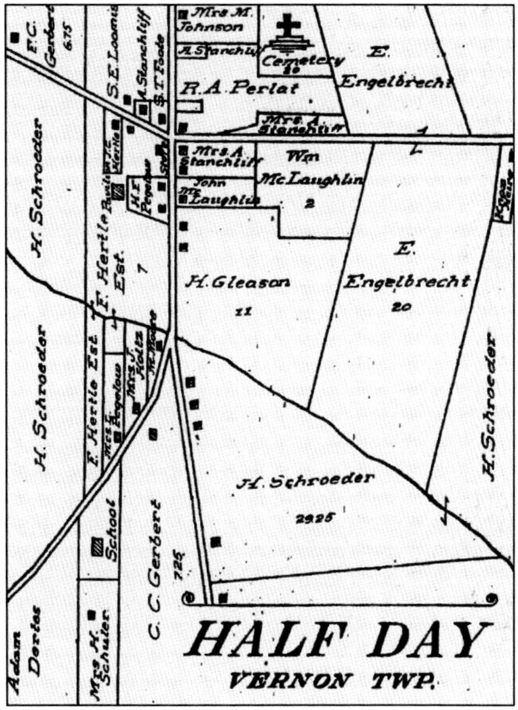

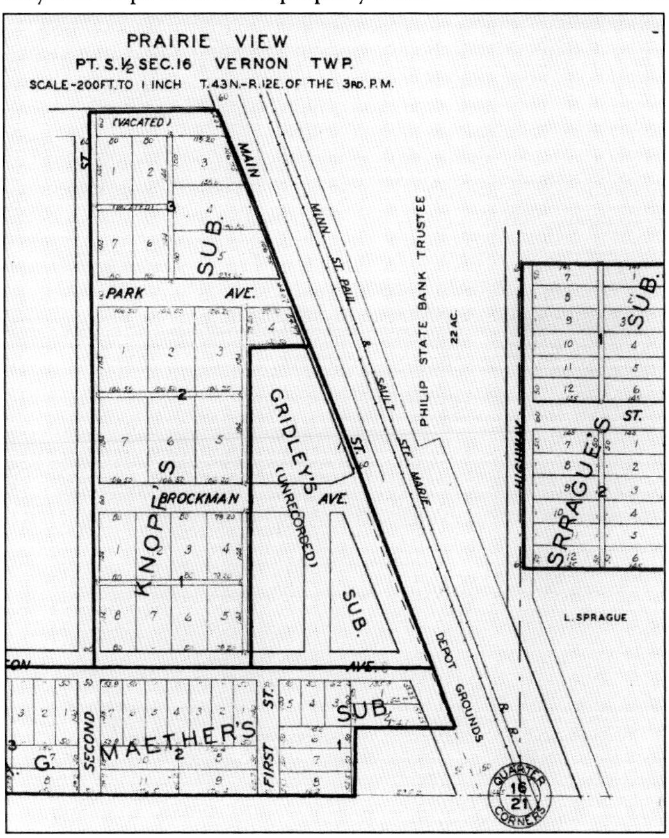

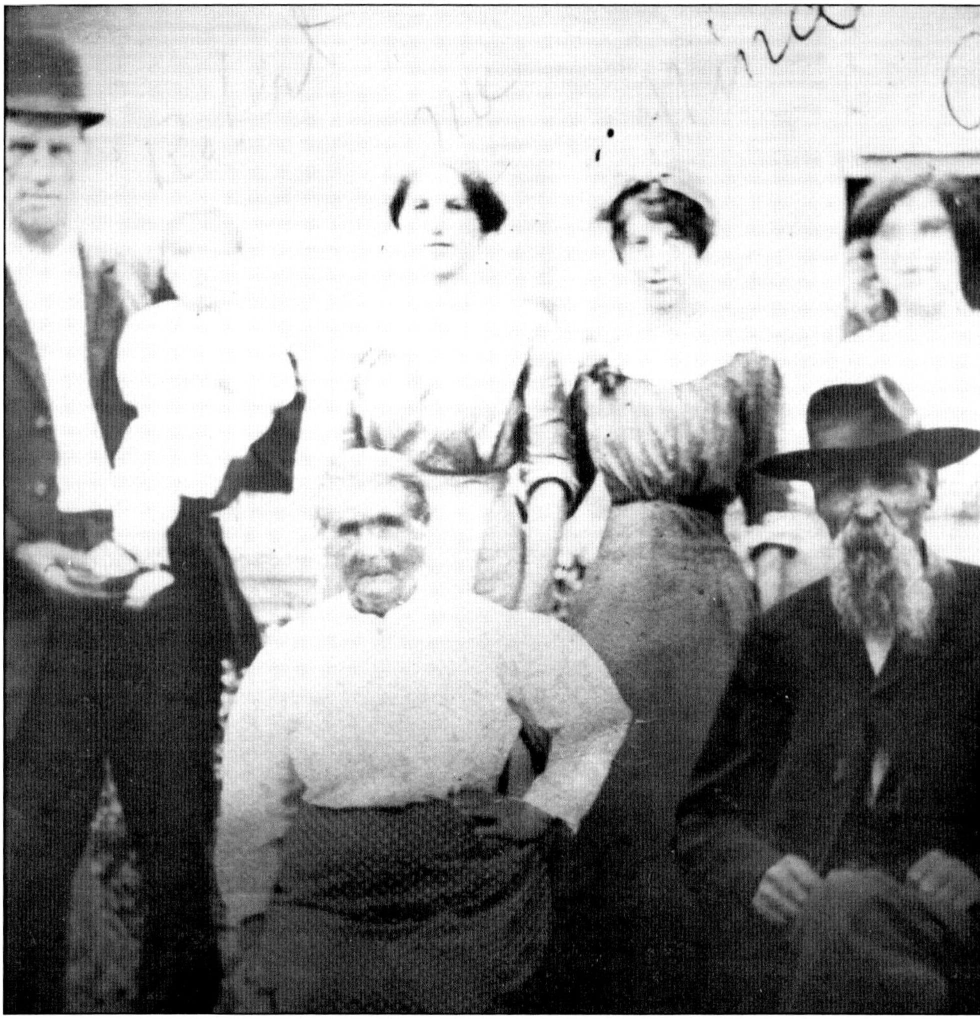

Robert Gleason's family was one of the earliest in the area. Gleason was born in Half Day in 1911, and his great-grandfather Emmett Gleason was a sawmill operator at the first mill in the county, owned by Hiram Kennicott. Robert's grandfather Enos, seen here, was a child when the mill was in operation in the 1830s. The Kennicott mill was located one mile south of Half Day on the Des Plaines River. Most of the mechanisms in the mill were made from wood, since metal was very rare at that time. Even the cogwheels, which were important components of the mill, were made of hickory and turned very slowly because of the crude design. The Gleason family is pictured here around 1912. They are, from left to right, (bottom row) Robert's grandmother Anne Shapter Gleason and Robert's grandfather Enos Gleason; (top row) Robert's father, Ed; Robert; Robert's mother, Mini; cousin Nina Davidson; and cousin Amy Davidson.

John Ballard was born in Half Day on July 18, 1842. He volunteered to join the Union forces during the Civil War and was part of Company F of the 37th Illinois Infantry for three years until his discharge on March 28, 1866. He had a role in many important engagements, such as the battles of Pea Ridge, Prairie Grove, Chalk Bluff, and the Sieges on Vicksburg and Mobile, among others. He returned home and settled in Half Day in order to farm the land. He married Isabella Shapter, Robert Gleason's great aunt, and had three children. The photograph at right is of John Ballard, taken later in his life, and the photograph below is of the sawmill located on his property, one half mile north of Route 45 on the east side of the road and north of the Gleason homestead.

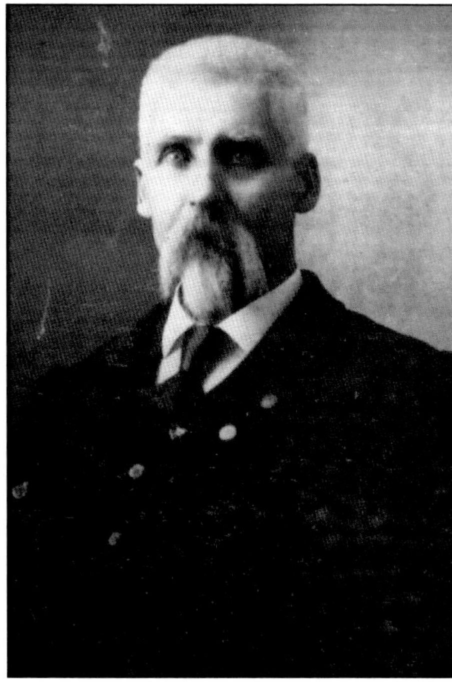

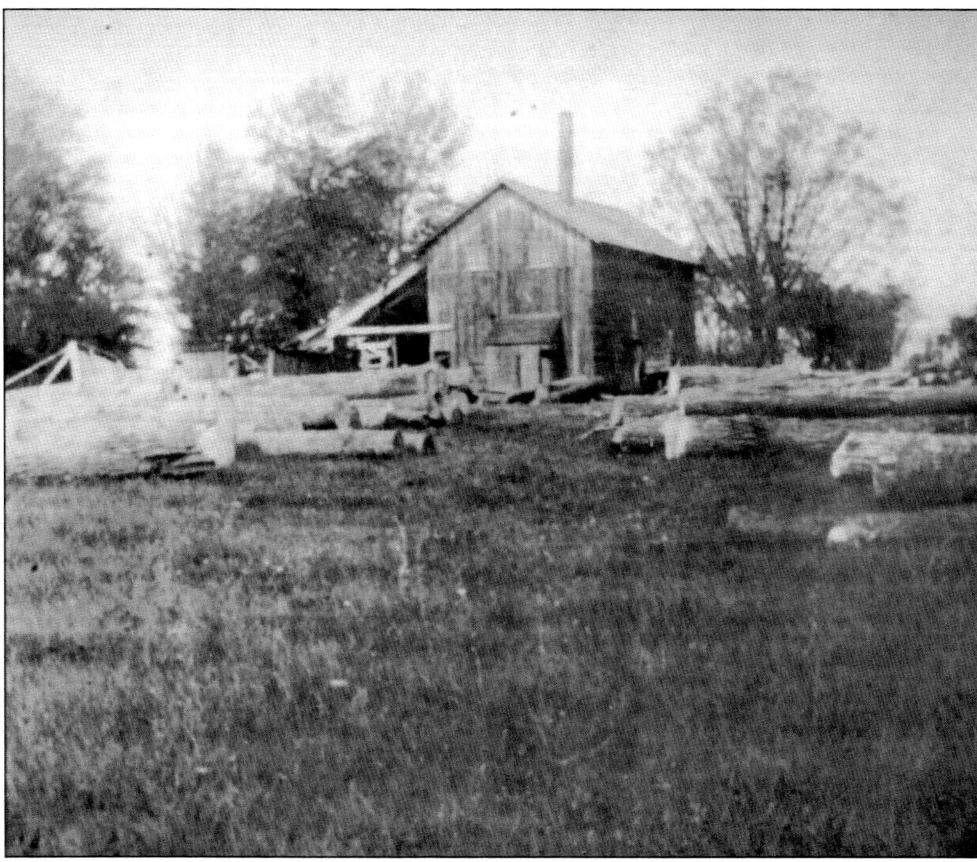

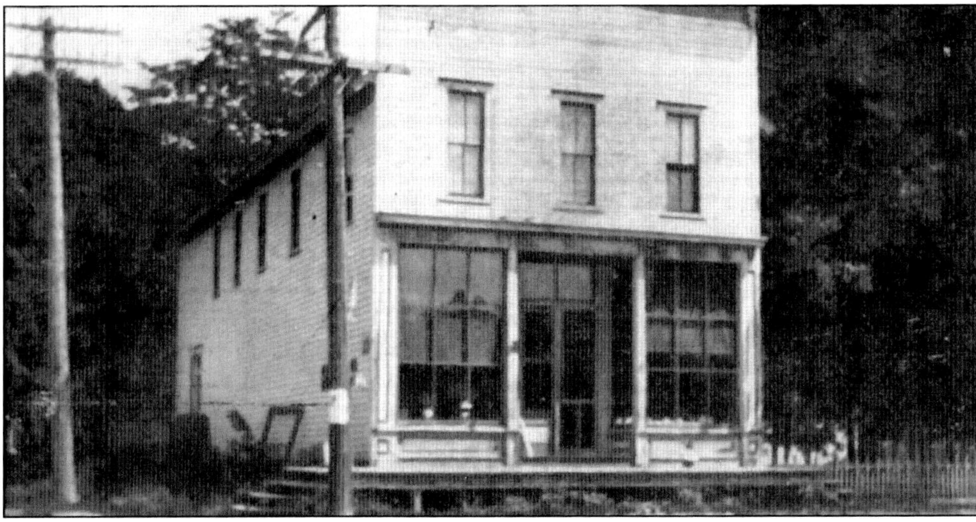

The Half Day General Store was located on Milwaukee Avenue just south of Route 45 on the west side of the road. The store was smaller than the neighboring Maether General Store in Prairie View but held a similar array of items. Products like hats, clothing, hardware, and food could be purchased from this friendly neighborhood establishment. Below, George Stancliff is pictured surrounded by an eclectic mixture of items. The store is seen here on a picture postcard marked April 27, 1908. Postcards were very popular at that time and were often sent through the mail as a casual means of communication. Some people had telephones, but they were party lines and had many households sharing one phone line, and turns had to be taken when someone needed to use it. (Above, courtesy of Vernon Township.)

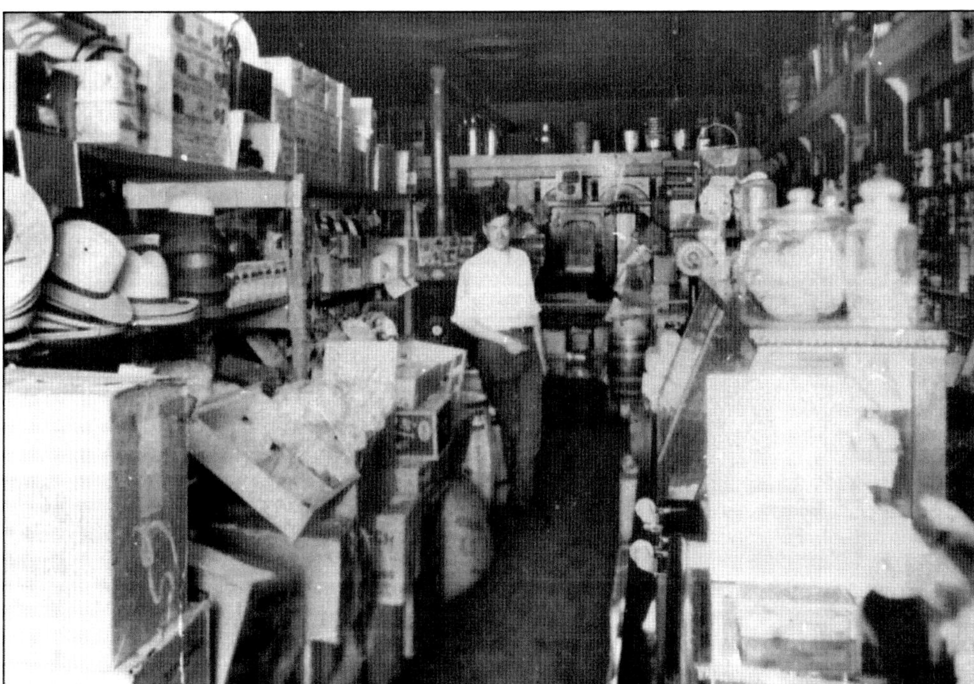

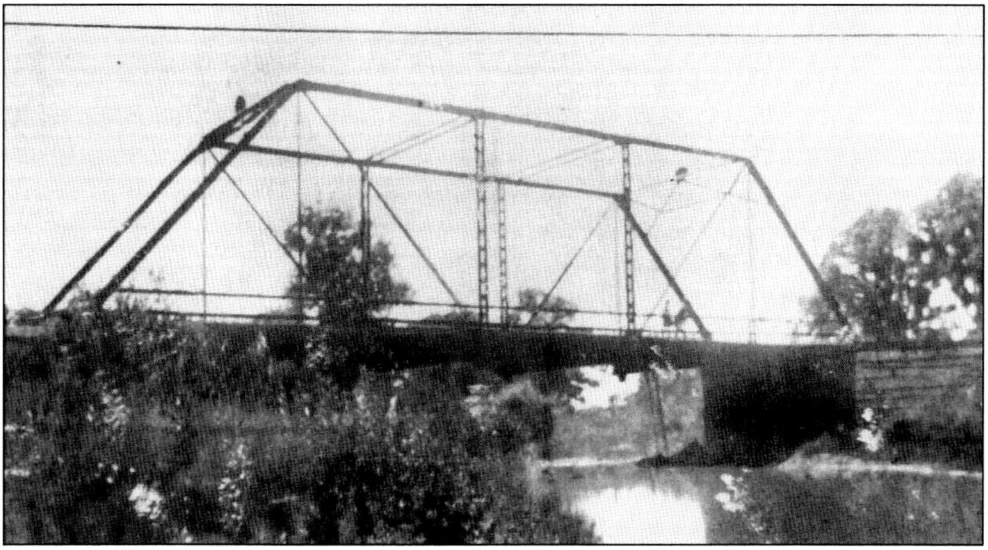

The very earliest bridges in Vernon Township were constructed of wooden pilings and logs or planks. There were many problems with wooden bridges. Many became unsafe and washed away in severe storms or floods. Some even collapsed under the weight of a horse and wagon while the unfortunate riders plummeted into the creek or river below. Steel bridges, such as this first one over Indian Creek, were much safer and longer lasting.

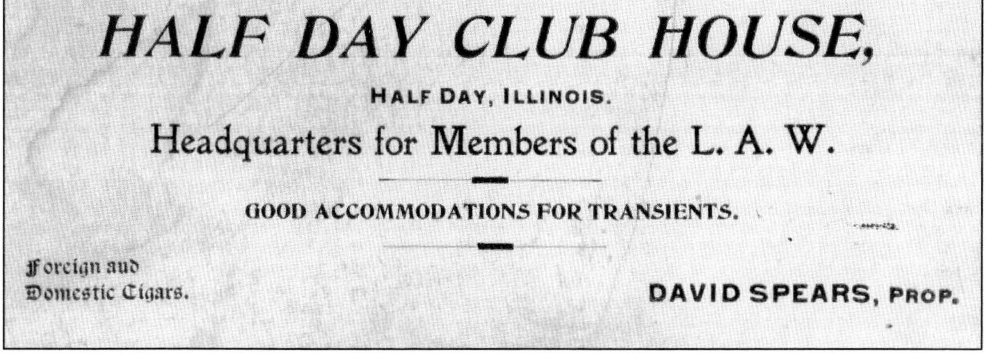

Cycling was a popular activity in the later part of the 19th century and the early part of the 20th century. It was not uncommon for people to take multiple day trips. This card is appealing directly to members of the national organization for cycling enthusiasts, the League of American Wheelmen (LAW), who were looking for a place to stay while traveling. (Courtesy of Vernon Township.)

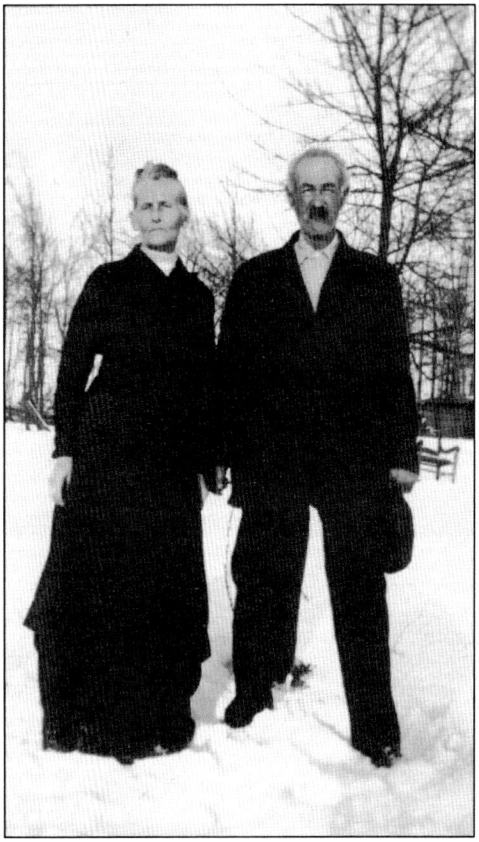

Elijah and Alice Courtney Keough were two early residents of Half Day. The Keough family moved to the area in 1899 and lived in a home on Elm Road. Alice Courtney Keough was born and raised in nearby Wauconda while her husband was from Buffalo Grove. He was reported to have had dinner as a child with Daniel Wright after the then-14-year-old had finished helping with a day's work. The Keoughs farmed the land, and Alice raised turkeys as well as seven children. Elijah died in 1924, and Alice carried on as a widow for the next 43 years, serving as the family matriarch until she passed away in 1967 at the age of 105. Elijah and Alice are pictured at home on Elm Road (left), and Elijah with his son Henry are pictured below around the same time. (Courtesy of Gertrude Moon.)

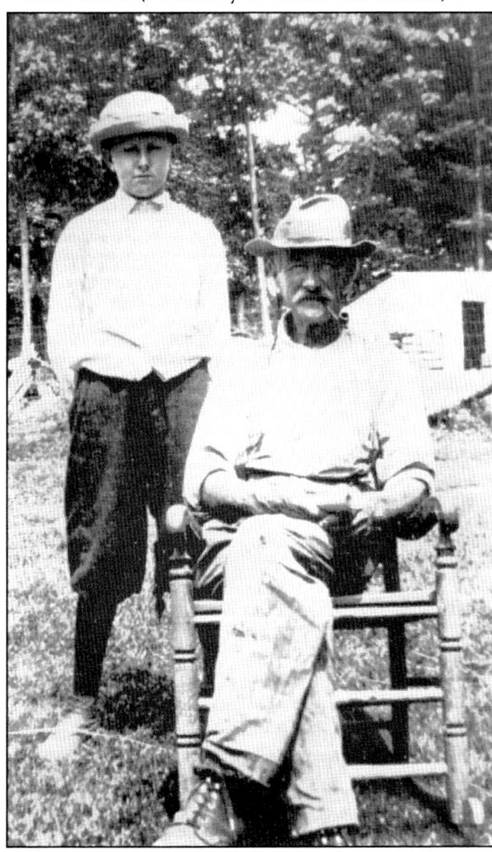

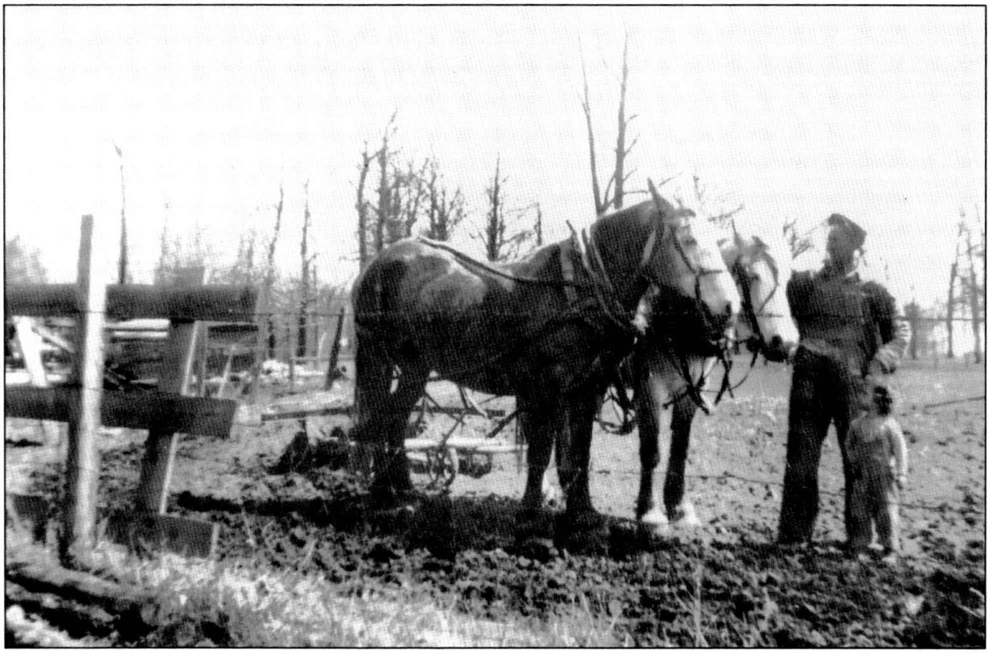

Farming the fields has never been easy work, but the invention of the polished steel plow by John Deere in 1837 was an important step forward in agricultural technology. While the plow was certainly an innovation, horses still provided a great deal of the muscle for years to come. Edd and young Laurence Keough are pictured in the field with their trusty horses Polly and Molly. (Courtesy of Gertrude Moon.)

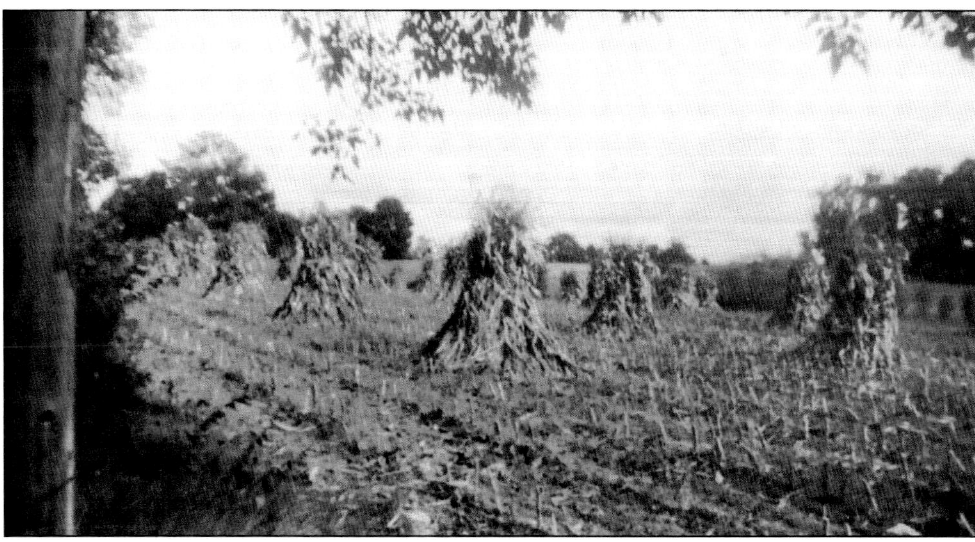

Farmers would often need to remove moisture from their corn stalks before harvesting the ears off of them. In order to do so, they would be cut and stacked in bunches to dry. After drying for a few days, the ears of corn would be taken off by hand, often by the farmer's children. (Courtesy of Gertrude Moon.)

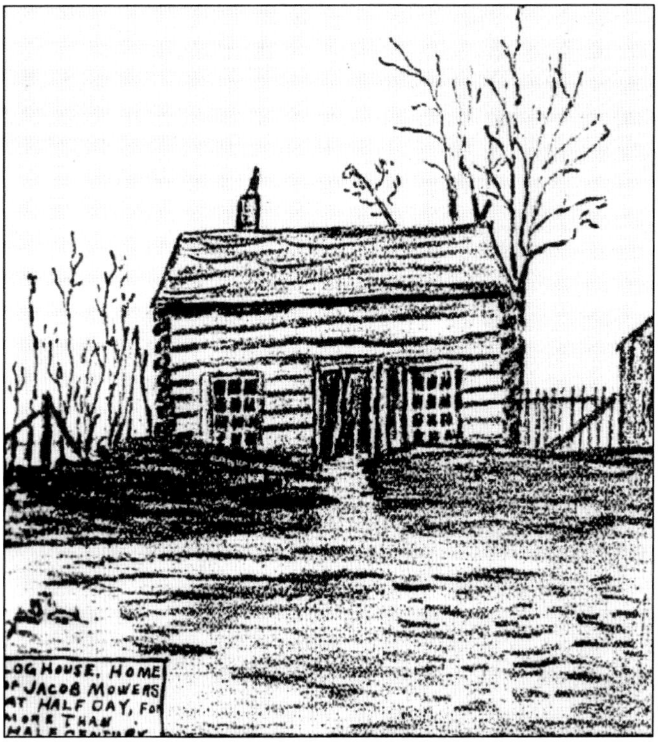

Jacob Mowers was a very early resident whose house was located on Milwaukee Avenue just south of Half Day. He was known as a reputable blacksmith as well as a man who could fix anything, due to his innate mechanical abilities. Perhaps he was best known for his beekeeping, hunting, and trapping skills. The animal traps he fabricated were renowned in the county, and people from all over came to purchase them.

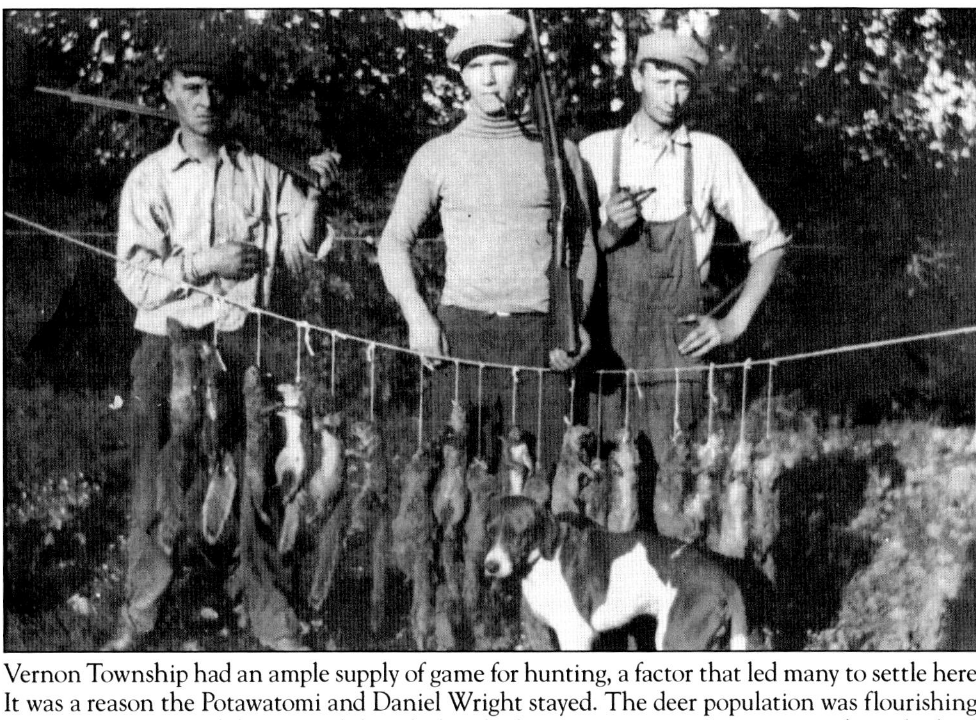

Vernon Township had an ample supply of game for hunting, a factor that led many to settle here. It was a reason the Potawatomi and Daniel Wright stayed. The deer population was flourishing, and hunting parties did not search long before finding success. Large game wasn't the only thing that was sought after, however. This Prairie View hunting party attests to the fact that squirrel was a desired quarry, as well. (Courtesy of Vernon Township.)

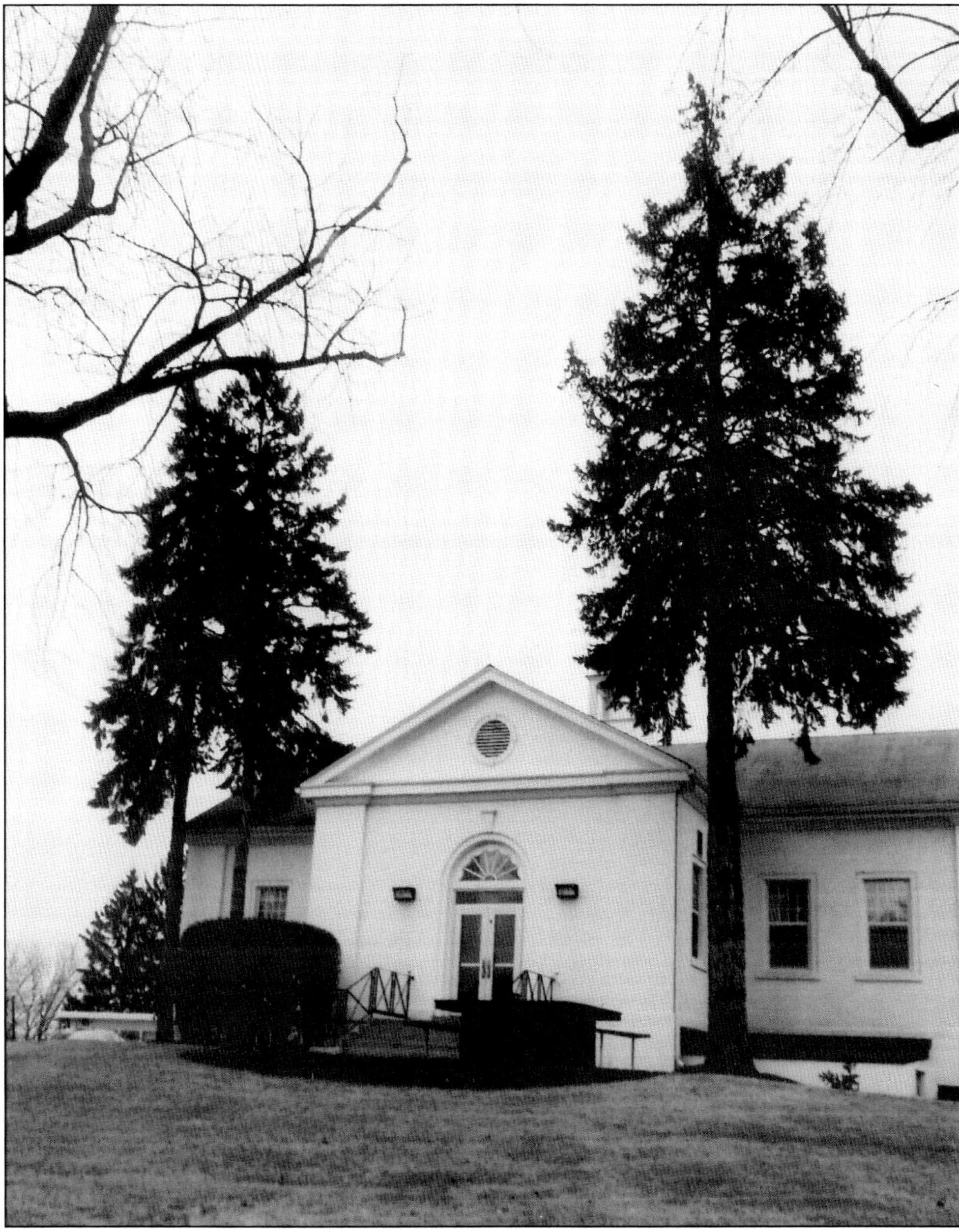

As the school-aged population grew, the need for a larger school became evident. A bigger one-room schoolhouse, which was built on the site of the present Half Day School building, replaced the log schoolhouse on Milwaukee Avenue. The population climbed, and the single-room school was replaced by a two-room structure, which itself was ultimately replaced by a two-room brick building. The brick building has been added on to but is still standing and used by the school district today. An old story in the village claims that some mischievous students once stole the bell out of the belfry of the school. They did it so they could not be called back to school in the afternoon after lunch one day. It supposedly was thrown into Indian Creek, never to be seen again. (Courtesy of the author.)

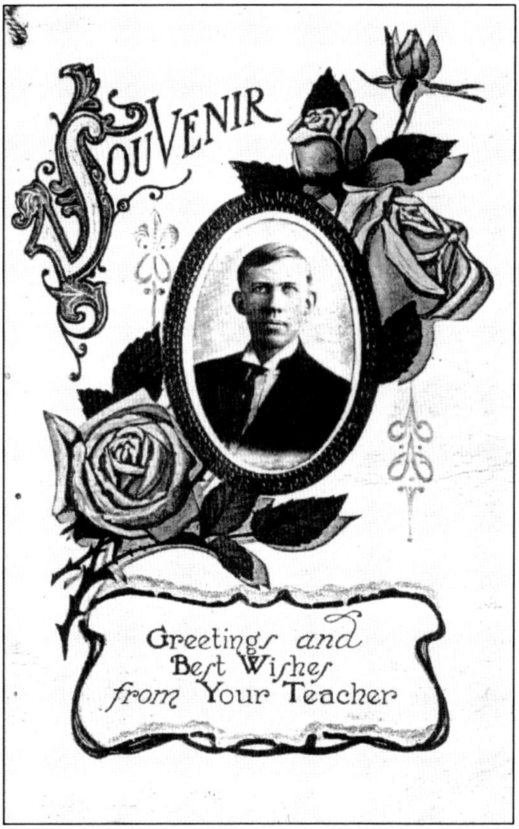

This attractive keepsake was given to the 29 students of Half Day School in 1912 by their teacher, S.D. Nelson, and included all of the pupil's names. Half Day School had students up through eighth grade. Once a student graduated, they had a choice of which high school to attend. The Half Day-Prairie View area was termed a non–high school district. The communities had no high school of their own, and students were entitled to go wherever they pleased for grades nine through 12 but had to provide their own transportation. Many students chose to go to Deerfield, Lake Zurich, or Libertyville. Others completed their education through correspondence or chose to go without any additional schooling.

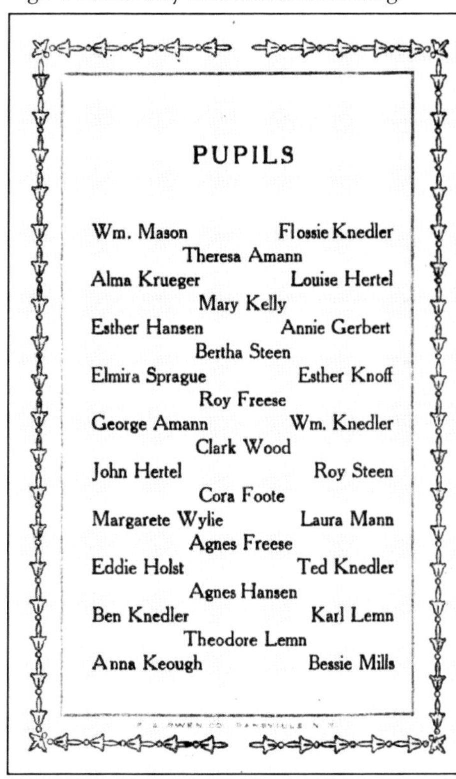
PUPILS

Wm. Mason Flossie Knedler
Theresa Amann
Alma Krueger Louise Hertel
Mary Kelly
Esther Hansen Annie Gerbert
Bertha Steen
Elmira Sprague Esther Knoff
Roy Freese
George Amann Wm. Knedler
Clark Wood
John Hertel Roy Steen
Cora Foote
Margarete Wylie Laura Mann
Agnes Freese
Eddie Holst Ted Knedler
Agnes Hansen
Ben Knedler Karl Lemn
Theodore Lemn
Anna Keough Bessie Mills

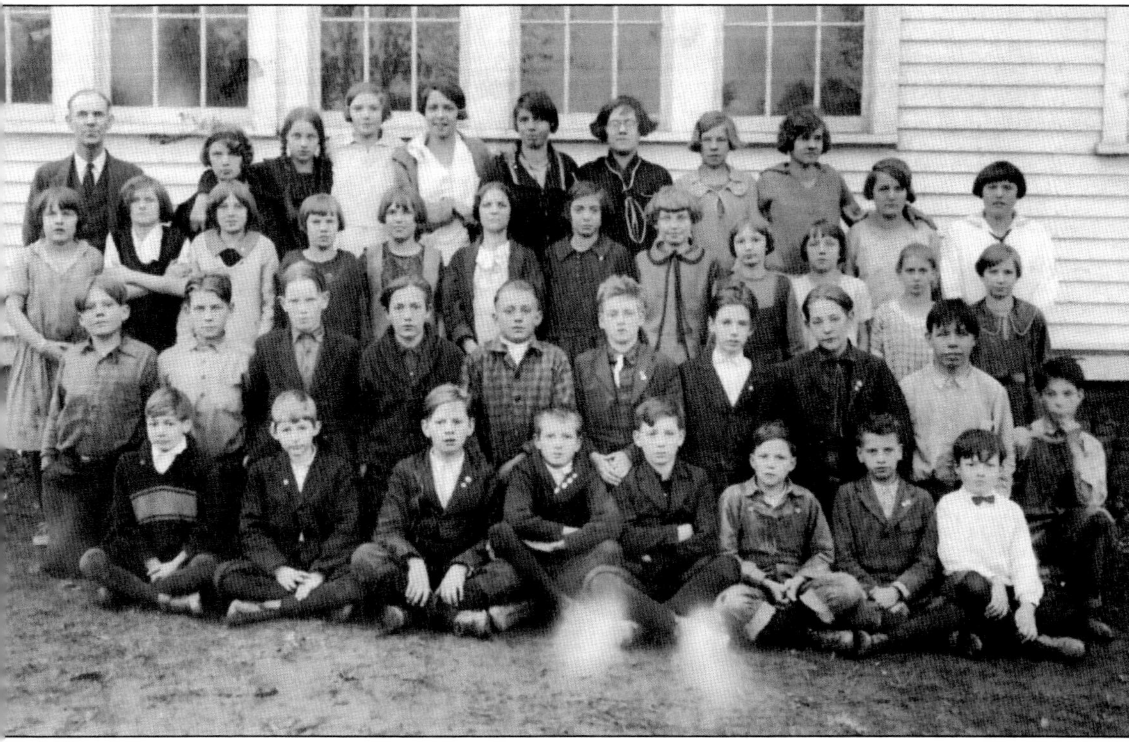

It was common to have class photographs taken during the school year. The students attending in 1926 proudly look into the lens of the camera. They are, from left to right, (first row) Earl Small, Robert Stahl, Orval Stancliff, Clifford Foote, Vincent Lynford, Edward Foote, John Lemm, and William Meyer; (second row) Russell Gilman, Alvin Stahl, Harold Peterson, Walter Lemm, Gordon Christenson, Lawrence Stancliff, Harold Stahl, John Schroeder, Charles Vanover, and Clyde Vanover; (third row) Kathryn Bock, Dorothy Stancliff, Della Anderson, Merle Collins, Ava Collins, Esther Prell, Helen Hans, Alice Peterson, Frances Foote, Madeline Christenson, Olive Prell, and Edith Sibley; (fourth row) teacher Fred Collins, Ruth Bubblitz, Lillian Lindstrom, Mabel Hans, Reva Gleason, Caroline Hans, Lavern Gilman, Evelyn Anderson, Grace Bock, Marannette Stancliff, and Kathryn Gabriel. Even with increasing enrollment, the two-room schoolhouse expanded for the first time in 1955 with four additional rooms and then again in 1958 with six more classrooms and a gymnasium. (Courtesy of Vernon Township.)

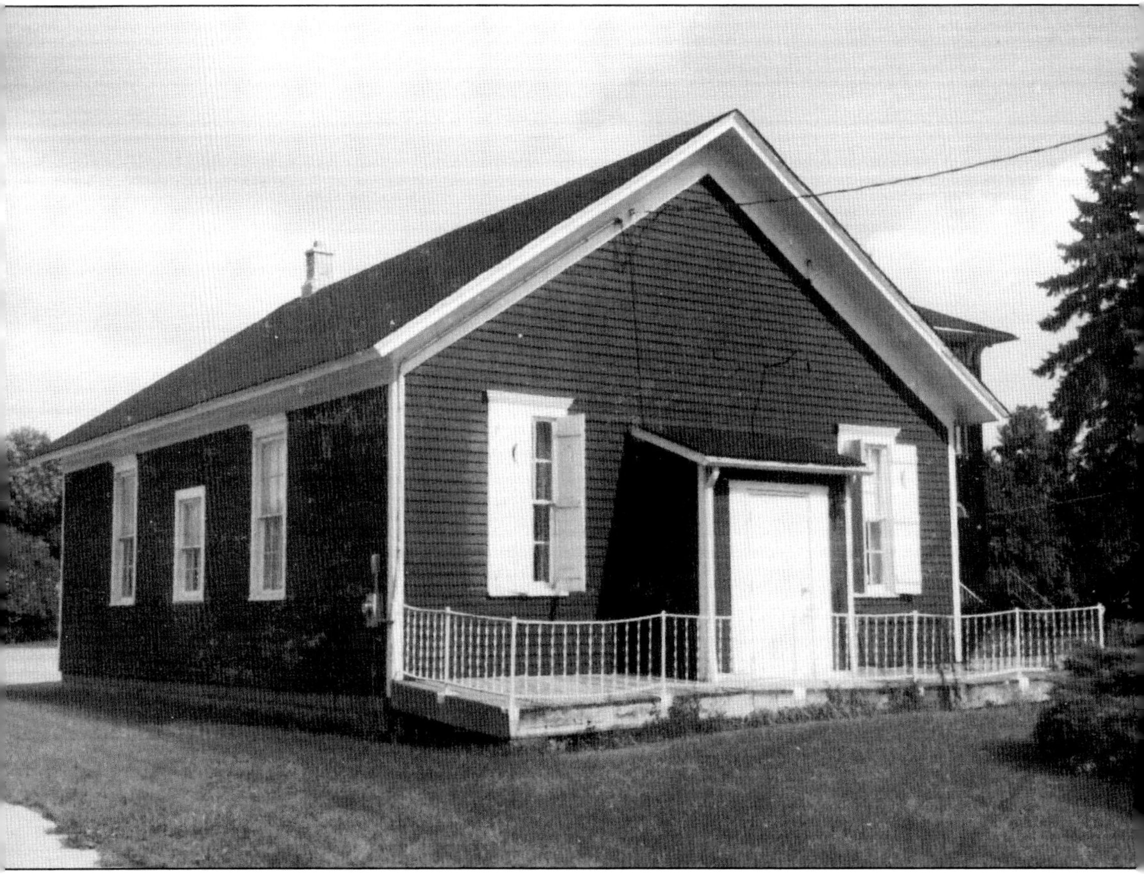

The congregation at Half Day began in 1836 when it was one of four preaching spots around the county. Services were held in a home on Milwaukee Avenue until a building was constructed in 1844. It remains standing on the corner of Indian Creek and Old Half Day Roads. It has been used in many capacities over the years, such as a church, Sunday school, meetinghouse, town hall, and even a polling place. It took several years to construct and was designed in a New England style, since most pioneers were from that area of the country. It was built with two separate doors, one for the men to enter and the other for the women. There was even a choir loft, and baptisms were done in nearby Indian Creek. Lake County's first postmaster, Seth Washburn, donated the land for the expressed purpose of building a house of worship. The first town meeting was held there in April 1850 for the purpose of electing officers.

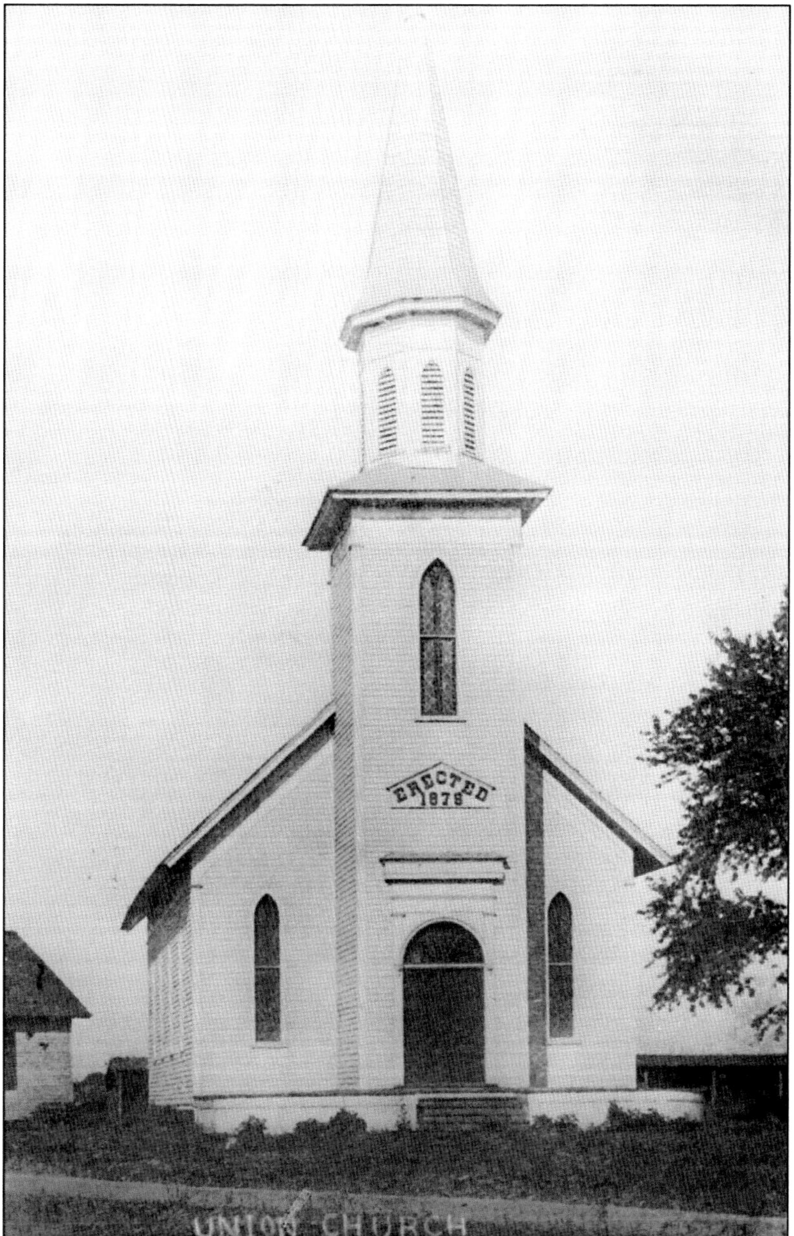

It was common for denominations to change in churches, and such was the case here. In 1870, a Presbyterian church was organized, and a new building was built. Union Church was constructed next to the town hall and dedicated in 1876. The next several decades saw change, and the church was closed from 1899 until 1914. A drifter named Elder Tohman was passing by in July of that year when he saw the closed church. He went in and began to ring the bell incessantly, summoning people from miles around. When people had begun to gather, he brought them inside and preached a sermon to them. The 80-year-old claimed that it was his mission in life to reopen closed churches. He stayed on until the fall, when a permanent minister was found, and the drifter disappeared as quickly and quietly as he had arrived. The church continued but was struck by lightning and burned to the ground in 1919.

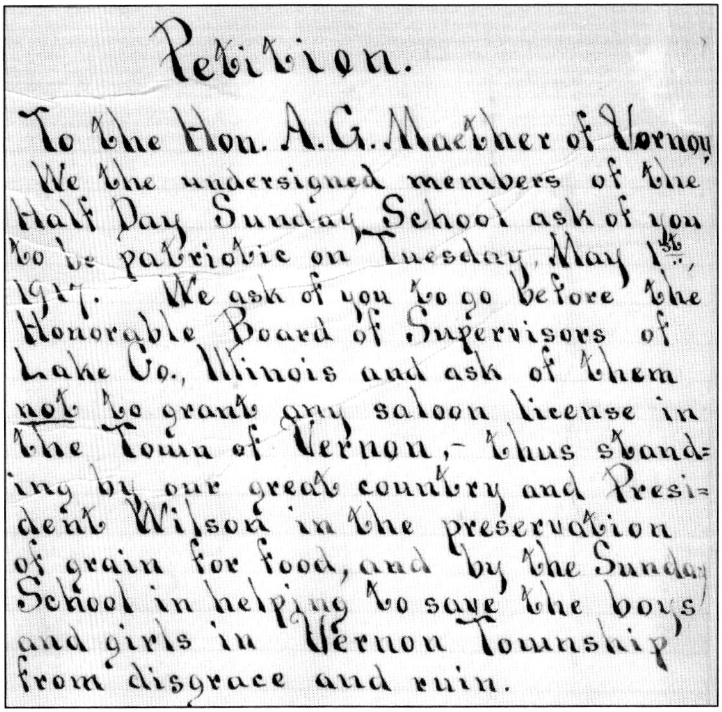

Petition.

To the Hon. A.G. Maether of Vernon

We the undersigned members of the Half Day Sunday School ask of you to be patriotic on Tuesday, May 1st, 1917. We ask of you to go before the Honorable Board of Supervisors of Lake Co., Illinois and ask of them not to grant any saloon license in the Town of Vernon, - thus standing by our great country and President Wilson in the preservation of grain for food, and by the Sunday School in helping to save the boys and girls in Vernon Township from disgrace and ruin.

America's involvement in World War I affected Vernon Township just like every other community. The United States entered the "war to end all wars" on April 6, 1917. During the war, there was a government campaign called "Food Will Win the War," which encouraged people to voluntarily conserve food. This petition was sent to township supervisor A.G. Maether in support of those efforts. (Courtesy of Washburn Church.)

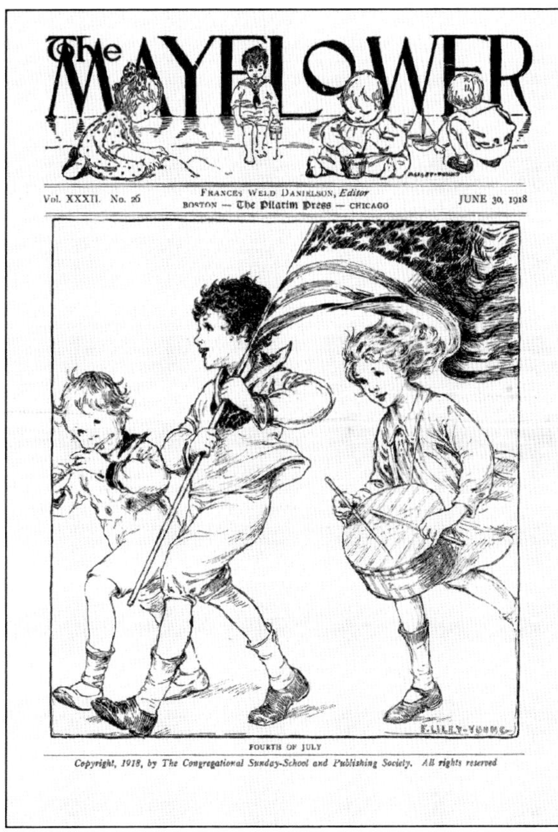

This church handout, titled the *Mayflower*, is reflective of not only its date of issue—the week of June 30, 1918—but also of the general war effort. The patriotic feeling that was permeating the entire country at the time is evident as America's involvement in the "great war" was still ongoing. (Courtesy of Washburn Church.)

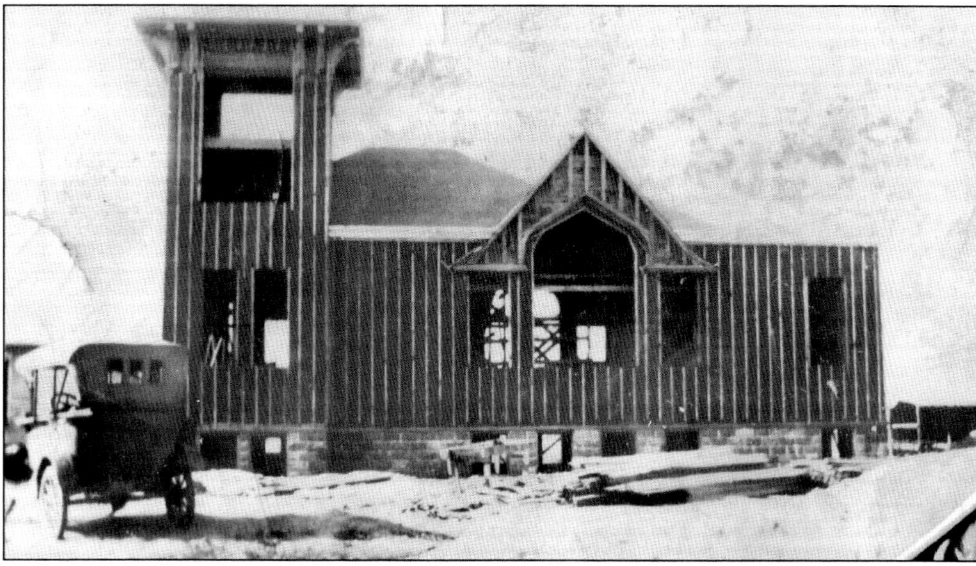

A brand new church was constructed on the site of Union Church. The name was changed to the Washburn Congregational Church in honor of Seth Washburn, who donated the land on which the church stood. Construction began in August 1921, and a cornerstone was laid that contained several objects, including newspapers, coins, arrowheads found in the area, a history of the church, an American flag, a Bible, and a township history by Seth Washburn himself. The ceremony was presided over by the Washburn pastor, Reverend Keithan, and Reverend Laidman from Chicago. At right, the bell is being raised into the bell tower. Note the temporary rails for dollies to help bring in building materials. (Both, courtesy of Washburn Church.)

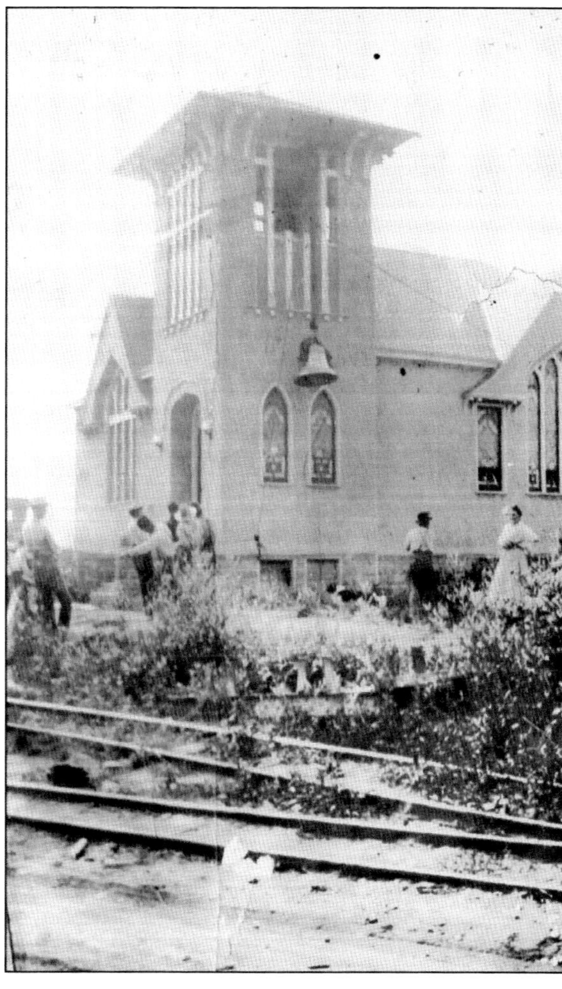

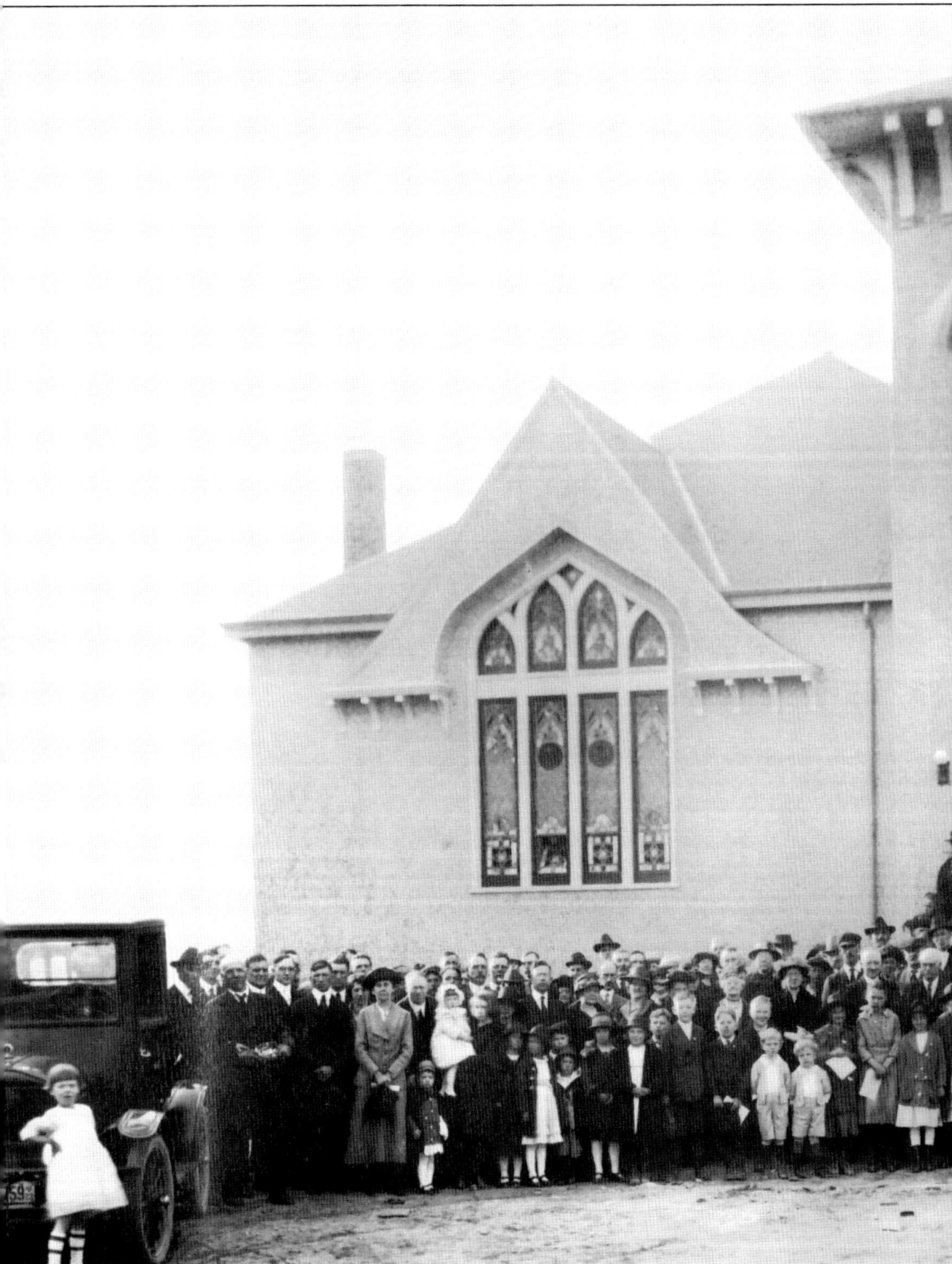

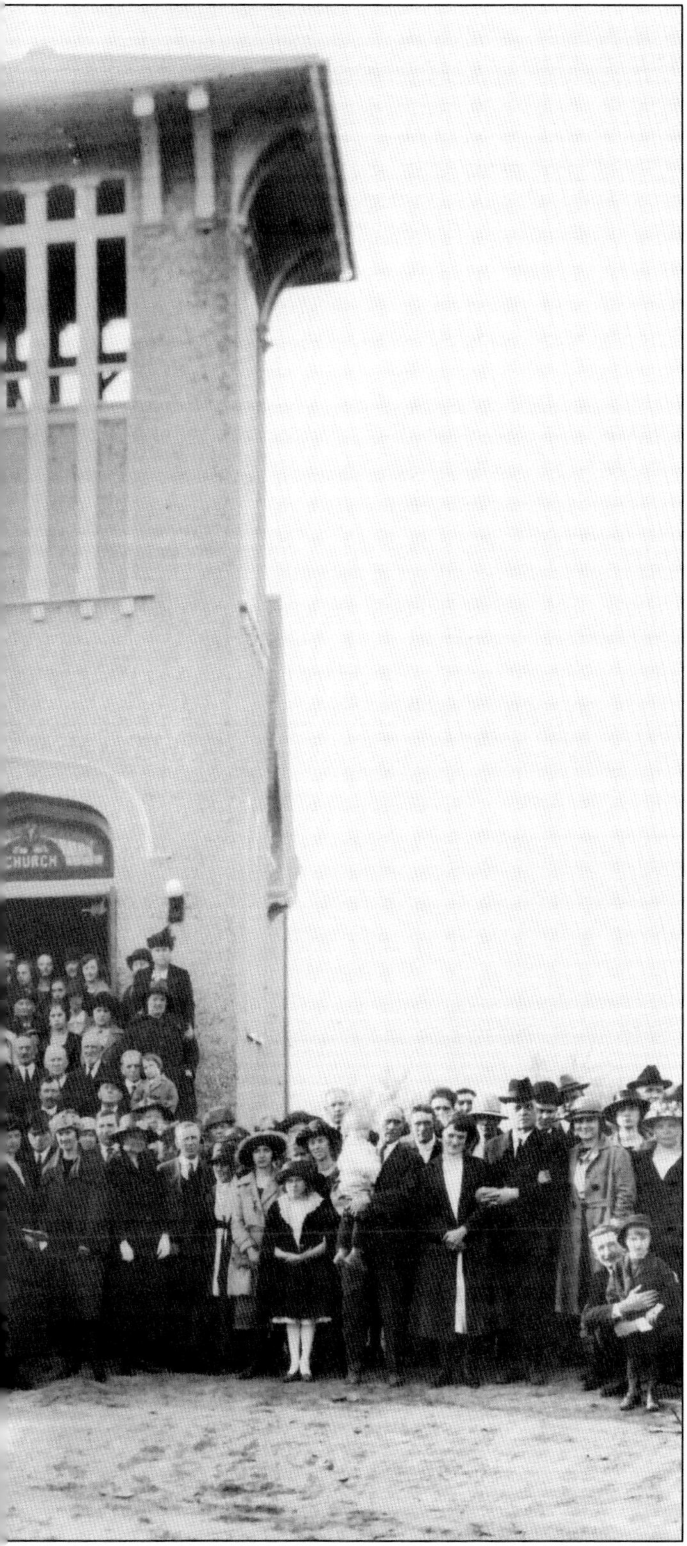

The dedication of the new Washburn Congregational Church occurred on April 30, 1922, and was attended by hundreds of people. The group of attendees is seen in the photograph, taken on a cool Sunday afternoon. There were many guest speakers, a service, transference of the keys from the building committee to the trustees, and a performance by the visiting Ivanhoe Church choir. It was a momentous occasion with visitors coming from near and far. There was even an automobile pick-up and delivery service for guests who were arriving by rail at Highland Park. Accommodations were provided for out-of-town guests by members of the congregation. A special lunch provided by the Ladies Aid Society was served after the two o'clock dedication. That evening, there was another regular service at eight o'clock, and the next evening saw a fellowship meeting for all, including a visit with three former pastors. That weekend, the church saw the largest increase of enrollment of new members at one time. Washburn became the central part of Half Day at that moment. (Courtesy of Washburn Church.)

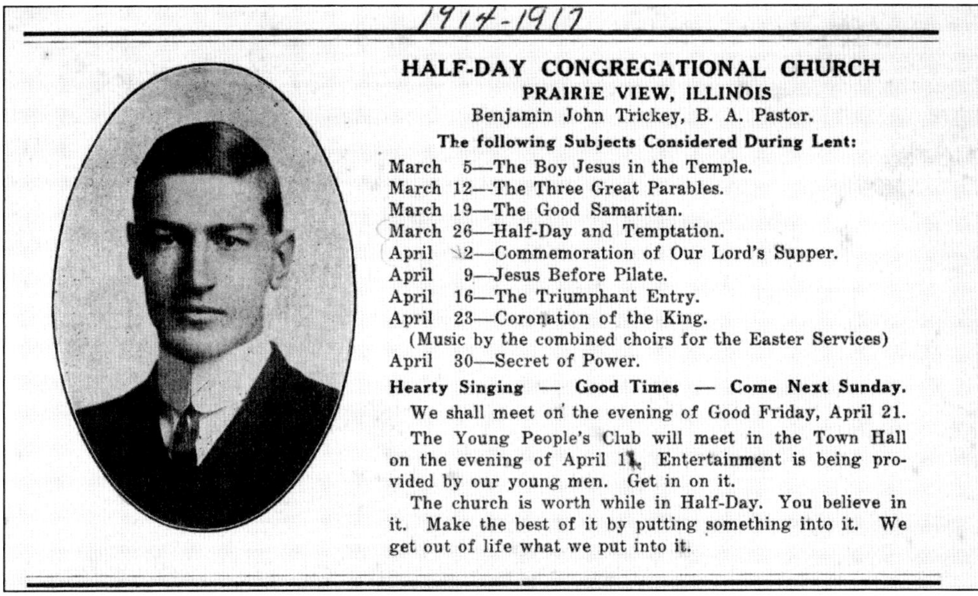

1914-1917

HALF-DAY CONGREGATIONAL CHURCH

PRAIRIE VIEW, ILLINOIS

Benjamin John Trickey, B. A. Pastor.

The following Subjects Considered During Lent:

March 5—The Boy Jesus in the Temple.
March 12—The Three Great Parables.
March 19—The Good Samaritan.
March 26—Half-Day and Temptation.
April 2—Commemoration of Our Lord's Supper.
April 9—Jesus Before Pilate.
April 16—The Triumphant Entry.
April 23—Coronation of the King.
(Music by the combined choirs for the Easter Services)
April 30—Secret of Power.

Hearty Singing — Good Times — Come Next Sunday.

We shall meet on the evening of Good Friday, April 21.

The Young People's Club will meet in the Town Hall on the evening of April 1[illegible]. Entertainment is being provided by our young men. Get in on it.

The church is worth while in Half-Day. You believe in it. Make the best of it by putting something into it. We get out of life what we put into it.

The pastor who presided over Union Church after it reopened was Benjamin John Trickey. He led the congregation there from 1914 until 1917, when he moved on to Albion, Nebraska. Reverend Trickey is shown above on this handout, which was designed with information intended to entice visitors to come to the church. The institution became an important part of life again in the community after its rebirth. The photograph below has Reverend Trickey standing next to the Sunday school class in front of the building. The congregation remained consistent, and the church got a reputation for being an excellent place for up-and-coming pastors to hone their skills. Consequently, there have been a large number of pastors who have made their way through Half Day before moving on to other congregations. (Both, courtesy of Washburn Church.)

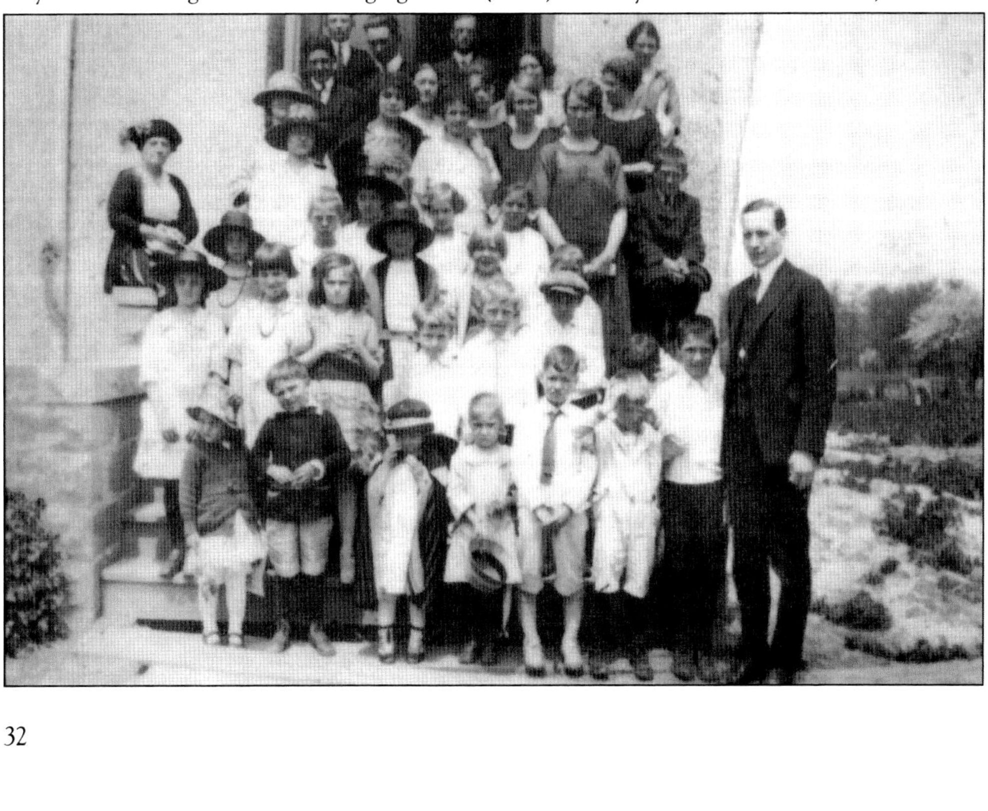

Washburn offered programs for all ages in the congregation. Children, such as these two members of the church pictured at the right, were enrolled in Sunday school. There was a Cradle Roll Program for newborns and different levels of Sunday school. Below is a certificate awarded to Evalyn Small, daughter of Bert and Eva Small of Half Day, on October 3, 1926. At age five, she successfully completed the Beginner's Department and was promoted to the Primary Department of the program. There were other religious and social programs available, such as the Young People's Christian League for young adults. (Both, courtesy of Washburn Church.)

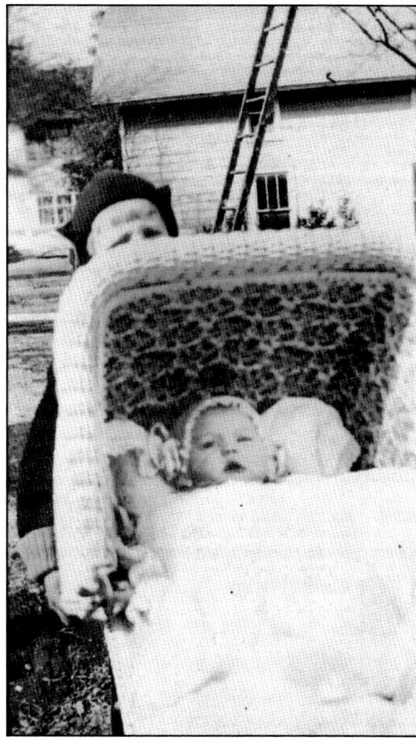

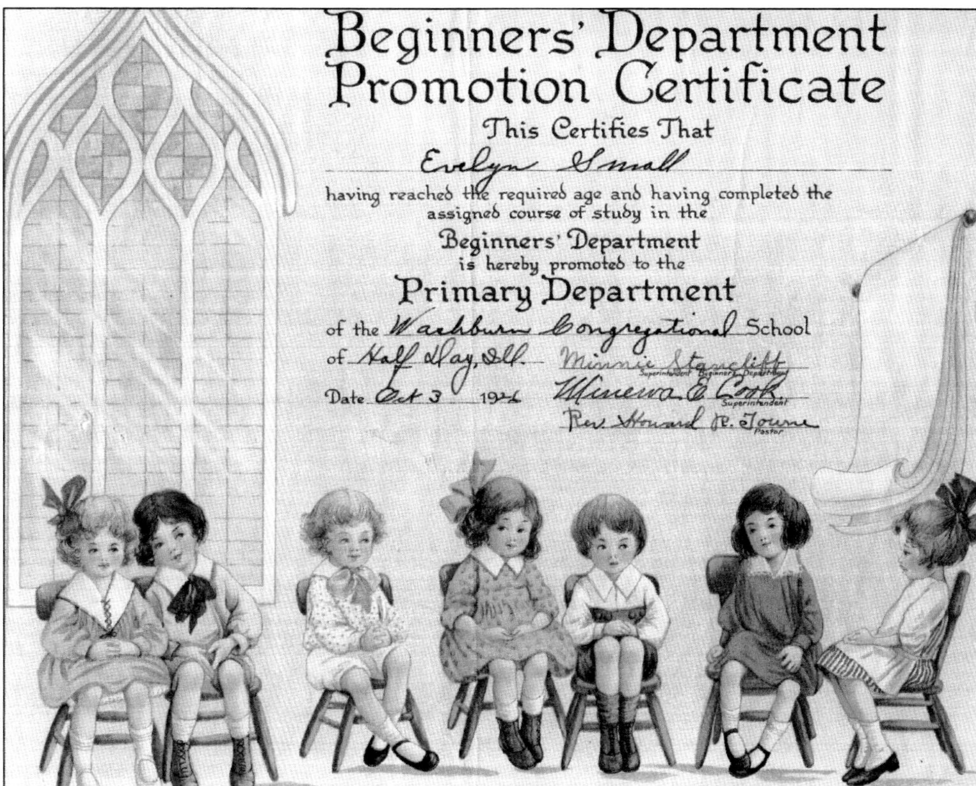

Beginners' Department Promotion Certificate

This Certifies That

Evelyn Small

having reached the required age and having completed the assigned course of study in the

Beginners' Department

is hereby promoted to the

Primary Department

of the Washburn Congregational School

of Half Day, Ill.

Minnie Stancliff
Superintendent Beginners' Department

Date Oct 3 1926

Minerva E. Cook
Superintendent

Rev. Howard R. Towne
Pastor

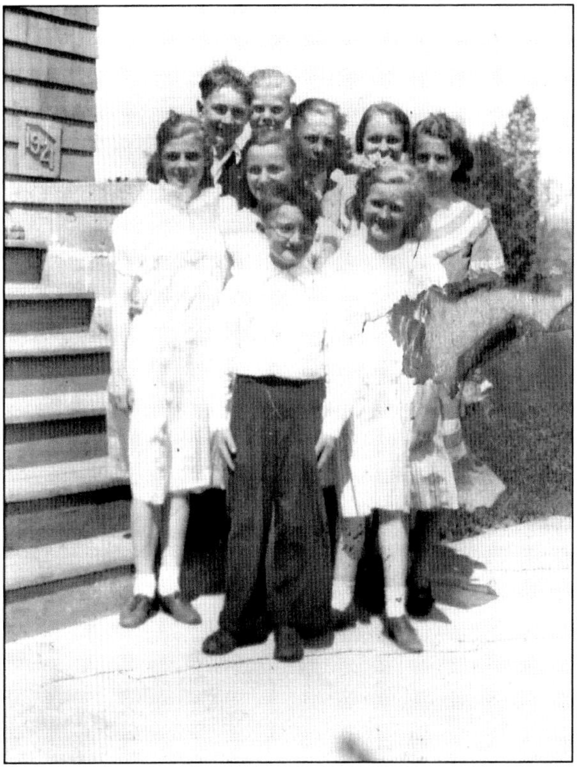

The children who attended Washburn Church found themselves involved in many different church-based activities. Sunday school was well attended, and there was even a junior choir that was directed by Pastor Davis. This photograph of the 1934 junior choir was taken on the front steps of the building and shows a balance between both boys and girls participating. (Courtesy of Washburn Church.)

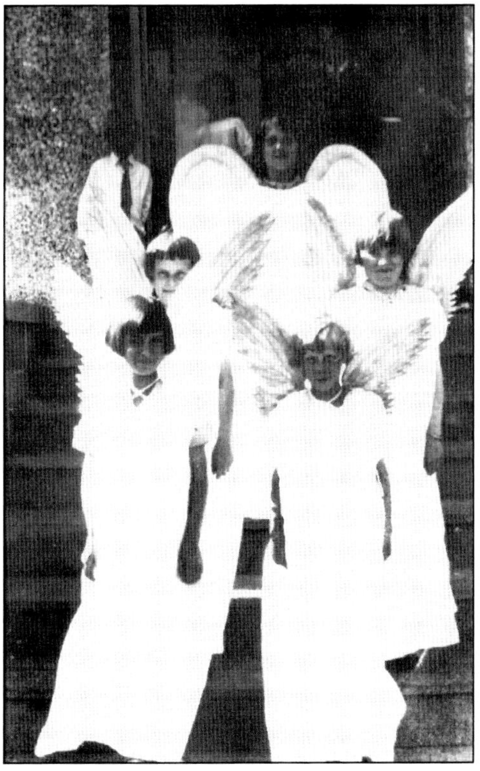

Many other activities took place at Washburn for children in the congregation. There were seasonal activities, such as Christmas pageants, but also year-round activities like the Boy Scouts and Girl Scouts. The church also had a special Children's Day Program. Children's Day predates Mother's and Father's Day and is an international celebration of the child. It is observed at different times of the year in different countries. (Courtesy of Washburn Church.)

Patriotic parade participants marched from Washburn Church to the Vernon Cemetery on May 30, 1923, to honor veterans during the annual Decorations Day ceremony. Decorations Day, the former name for Memorial Day, involved all members of the church. The day before the event, the children of the congregation would collect wildflowers from the fields off Elm Road and return them to the church basement, where they would be placed into tubs filled with ice water to keep them fresh. Over the course of that evening, the flowers were woven into decorative flower chains by the ladies of the congregation. A parade involving all members commenced the next day and culminated in a graveside service. The parade is pictured traveling northbound on Milwaukee Avenue past Hertel's Park, the popular dance hall and picnic grounds, on its way to the Vernon Cemetery.

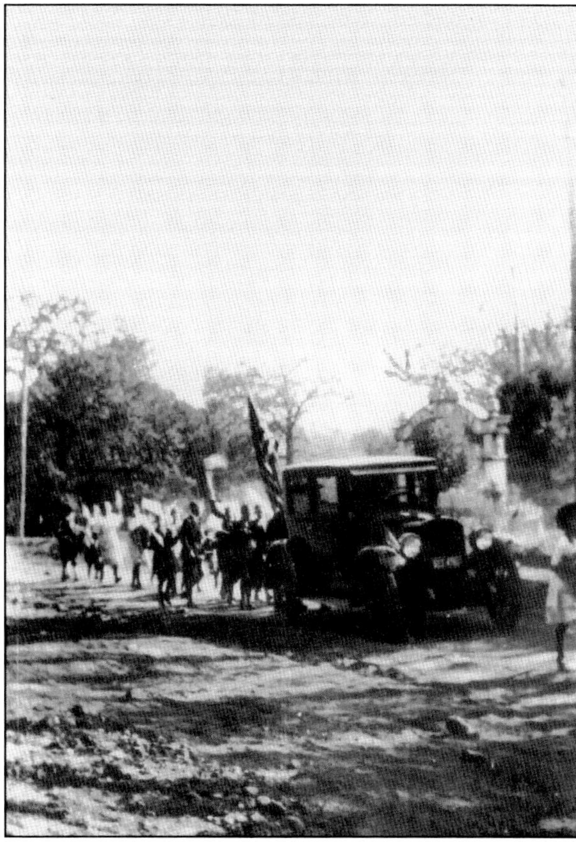

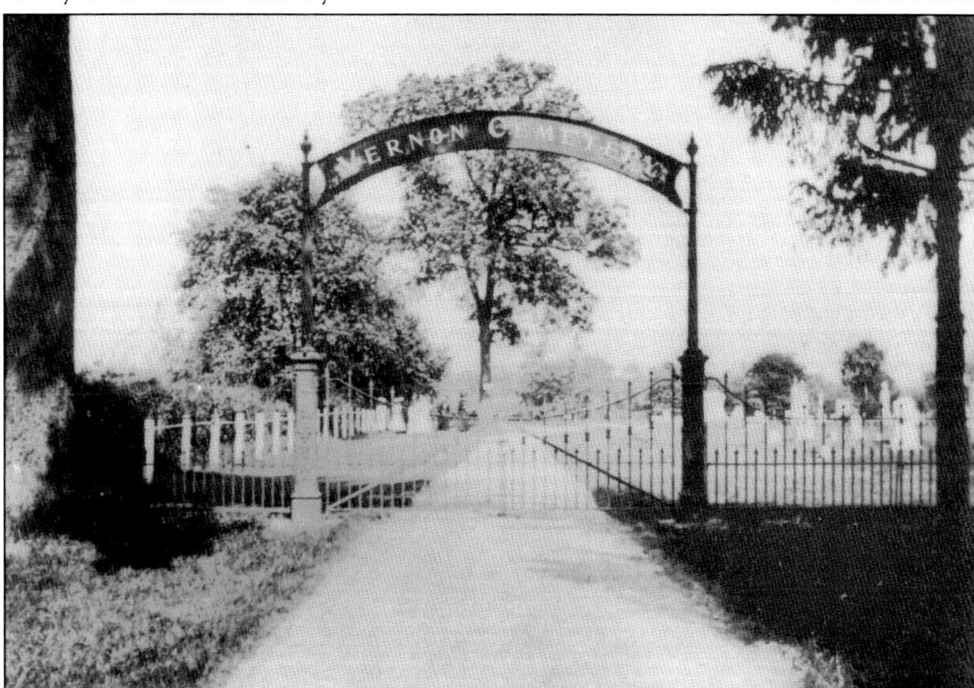

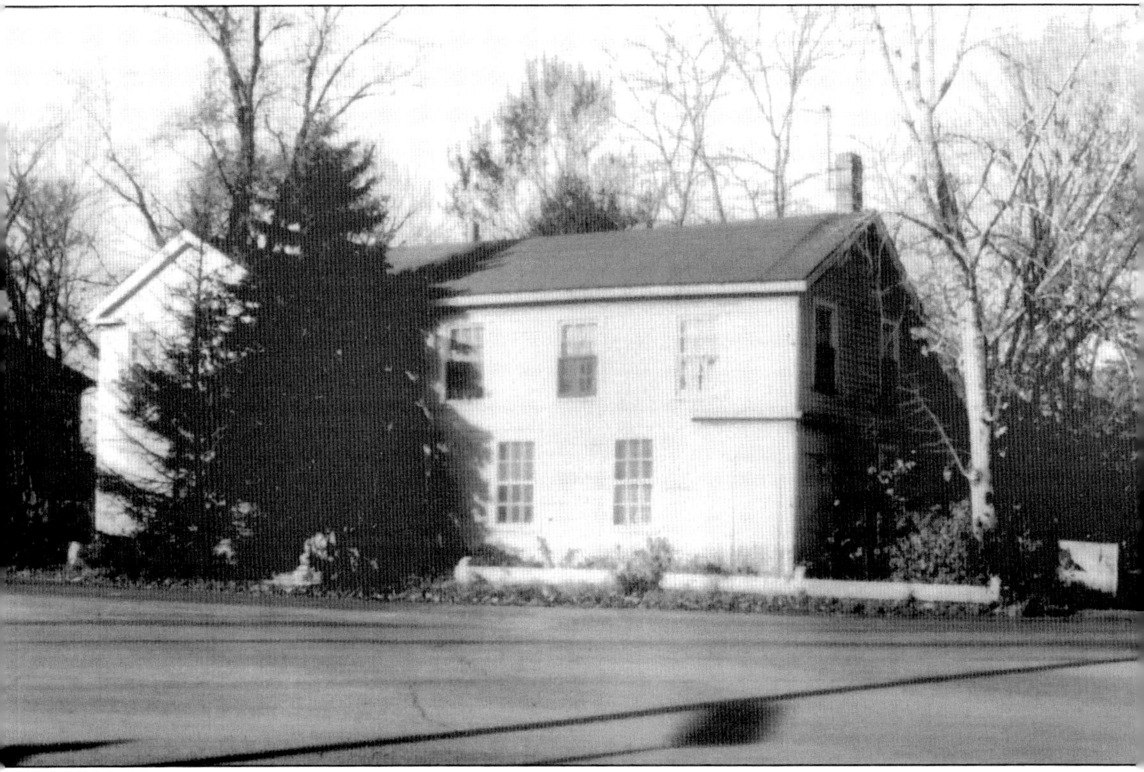

The Half Day Inn is a building that lives on in infamy, even today. The house pictured was the original Half Day Inn, which was built in 1843 by John F. Hertel one year before the original Half Day Town Hall and church. Its former location was on the northwest corner of the intersection of Milwaukee Avenue and Olde Half Day Road, which was Route 22 at that time. A bypass has since rerouted the road connecting it to close to the present site of the Lincolnshire Village Hall. The Half Day Inn served many purposes during its long existence. Originally built as a boardinghouse and tavern, it has also been a private home, general store, ballroom, restaurant, pharmacy, and housed the Half Day post office until 1904, when the postal facilities were moved to Prairie View to be closer to the train and the incoming mail. The original Half Day Inn burned to the ground in 1964.

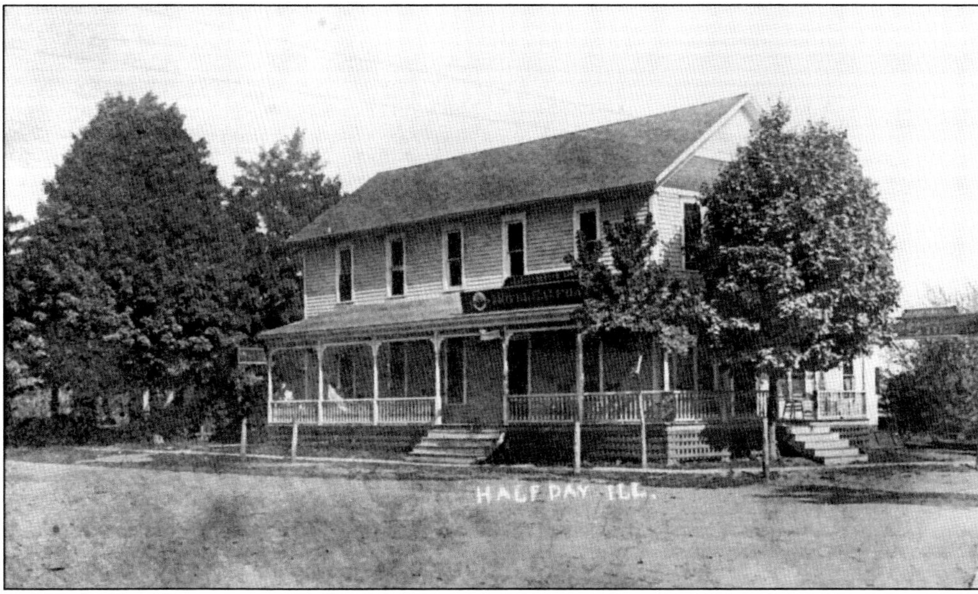

The building most people called the Half Day Inn was located on the northwest corner of Route 45 and Milwaukee Avenue, just one block away from the site of the original Half Day Inn. This building, demolished in 2007, has been known by many names and owned by many people. It was the Hotel Half Day, the Earle Mae Inn, the Half Day Tavern, and the Foote Brothers' Tavern before becoming known as the Half Day Inn. One thing stayed consistent: it was always a popular place where one could share a libation. Originally serving as a stage stop on the line between Chicago and Milwaukee, the building survived natural disasters including blizzards, floods, tornadoes in the surrounding vicinity, and several world wars, but could not overcome the push of progress in the area.

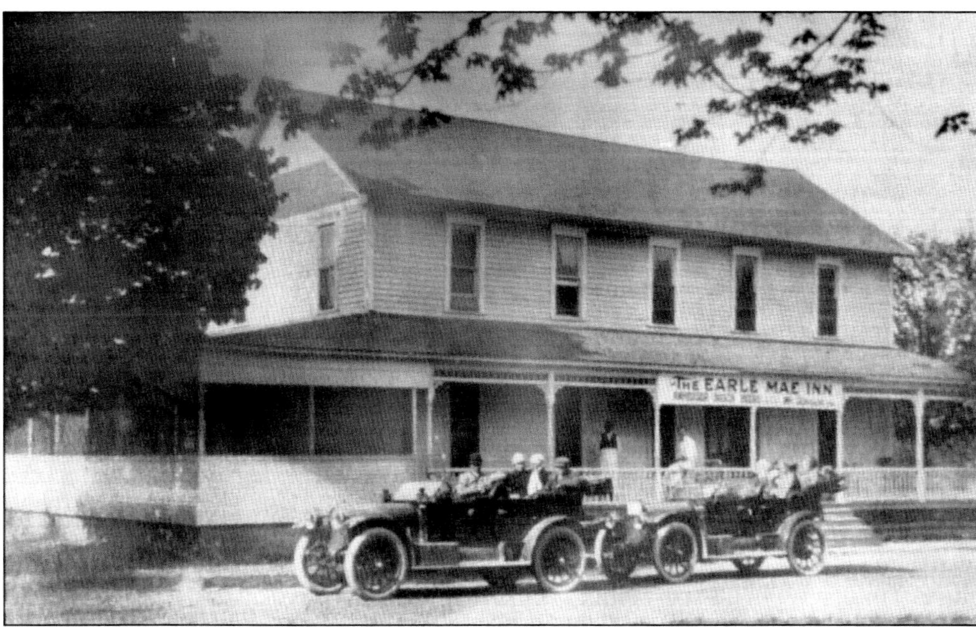

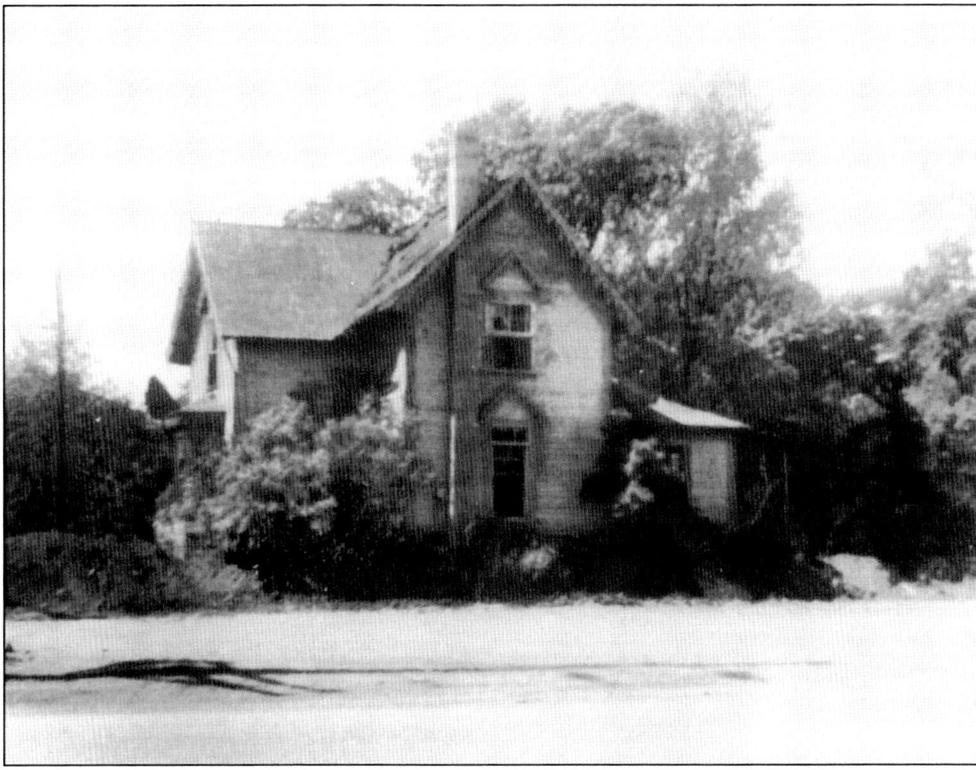

Hertel's Pavilion (below), built around 1898 in Half Day, was a dance hall popular with couples and families. The pavilion was located behind the present-day shopping center on the southwest corner of Route 45 and Milwaukee Avenue. It was a place where people came from miles around to hear orchestras from as far away as Chicago and to dance on a large 40-by-60-foot wooden dance floor. Additionally, cakewalks were big events held there, which were often advertised in local papers to attract crowds. The Hertel family lived in Half Day. The pavilion was burned to the ground in 1909 by an unknown assailant but was rebuilt and known as Hertel's Park. The business was eventually torn down sometime in the 1920s. The Hertel home is seen above in 1958. (Below, courtesy of Vernon Township.)

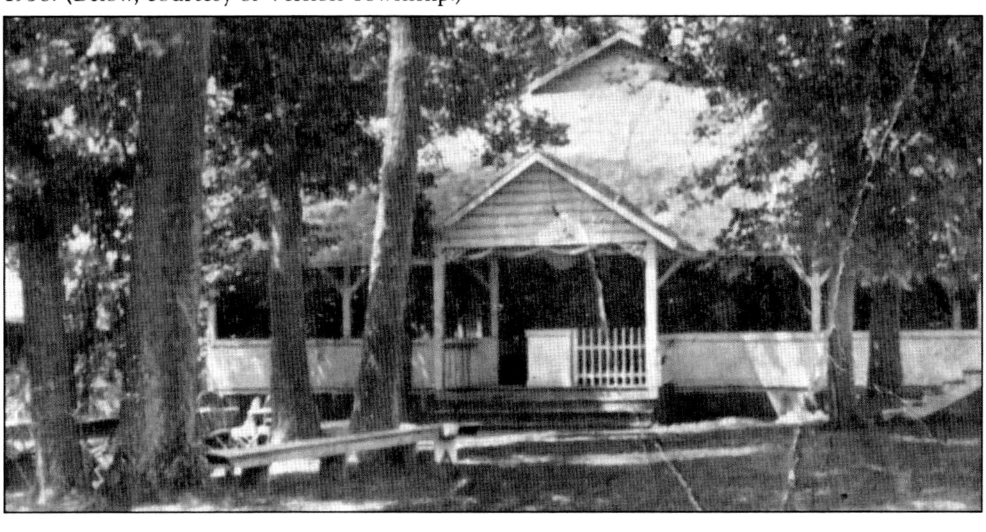

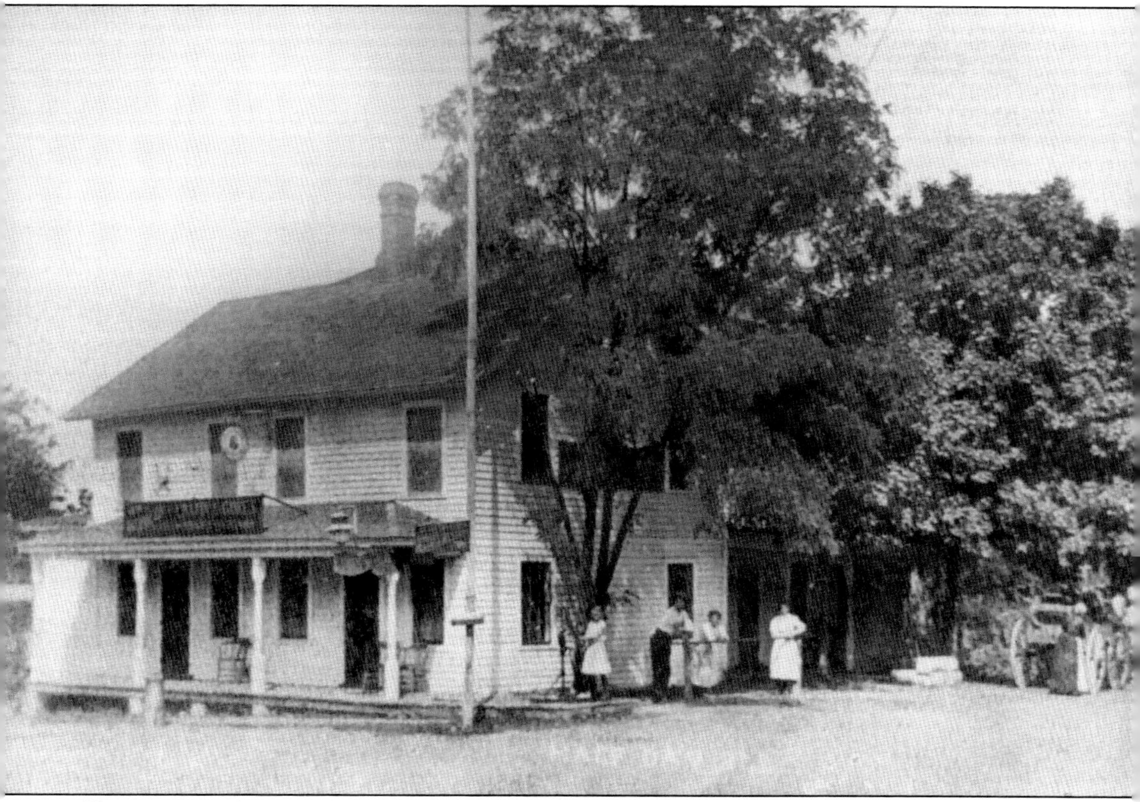

Half Day was a vibrant and bustling village for many years, and Milwaukee Avenue has always been a well-traveled thoroughfare. It began as a Native American trail and then evolved into a route for the stagecoach lines connecting Chicago with Milwaukee. In those early days of stage travel, people preferred to sit up front with the driver because the inside of the coach was always the roughest and could easily nauseate a person. The coaches would often bottom out on the unpaved, rut-filled roads and get stuck. Passengers were required to get out and help push the carriage out of the mud. Wagon wheels were also a problem and did not last long on the bumpy and uneven roads. Passengers were also expected to aid the driver when it came to changing them. The hotel pictured above is the William Schuler Hotel, located on the northeast corner of Route 45 and Milwaukee Avenue. Note the people leaning on the horse rail on the side of the building.

* Vernon Athletic Club*
Instructions to
Baseball Players on Team

1

All players on team must become a member of The Vernon Athletic Club by June 1st. of each year. Membership is Fifty Cents per year and no Dues. Membership in Club entitles you to all the rights of Voting power in Club. Regular meetings are held on the last Tuesday of each month and are held at Town Hall at Half Day, Ill.

2

Club's standing rule for years past and will continue. Players are not to use Profane Language on Field and during a game conduct yourself gentlemanly and when an argument arises over some decision show your opinion in a decent manner and if further discussion is needed have Team Manager argue it out. There never should occur a instant where one player is bawling another player out for a misplay, it is better to talk it over in a friendly manner after a game or some evening when practice is on.

3

All Uniforms are numbered on shirts sleeve,except one or two of a different material, Dont wash shirts on account of advertisement on same unless it is necessary and then only in cold water,as lettering will be damaged in hot water. At close of season or if player quits team before close of season all players must return their complete baseball uniform, except for natural wear to same, to me as it was given to you.

4

Some players have their personal bat, dont use it without given permission from owner,as Club will not be responsible for it,this applies to other personally owned baseball equipment.

5

There will be baseball practice on Tuesday and Thursday evenings of each week,except later on will have Twi-light games which will take place of regular practice. There will be games every Sunday & Holiday unless weather interferes. If you wish to be absent from practice or games notify Manager R. Gilman what nights you cannot practice and as to absent from games,leave him know at least a week ahead of time so he can arrange accordingly,dont just say I wont show up,that is the wrong attitude and not fair to Manager nor your fellow players.

6

I have given each player another sheet with SIGNALS ON IT, and some other instructions. Besure you MEMORIZE the Signals and WATCH for them during a game, because with a miscue on Signals it spoils plays which will be worked out and may loose games for us. If players slip too many times on Signals it will be a reason for taking points off of your batting average ETC.

7

We are members of the Illinois State Amateur League which cost CLUB $ 10.00 and of course Club expects a team they can be proud of at the end of season, so lets all get in there and give our best all the time and get the CHAMPIONSHIP of our BRACKET and then go further in the play offs at end of the season. Wide awake at all times speed and VERY BEST EFFORTS WILL BE OUR REWARD,So HUSTLE.

8

If you have any complaints or Construcative Information give it to Manager because we all are working for one end and that is the Bracket Championship.

Very truly

C. Gilman   Russell Gilman

The Vernon Athletic Club (VAC) was a group of young men who got together to participate in the state amateur baseball league, which competed against other communities. Some of the other communities they played were Libertyville and Lake Forest. The team was managed by Chester Gilman. The group was serious about the sport, and the team was very successful. They practiced twice a week during the entire season, and players were charged a membership fee of 50¢ to belong to the club. They had local businesses sponsor the team and wore the sponsor's names on the backs of their jerseys. The instructions that the 1938 team received reveal just how serious the game was taken. The team was quite successful and ended up with a winning record that year. The team continued until the beginning of World War II. (Courtesy of Vernon Township.)

The steal signs that players received reveal the earnestness of these young men, who held both games and practice in a field on the northeast corner of Route 45 and Milwaukee Avenue. The entire ball club had to verify they had received their uniforms and understood the rules that were to be followed. The other teams saw the VAC as a serious threat, and one team from Waukegan actually hired a pitcher to play them. The players on the Vernon Athletic Club were lifelong friends, many of whom went on to form the core group of volunteer firemen in Vernon Township. (Both, courtesy of Vernon Township.)

Vernon Athletic Club

We the undersigned baseball players on Vernon Athletic Club 1938 season Baseball Team(Hard Ball) have receipted for and received the baseball uniform complete,consisting of one shirt,one pair trouser,one pair of socks and one cap, same is for use while playing on V A C Baseball team and will be worn only during practice or a regulation game and promise to return same without any legal action necessary to C.M. Gilman, Business Manager of team when he is dismissed from team, quits team and at end of 1938 baseball season of V A C.

Uniform Number on Shirt and exceptions as to uniform not complete name on uniforms	Signature of V A C Baseball team Receipting for uniform for use only.
Two(Mellody Farm 2)	
Three(Tripp Lbr. Co:) 3	J. Wr[illegible]
Four (Vernon Garage) 4	Ben Mayfield
Five (Herschberger Implt) 5	Eugene [illegible]
Six (Chief Half Day)	
Seven (Dietz's Stables) 7	Art [illegible]
Eight (White House Tavern)	[illegible]
Nine (New Way Laundry)	
Twelve (State Bank Mundelein) 12	[illegible]
Thirteen (Bernard Chev. Co.) 13	Vernon [illegible]
Fourteen (Libertyville Dairy) 14	Eugene [illegible]
Fifteen (Emil Geest)	15 Russell Gilman
Sixteen (Grande Cleaners) 16	[illegible]
Seventeen (Berghoff Brewery) 17	[illegible]
Eighteen (H. Tatge)	Alfred Kruger
Old Uniform No Number)	[illegible]
Old Uniform No Number)	[illegible]

Note any Exceptions below

DO NOT LOOSE OR SHOW TO ## OTHERS

SIGNAL	WHEN GIVEN TO YOU & WHAT TO DO
(Legs crossed by Batter or Coach)	(Lay down a Bunt)
(Place hand in Trouser Pocket) Take this signal from Coach	(Steal the next Base) Batter watch this so as not to Foul the Ball and try to hinder Catcher from making a good throw.
(Folding of Arms either by Coach (or party giving the Signal.	(Cancelling of any Signal given to (you, as some times it is necessary (to change a Signal,watch close.
(Raise Right Hand to side of (head or Cap.	(Acknowledging every Signal given (to you so coach as well as players (know you have got the Signal.Do (this after every Signal you receive
(Coach will hold up right hand (with fingers spread apart.	(Pitcher to walk Batter purposely.
(Batter will rub End of his Bat.	Squeeze Play (Batter and runner must work (together on this otherwise it (is of no value. Batter will lay (down a Bunt & Runner will go to (next Base.

Pitcher, Catcher and Basemen will arrange their own Signals, such as Catcher gives Signal to Pitcher to throw to a base to catch a base runner, also First, Second & Third Basemen want pitcher to try to catch a runner off of base, or Catcher attempting to catch a runner. We will get together and arrange these simple plays & signals. Always run out every ball hit in fair territory as fielders may make an error and then it would be too late, even a fly ball near foul line may blow fair before it hits ground, further making a fielder hurry to get you on a base might cause his to error or fumble in his haste to field the ball. Each player should back up another player near you not watch to see if he gets the ball. Help each other,both infield and outfield. Dont wait for the other fellow to get the ball, if you feel you can get it Call for It (Loud) and then the other player is to back him up.

If any Suggestions in your minds lets have them and we will all talk them over together.

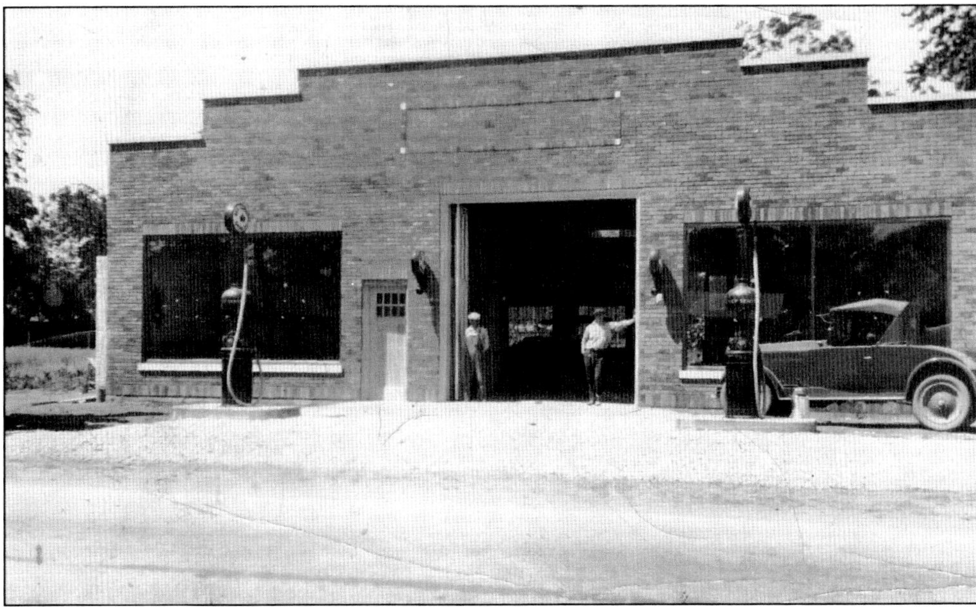

Half Day had several service stations on Milwaukee Avenue. The brick building pictured above was known as Holtje's Garage and located just south of the intersection of Milwaukee Avenue and Route 22. An attractive red crown painted on the glass globes of the gasoline pumps signified that this station carried the Red Crown brand, a subsidiary of the Standard Oil Company. Frank Holtje owned the garage and was a member of the volunteer fire protection district. He was the organization's first fire chief and the only one to have the keys to the garage. The district rented garage space to store its 1941 International Fire Truck, until a permanent firehouse was constructed across the street. The photograph below is the same station in its later years. (Above, courtesy of Vernon Township.)

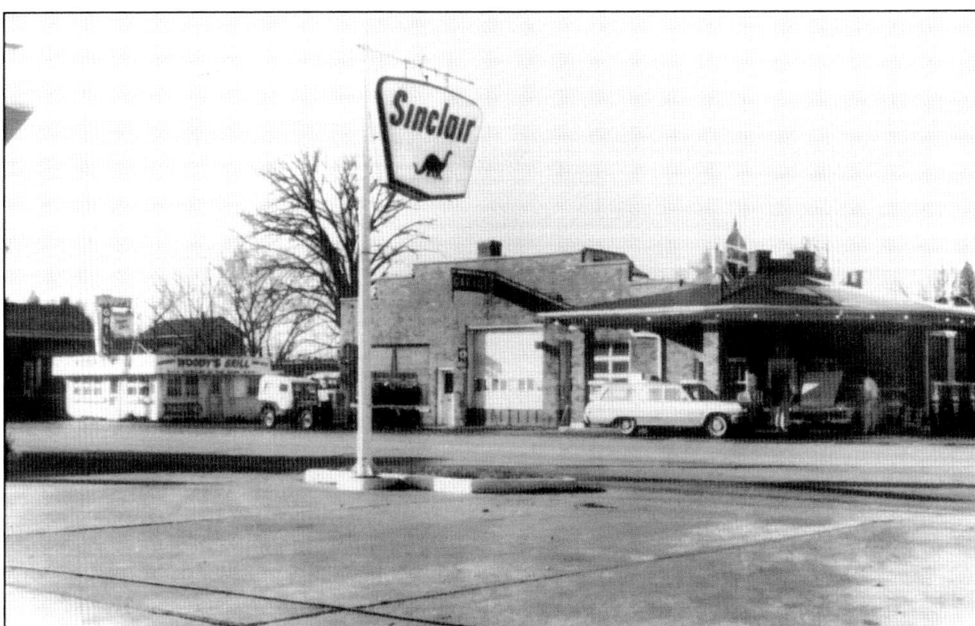

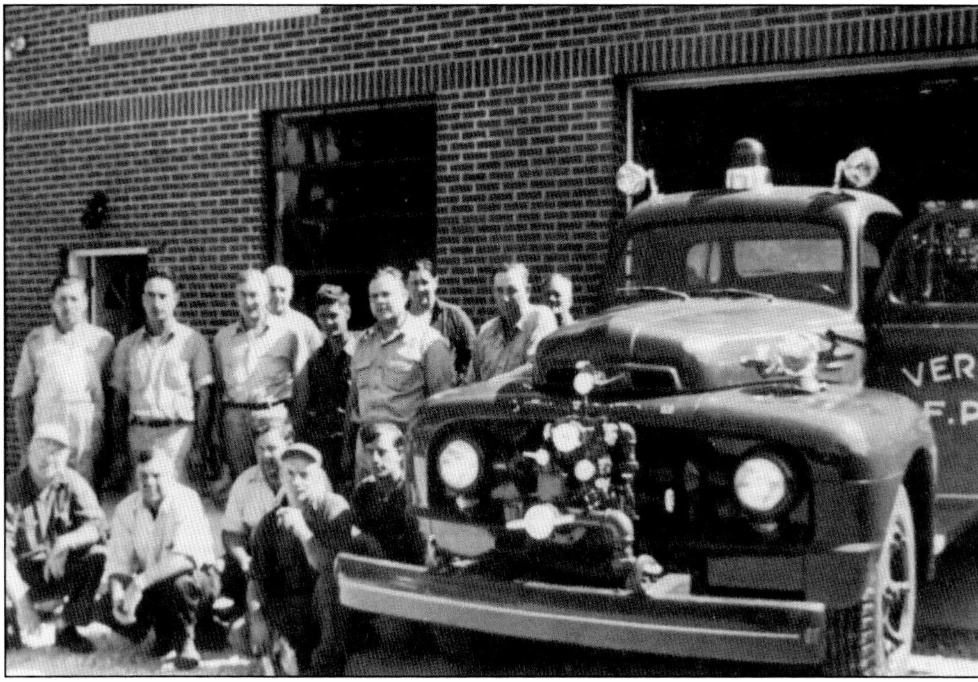

Vernon Township did not have a regular volunteer fire department until 1941. The brave men who volunteered did so at their own peril and cost, as they often sacrificed time and wages from their regular jobs when fighting a fire. Some members are pictured with their second truck, a 1953 Ford. From left to right are (first row) Frank Holtje, Gus Stoerp, Walter Gerbert, Fritz Farner, and Clarence Raasch; (second row) Art Schar, Harry Farner, George Stancliff, Fred Kruger, Stu Mattson, Russell Gilman, Alfred Kruger, Eunice Ladd, and Joe Wolf. In the beginning, the men had to live close to the firehouse in order to hear the fire bell and answer the call. Eventually, the department became official and a regular firehouse was built in 1951 on Milwaukee Avenue. (Below, courtesy of the Lincolnshire-Riverwoods Fire Protection District.)

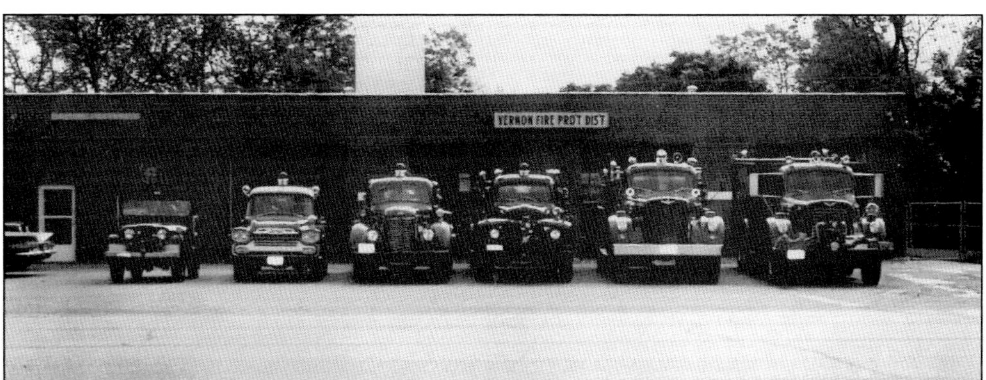

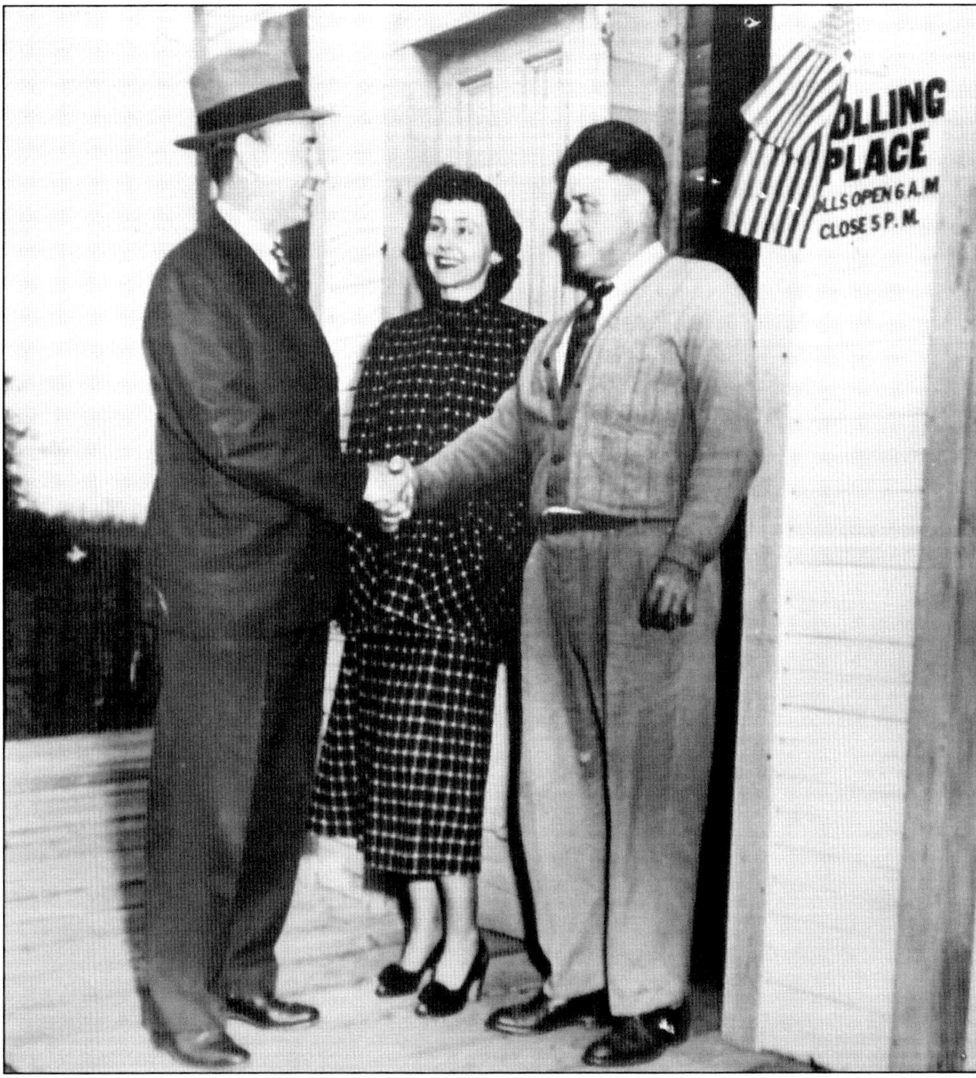

Adlai E. Stevenson II was a well-regarded statesman and politician who owned a farm in Vernon Township, having moved there in 1935. Stevenson came from a family with a long history of public service. His paternal grandfather, Adlai E. Stevenson, was vice president of the United States; his father, Lewis G. Stevenson, was Illinois Secretary of State; and his maternal grandfather, Jessie W. Fell, was Abraham Lincoln's campaign manager. Stevenson was governor of Illinois and ran for presidency in 1952 and 1956, losing to Gen. Dwight D. Eisenhower. He is pictured arriving at his polling place in the Half Day town hall to vote in 1952. Stevenson was a noteworthy intellectual and a gifted orator who was appointed US ambassador to the United Nations by Pres. John Kennedy. Stevenson considered the farm in Vernon Township to be his family home, until his sudden death in 1965. (Courtesy of Adlai E. Stevenson High School.)

Two

Prairie View and the Railroad

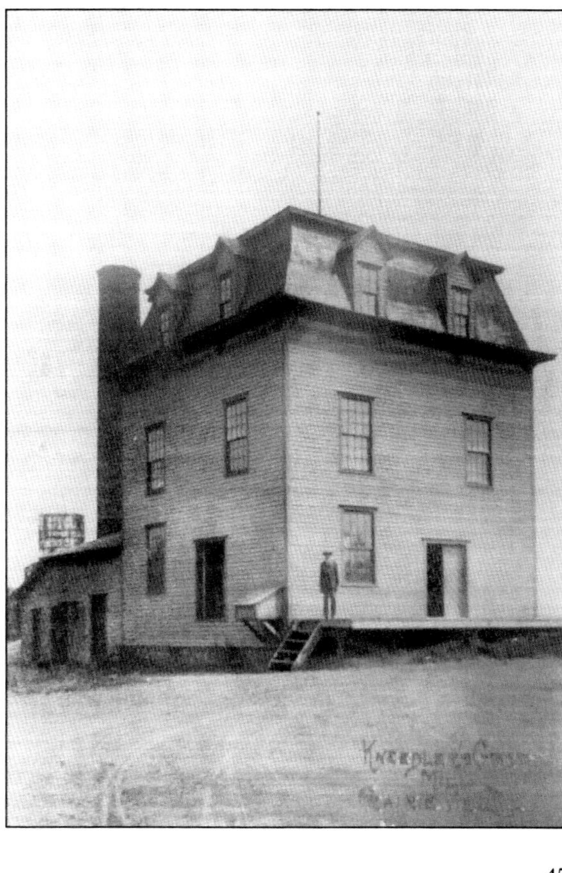

Prairie View is a town that grew up around the railroad. It got its name from John Gridley's wife, Lillie. It had many buildings, including a train depot, general store, blacksmith's shop, saloon, and pool hall, but none as iconic as Knedler's gristmill. The mill was a three-story building with an enormous brick chimney. The mill became synonymous with the town and a vital part of the community.

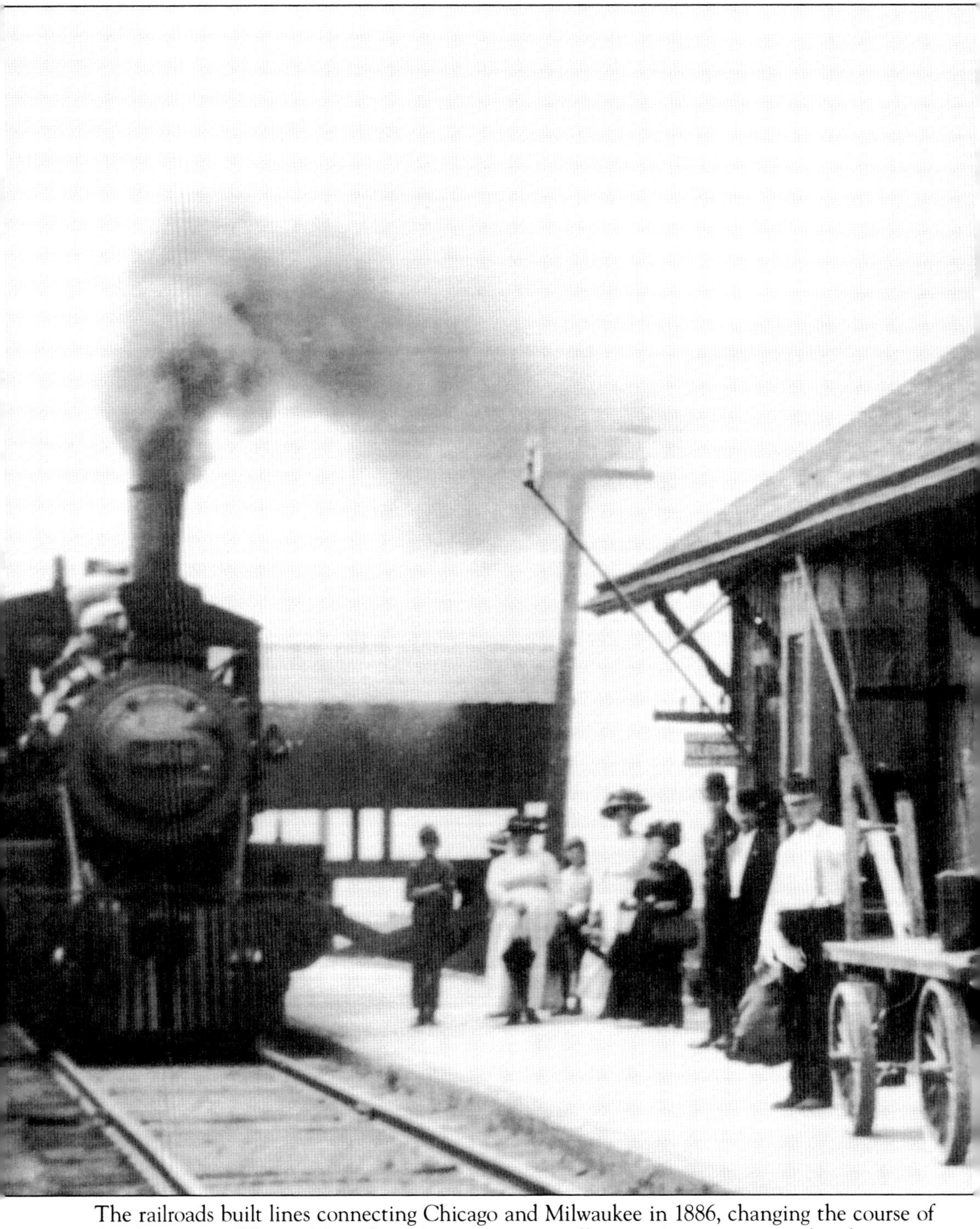

The railroads built lines connecting Chicago and Milwaukee in 1886, changing the course of development in Vernon Township. Towns sprang up all across America near railroad stations, and Prairie View was no exception. The Wisconsin Central Depot was a hub of activity, with trains carrying both freight and passengers. The rail lines quickly started supplying everything that came into town, such as clothing, dry goods, milk, produce, newspapers, and visitors. Prairie

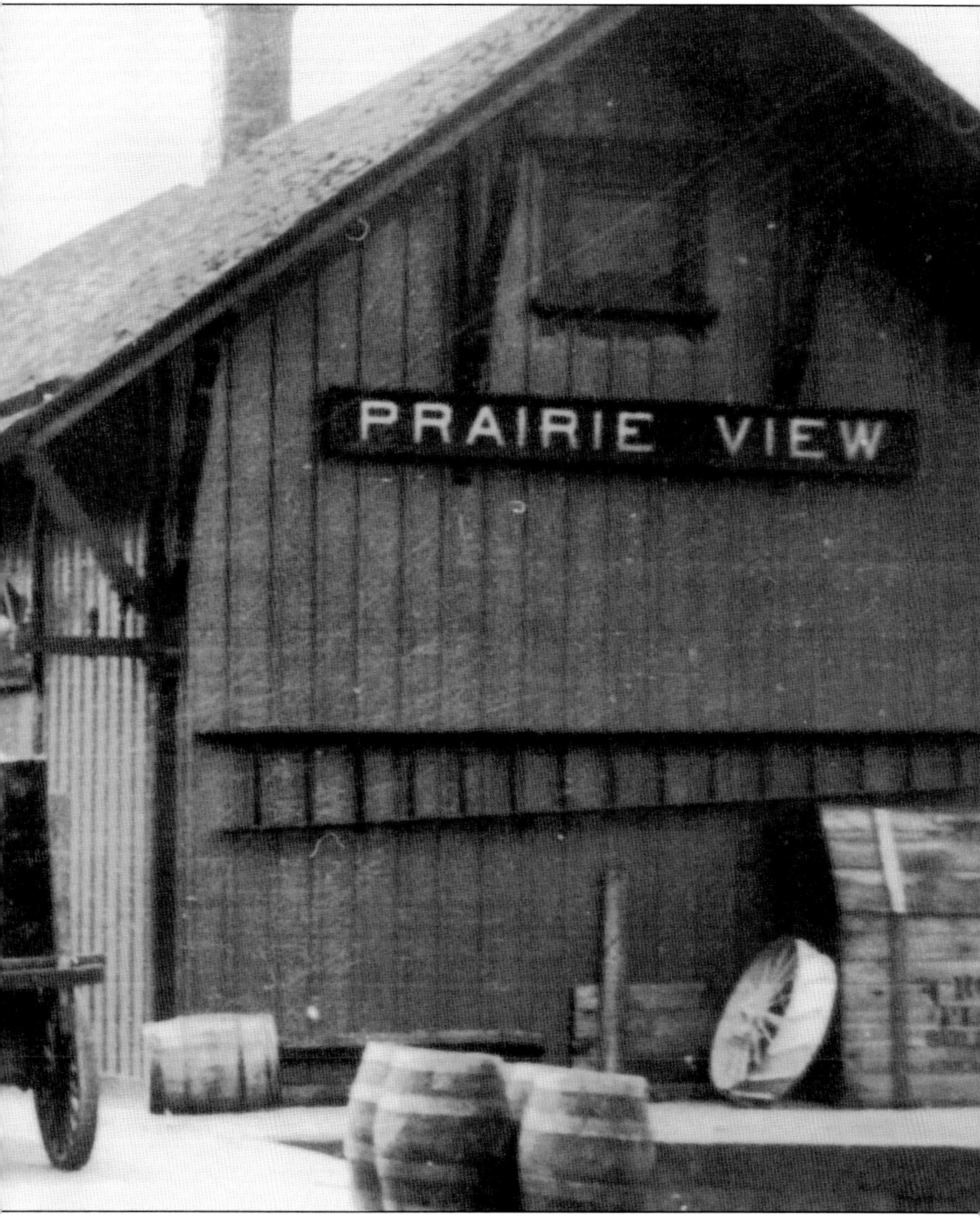

View quickly became an important point for farmers shipping and receiving their goods, and the depot became the area's nerve center. In 1892, train travel was so prevalent that the town had three northbound and four southbound trains stopping there daily, and another three express trains that traveled right through the station. The Golden Age of rail had begun and would last until the mid-20th century.

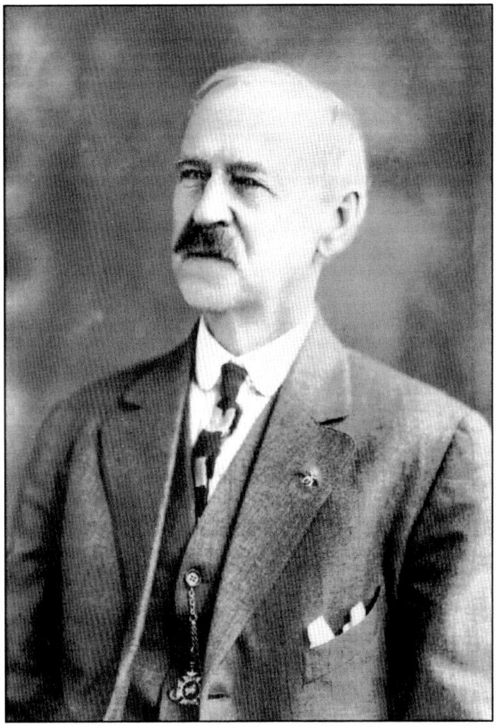

The Vernon Township supervisor position has been around since the township was created. There are 18 different townships in Lake County and hundreds of others all around Illinois. Many different men have held the office of township supervisor over the years while also holding a variety of different occupations at the same time. Some have been farmers, store owners, businessmen, or politicians, but all have had one common trait—they desire to serve their fellow citizens. Judson Mason is pictured at left and served from 1898 until 1904. C.A. Sauer, pictured below with his wife, also served as supervisor from 1877 until 1880. (Both, courtesy of Vernon Township.)

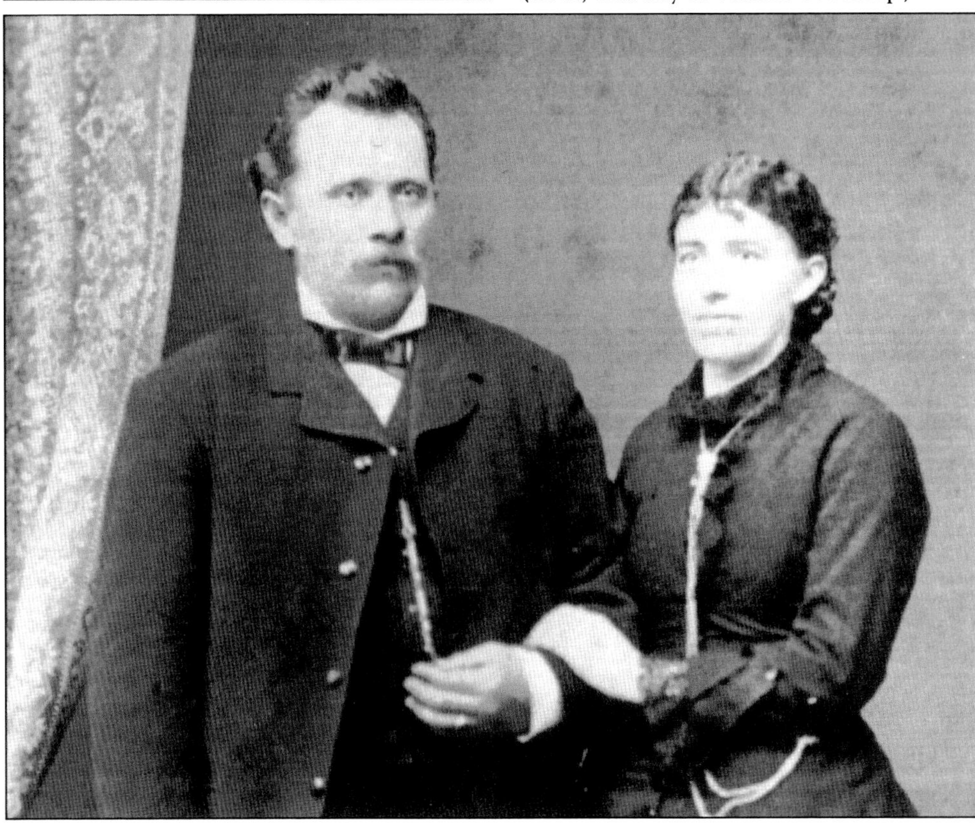

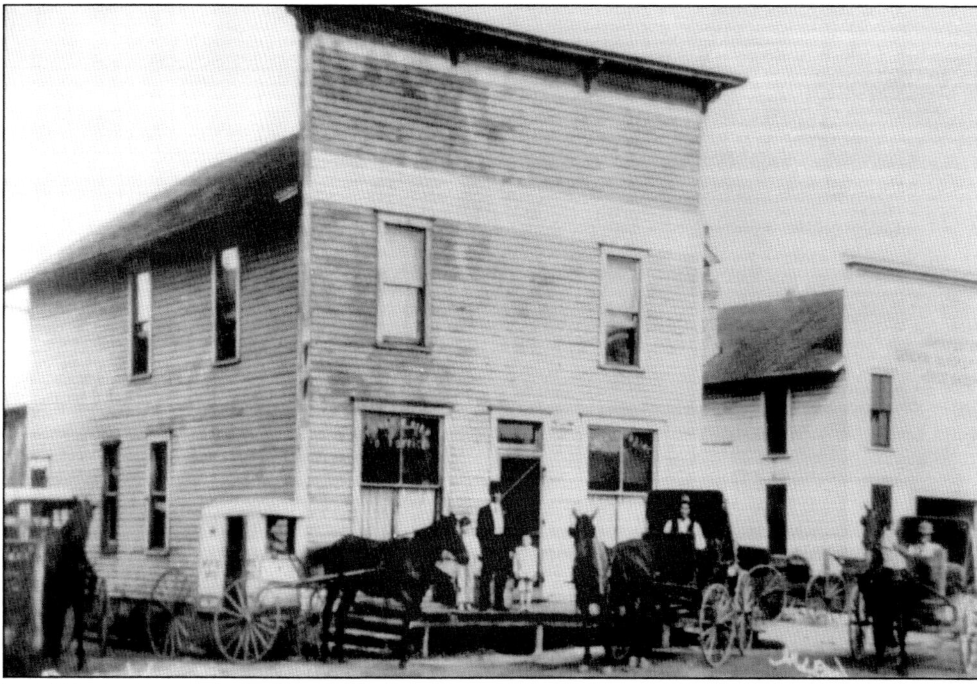

In 1903, the Prairie View Post Office was located on Main Street. The white carriage in front of the building displays "R.F.D. No. 2" on the side, which stands for "Rural Free Delivery." The postmaster at the time was John Seely Gridley, who served from 1889 until 1905. The building to the right is the blacksmith's shop. Both buildings were destroyed years later in the fire of 1920.

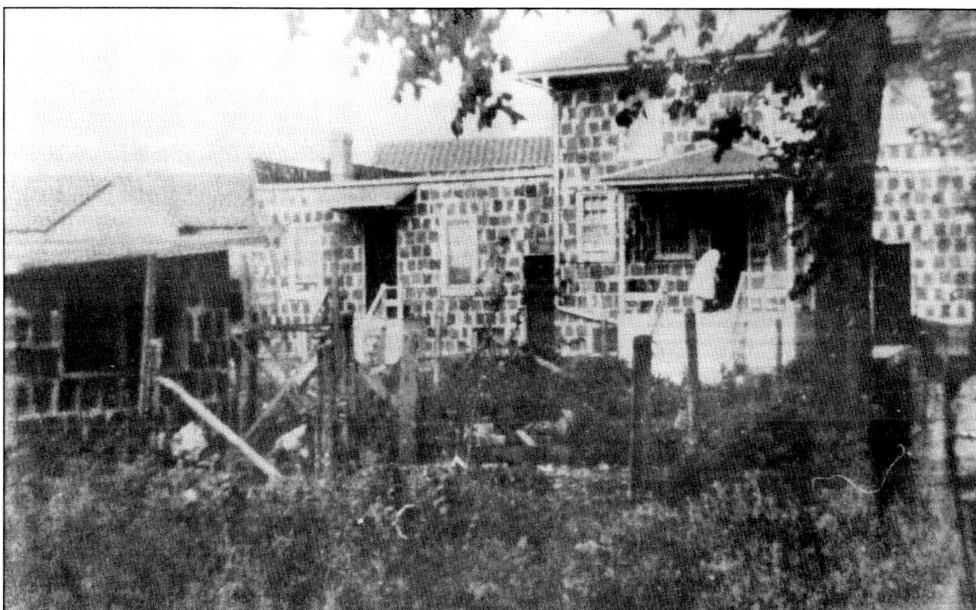

Ferd Priess and his family owned and operated a hotel and tavern on Main Street. The devastating fire of 1920, which almost destroyed the entire town, was thought to have begun in the combustible sawdust used in an icehouse that was located behind the establishment. The building was a total loss but was rebuilt and is now where the Prairie House Restaurant is located.

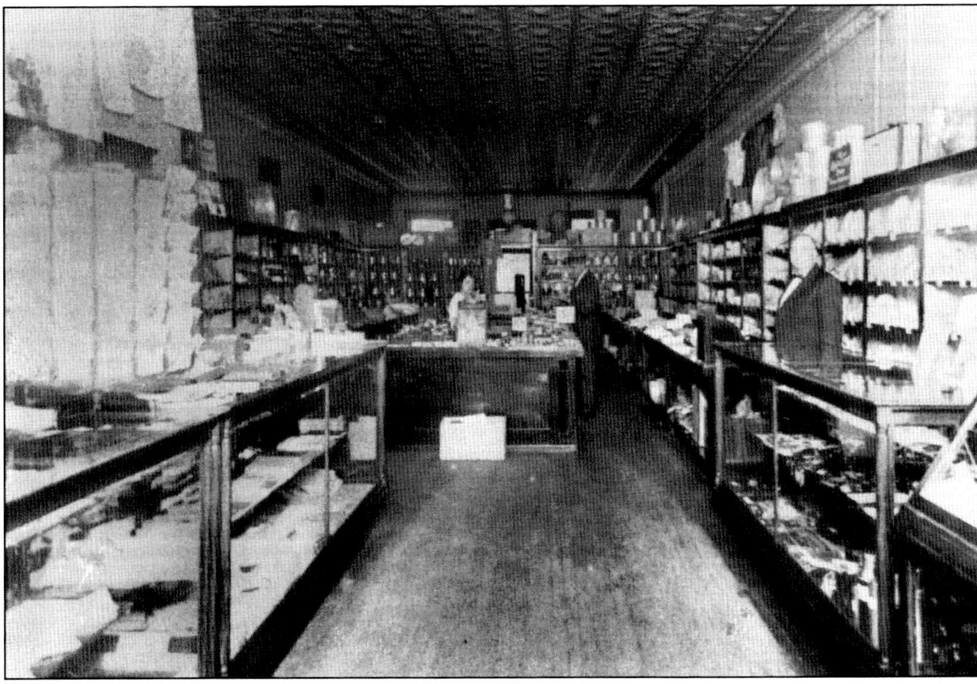

The Sauer brothers of Long Grove built the general store that was in Prairie View. The brothers, along with another partner, also built a successful store in Long Grove. The Prairie View store was eventually sold to one of their clerks, Alfred George Maether, in 1889. W.V. Sauer can be seen on the right of this photograph.

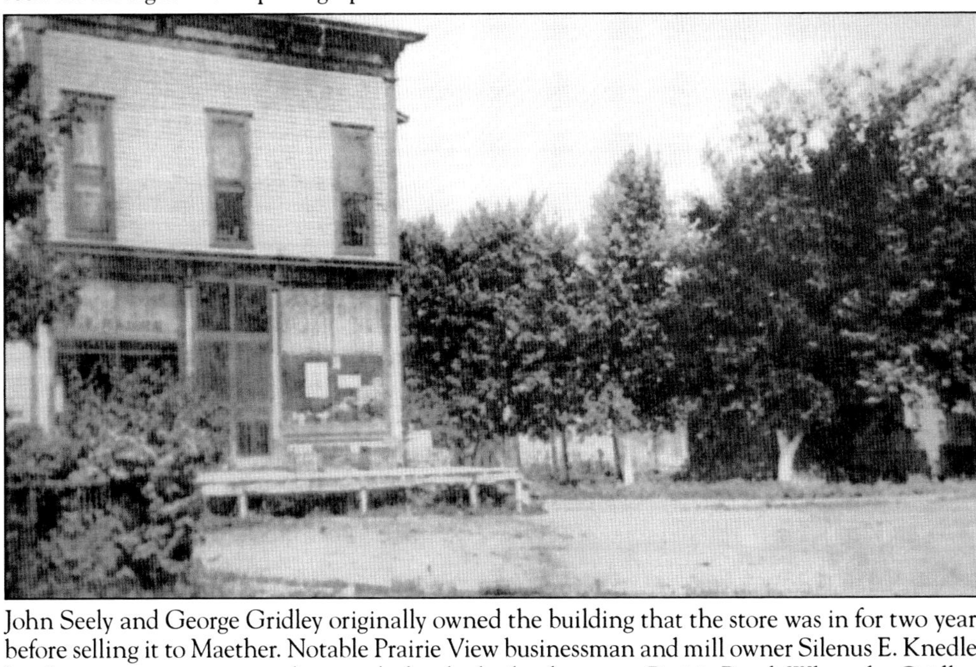

John Seely and George Gridley originally owned the building that the store was in for two years before selling it to Maether. Notable Prairie View businessman and mill owner Silenus E. Knedler lived in an apartment over the store before he built a home on Prairie Road. When the Gridleys were owners, the Knedler home was located on the east side of the tracks. The store is seen here in 1906.

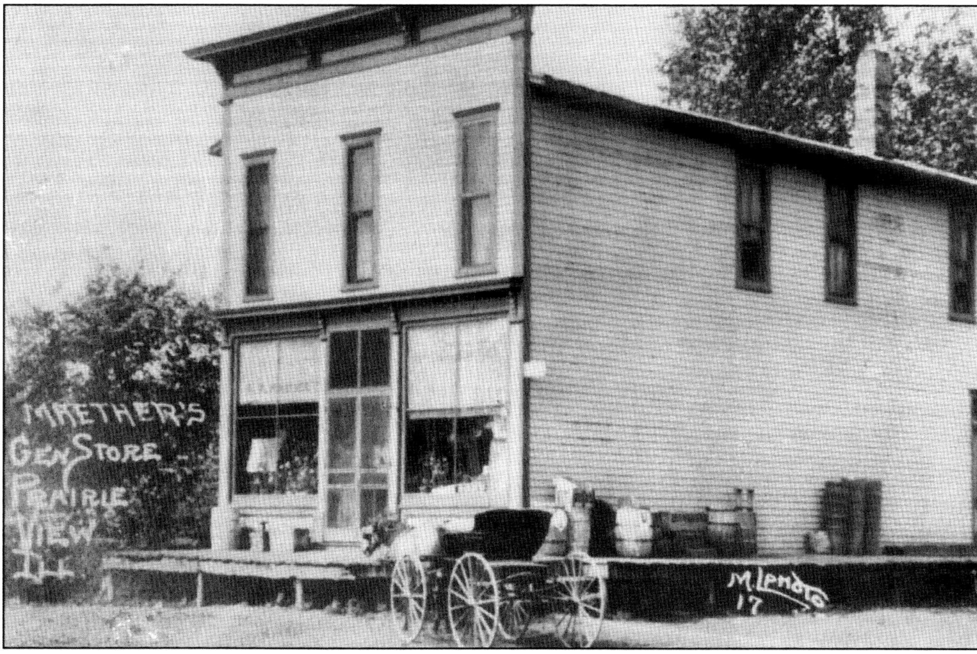

Maether's Prairie View General Store, located on Main Street, was a mainstay in the community for over 60 years, with Alfred G. Maether acting as proprietor for 50 years. The store remained in the family afterward with Florence Maether Stoerp and her husband, Frank, running it for the next 10 years. Florence Stoerp also served as postmaster of Prairie View from 1933 until 1940.

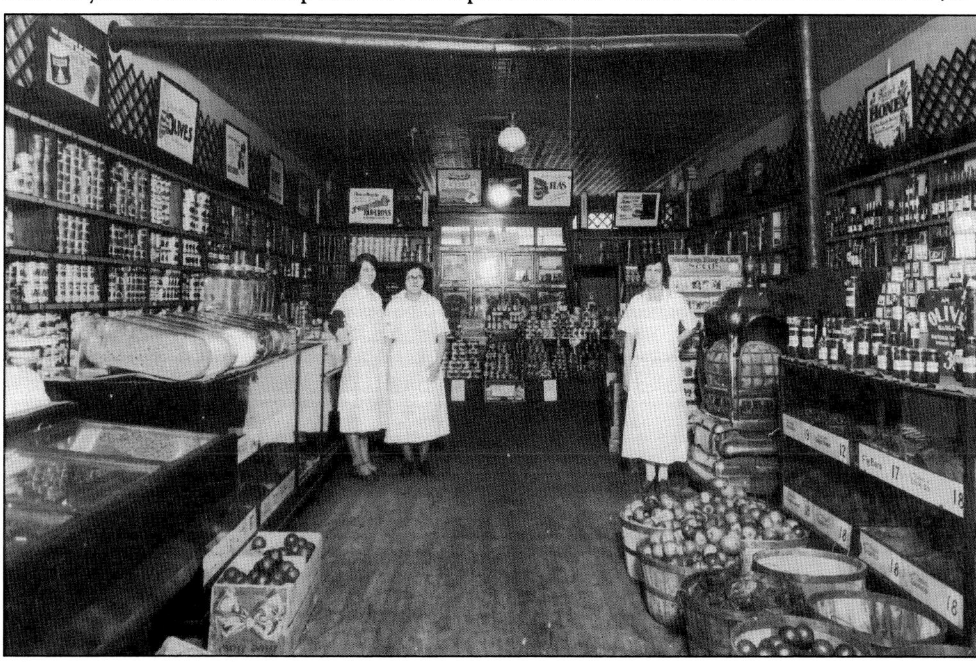

The store was a typical general store of the day and housed everything under the sun, including produce, dairy, baked goods, hardware, nails, and building supplies, as well as clothing and furnishings for the home. Small stores like this one provided all the essentials of everyday life before the days of supermarkets and shopping malls. (Courtesy of Vernon Township.)

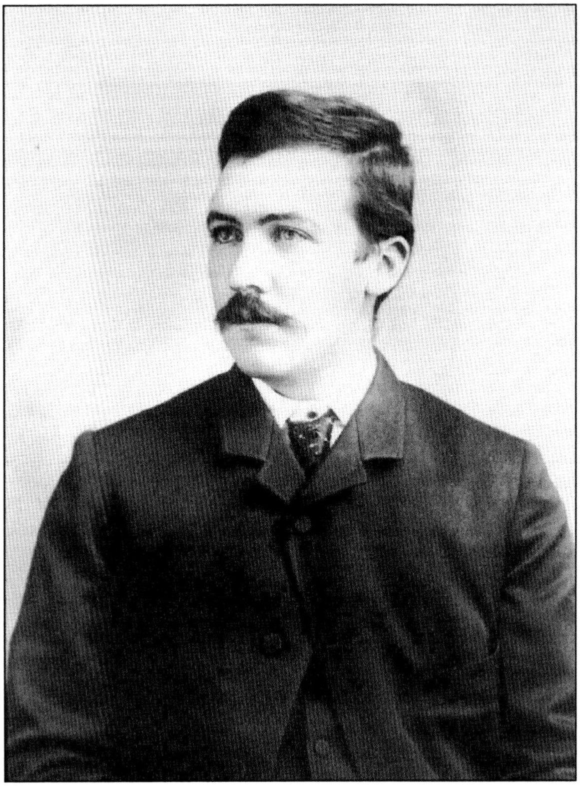

Alfred G. Maether was a very civic-minded individual. As a successful business owner, he got involved in local politics and became Vernon township supervisor from 1918 until 1926. After that time, he ran for county wide political office but was unsuccessful. (Courtesy of Vernon Township.)

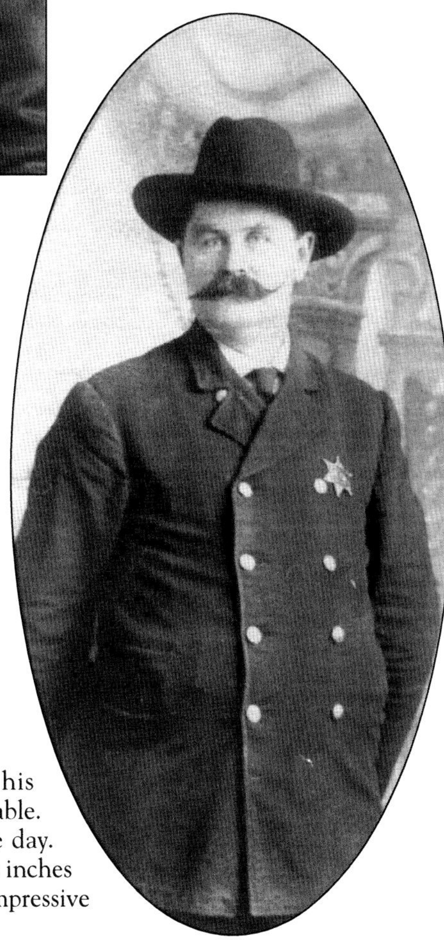

Maether had a wide variety of occupations in his lifetime, and here he is pictured dressed as a constable. Constables acted as the law enforcement of the day. Maether was a large man, standing six feet and four inches and weighing well over 200 pounds. He cut an impressive figure in his uniform.

Alfred G. Maether married Suzanna Sophia Hans of Quentin Corners, Illinois, in 1891. Suzanna's father was a cousin to John Hans, one of the original owners of the Sauer Brothers and Hans Store located in Long Grove, the site of Maether's genesis in retail. The Maethers had three children, Lloyd, Percy, and Florence, who they raised in Prairie View while they were living in an apartment above the store.

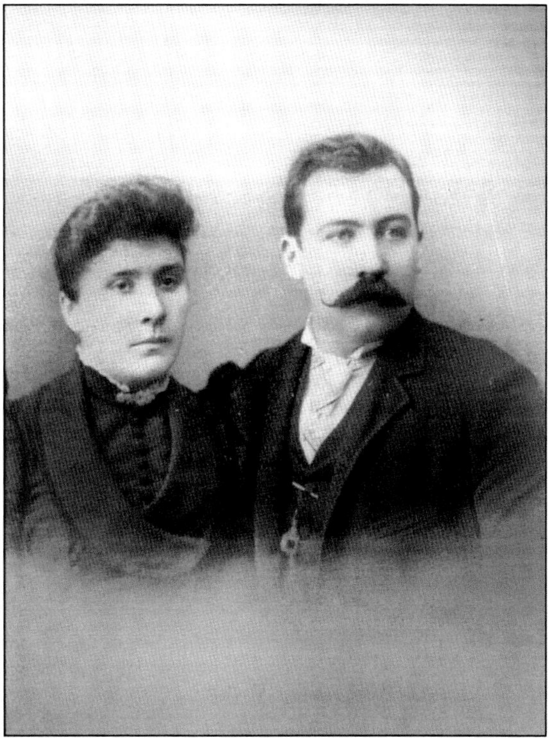

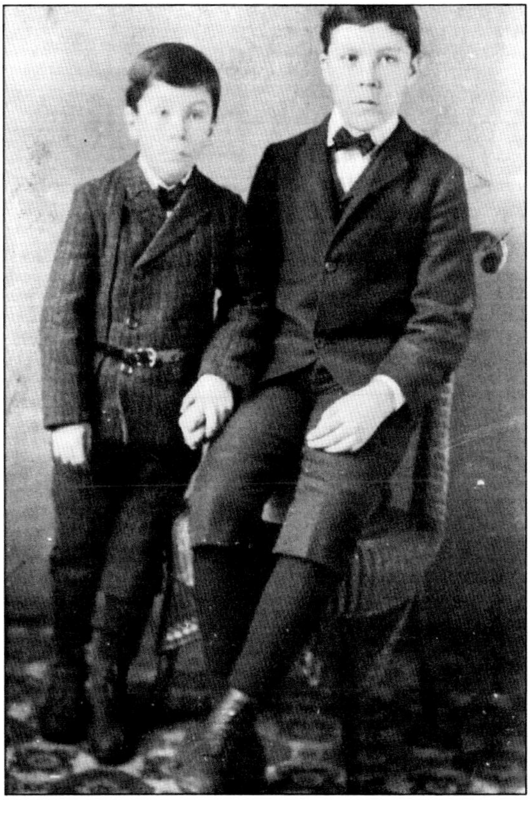

Percy (left) and Lloyd Maether (right) attended Half Day School as children. They traveled the one and a half miles to and from school each day. Percy remained a bachelor his entire life. Neither son went into the family business. Percy worked for Geest Lumber in Prairie View and nearby Aptakisic and for a time also on the Soo Line Railroad.

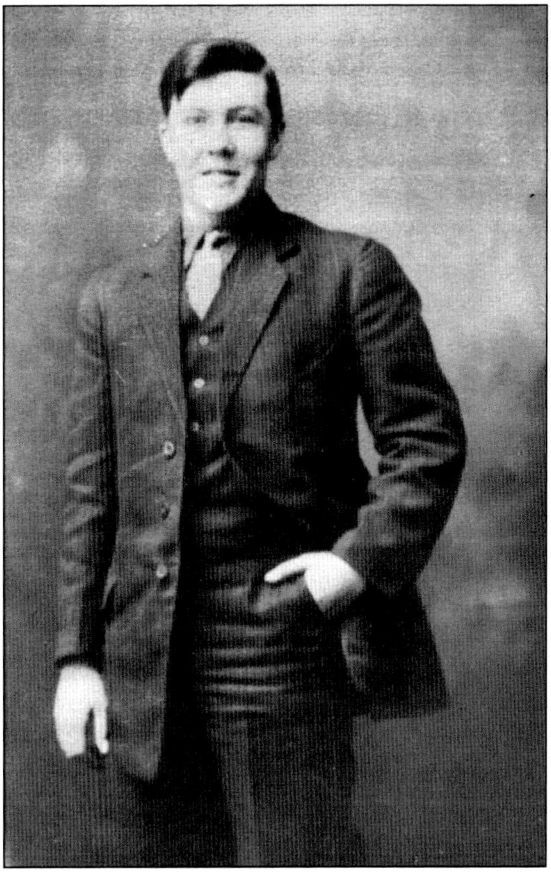

Lloyd L. Maether attended the Waukegan Business College on Washington Street in downtown Waukegan, Illinois. He graduated from the school in 1910. This photograph was taken at the time of his commencement when Lloyd was 17 years old. Ninety-six students were in the class of 1910. A young man by the name of Benny Kubelsky was among those in Lloyd's class. Kubelsky did not graduate from the school, instead opting to drop out and pursue a career in show business. He would later change his name to Jack Benny and go on to become a world-famous radio and television personality.

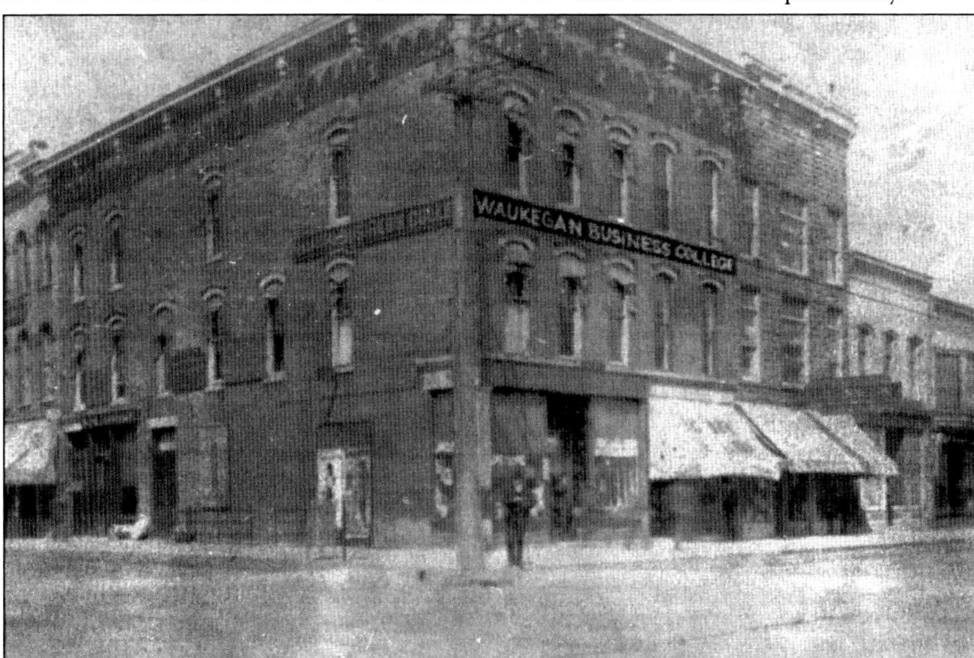

Lloyd Maether became engaged to Ruby Moline of Chicago in 1916. They were married three years later in Chicago, Illinois. The union produced two sons, Milton and Dwayne. The Maethers lived in a home in the family subdivision located behind the Prairie View General Store. Ruby Maether went on to become a long-time columnist for the *Independent Register* newspaper years later.

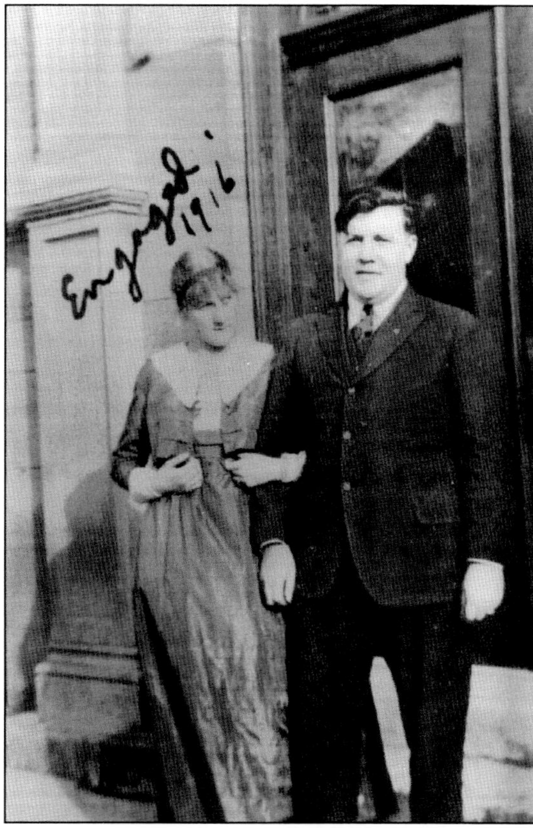

There was a well-known milk route along the Soo Line tracks that was an important source of income for local farmers for many years. In this photograph, Lloyd and Ruby Maether ride alongside milk cans being transported. The importance of the rail line to businesses in both large cities and rural towns cannot be overstated.

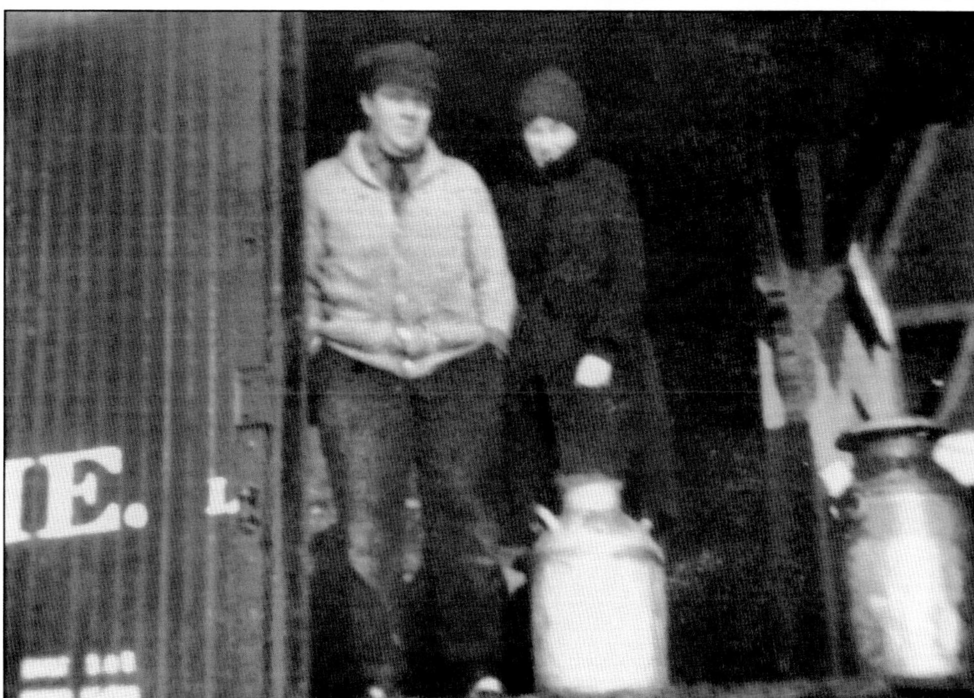

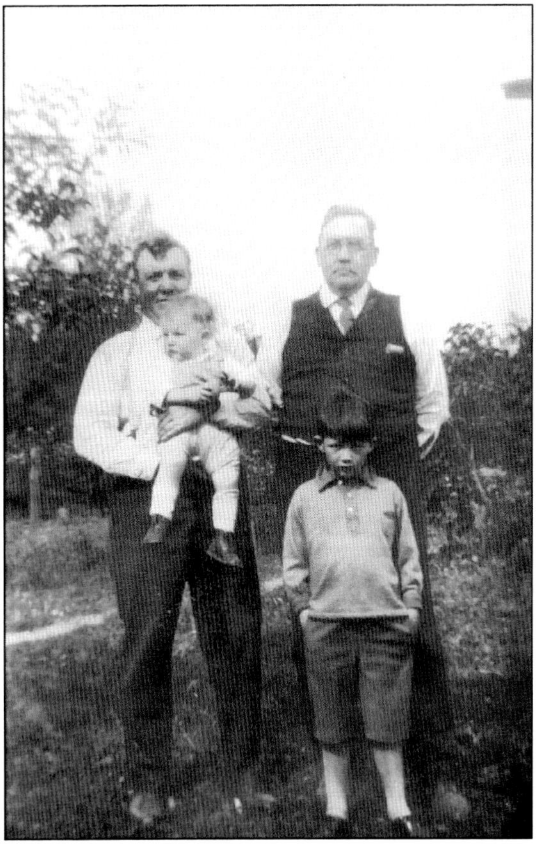

Three generations of men from the Maether family gathered for a family photograph in 1927. Lloyd Maether is holding his youngest son, Dwayne, age two, while his father, Alfred, stands behind his older grandson Milton, age seven. Alfred was born on the family homestead in Long Grove, while all others hail from Prairie View.

Alfred G. Maether relaxes at home surrounded by turkeys. In 1917, he purchased the land from the store to the next road west from E.E. Easton. Maether created a subdivision from his property where his heirs, among others, resided. The land was originally a 10-acre rectangular plot. The property contained a variety of trees, including fruit trees, from which the family grew their own produce.

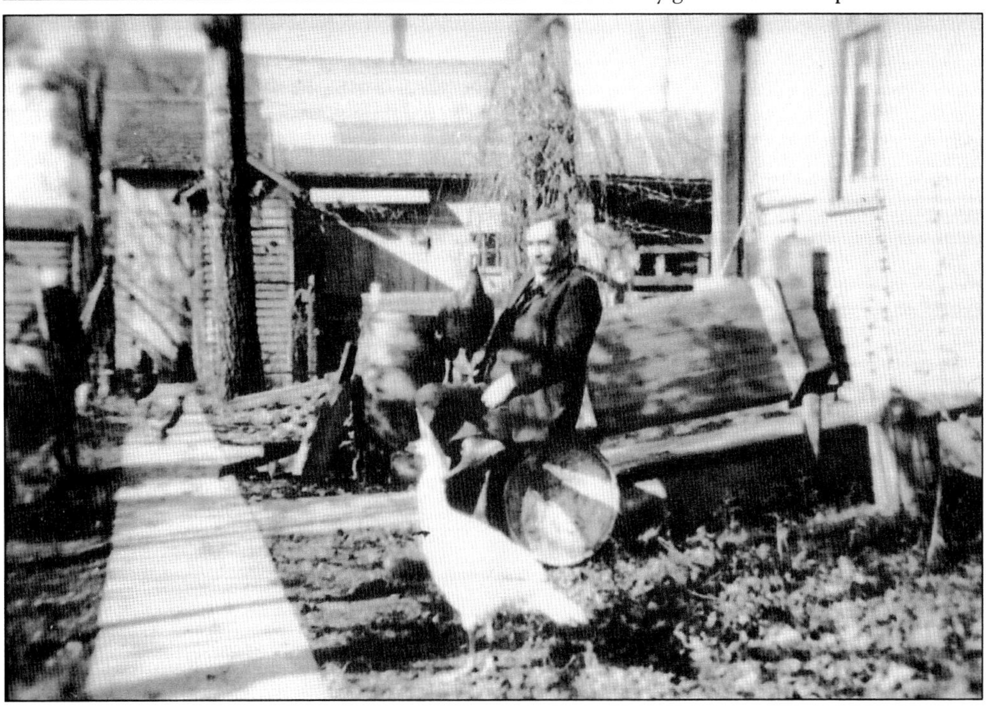

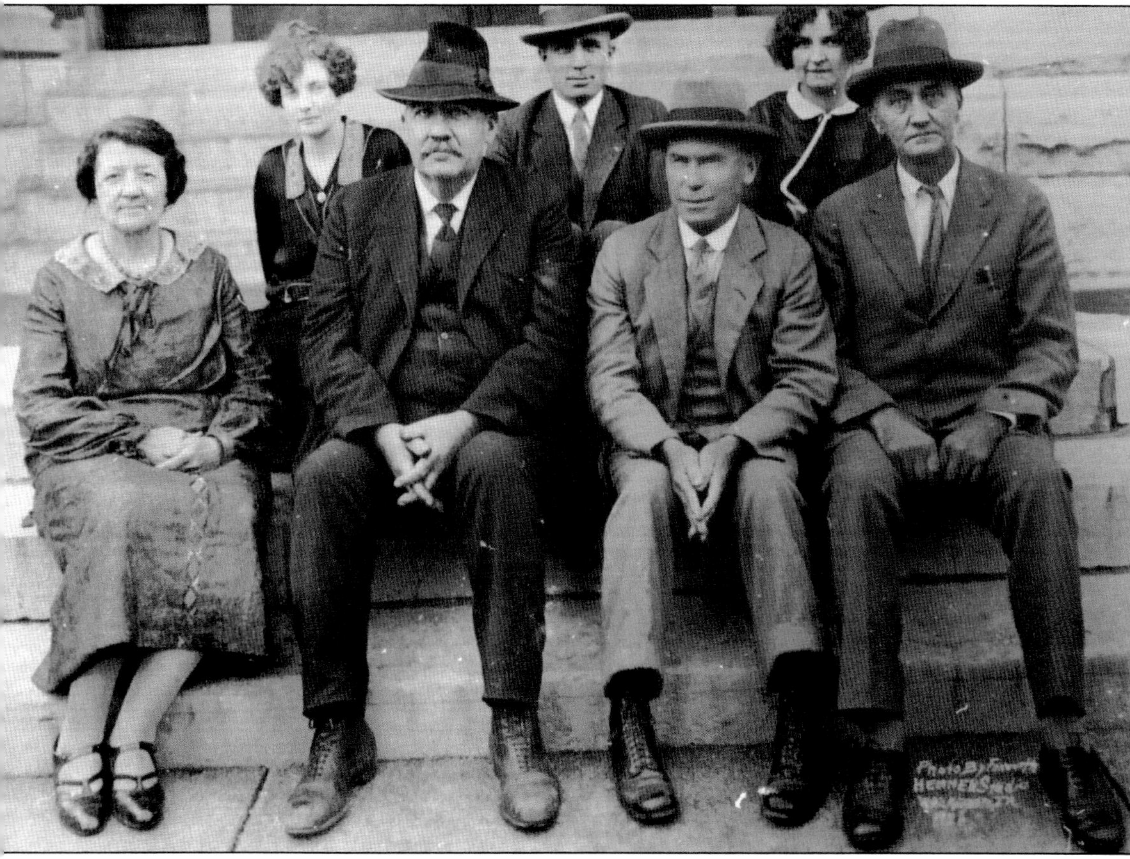

Alfred G. Maether was one of the few democrats in Lake County to be elected as township supervisor, but he was well liked by members of both parties. He served in that position for 16 years. He is pictured sitting on the steps of the Lake County courthouse in 1926 with other county officials. They are, from left to right, (first row) Vernon Township clerk Maude Kroll, Maether, Wauconda Township supervisor and chairman of the Lake County Board of Supervisors Ray Paddock, and unidentified; (second row) unidentified, commissioner of the Waukegan Water Department Robert Pearsall, and unidentified. In 1930, Maether served on the grand jury that indicted Al Capone. Having never owned or driven a car, he decided to commute back and forth one hour each way daily on the train to Chicago. During that period, he received many intimidating phone calls ordering him to get off the jury. Finally, tired of the threats, he told off the caller in no uncertain terms and never received another call again.

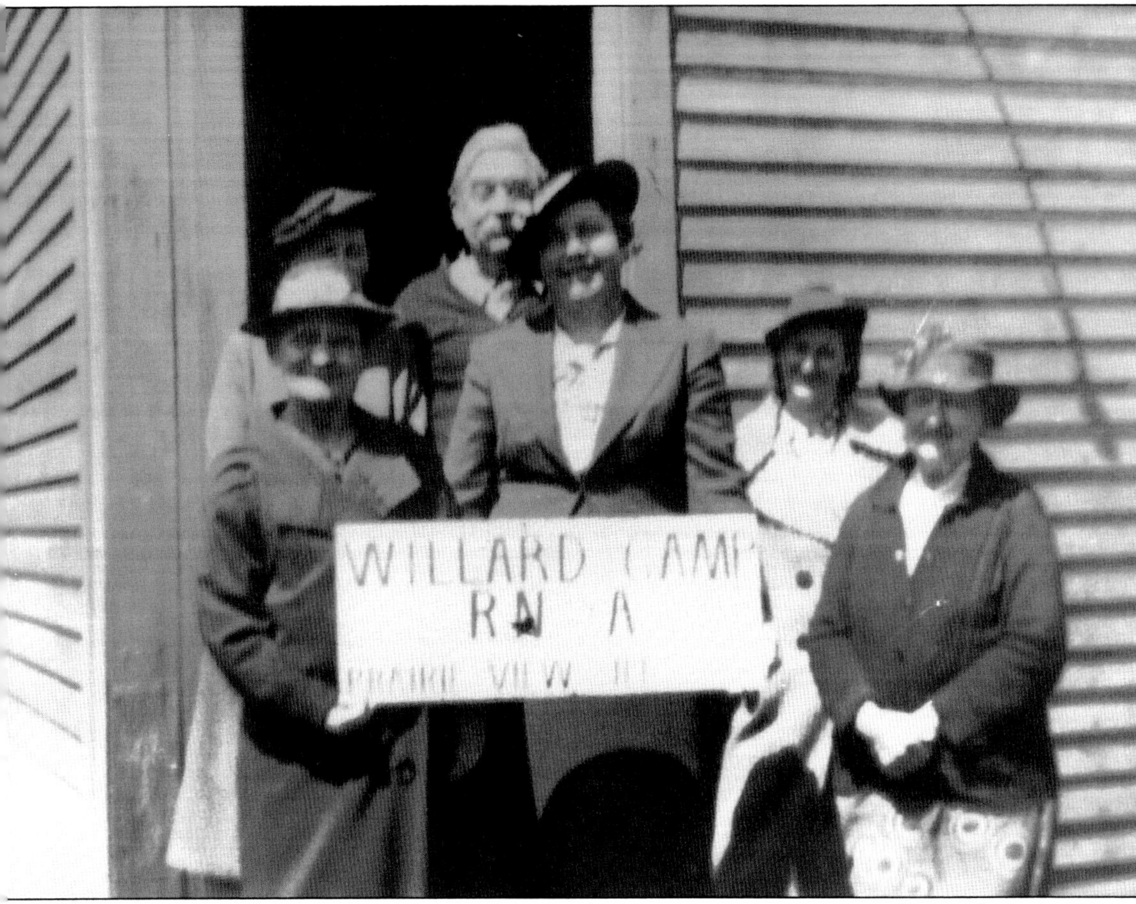

The Royal Neighbors of America was a fraternal woman's organization originally founded in Iowa in 1888. It originally provided only a social outlet but evolved to encourage community service and to offer women insurance policies. It was a forward-thinking group at a time when people's attitudes were beginning to change about women and their role in American society. At one time, it was the leading women's benefit agency in the United States. The Royal Neighbors were the ladies' counterpart to the men's organization, Modern Woodmen of America. The Royal Neighbors and the Woodmen supported women's suffrage issues in the early part of 20th century. The groups were organized into camps around the country. Pictured in 1938, members of the Royal Neighbors Willard Camp No. 507 met to celebrate the organization's 50th anniversary. The members pictured are, from left to right, (first row) Mary Stahl, Leonora Brockman Stoerp, and Maude Kroll Maether; (second row) Ruby Moline Maether, A.G. Maether, and Dorothy Stancliff Schar.

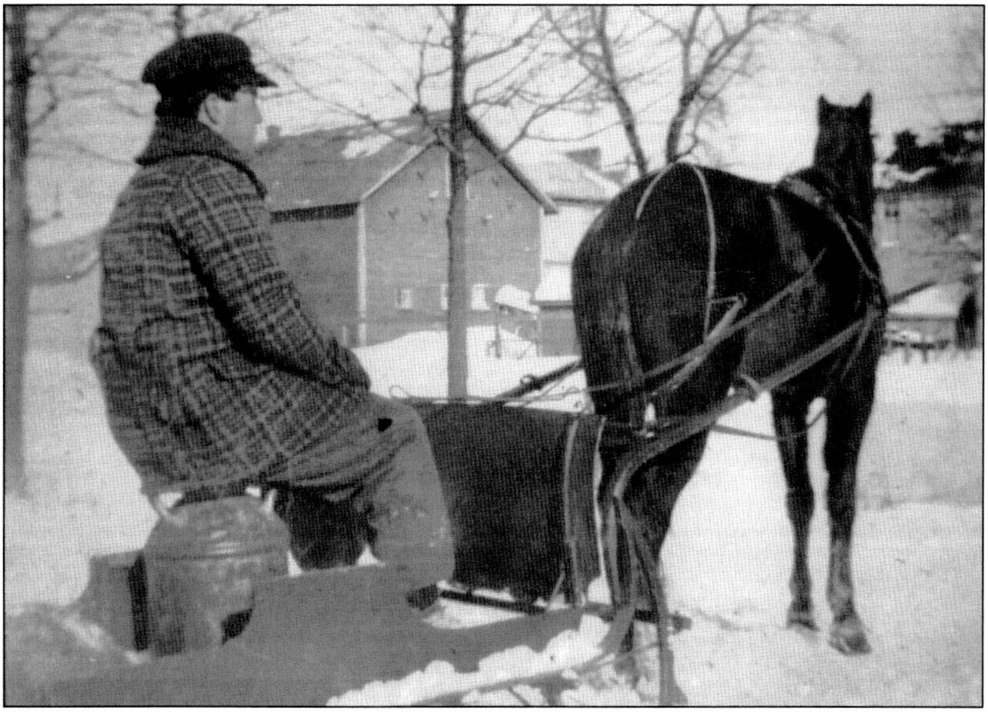

Lloyd Maether is seen here in his sleigh hitched and ready to go. Often, milk cans were used as seats in sleighs, buggies, and wagons. Horses provided for transportation needs year-round. During the remainder of the year, a buggy would take the place of the family sleigh. People did not let the elements stop them from doing things.

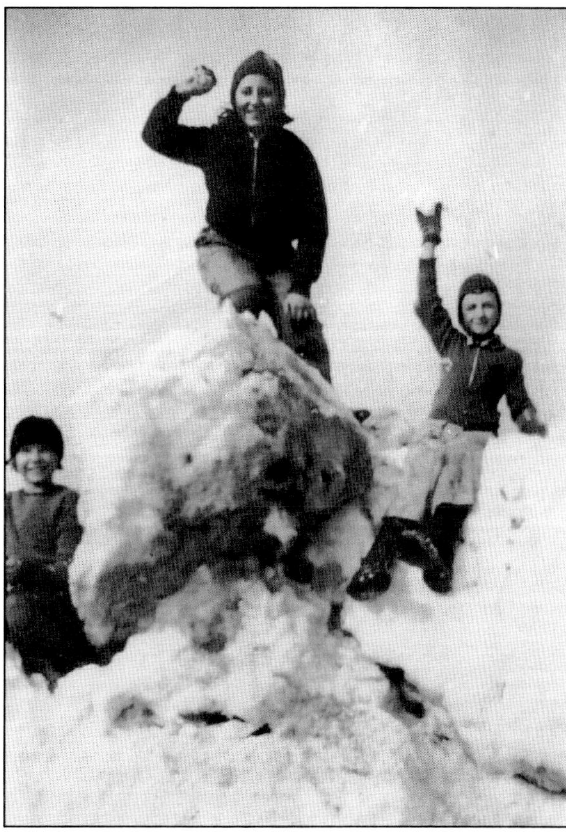

Winters in the area provided another opportunity for children to play. Mary Sue Link is pictured perched on top of an unusually large snow pile with Anna Sievers and Fred Draper. All three are ready for a snowball fight. In addition to playing in the snow, popular winter pastimes included skating and sledding. (Courtesy of Mary Sue Didier.)

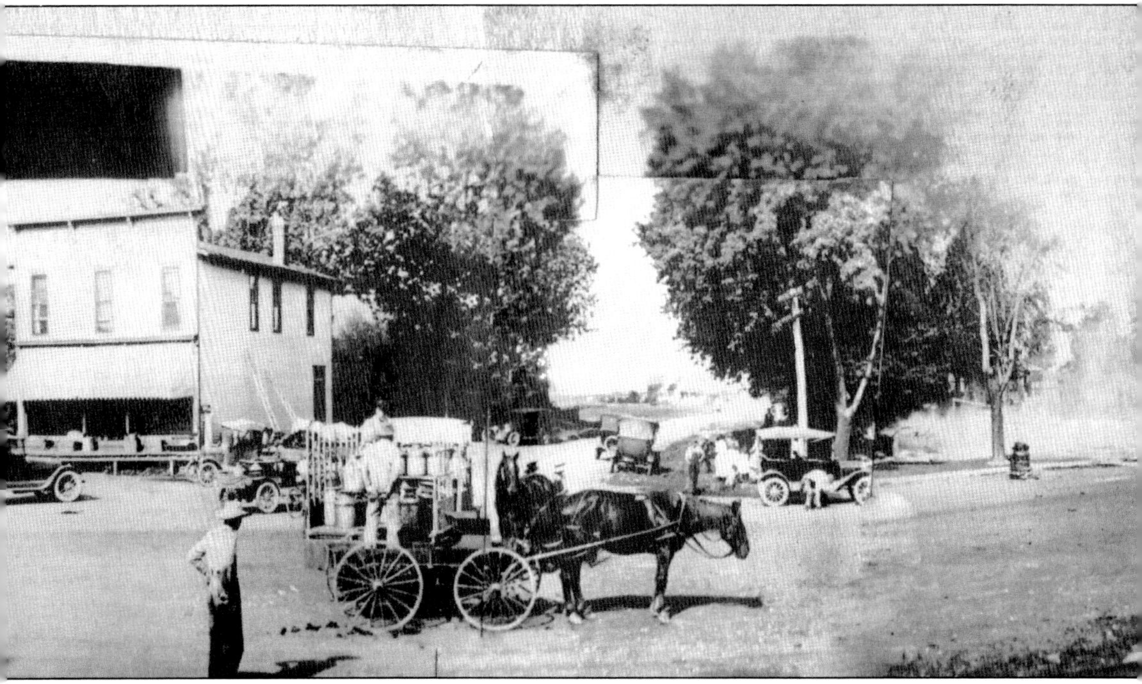

On the evening of Wednesday, July 28, 1920, the town of Prairie View was nearly wiped off the map by a horrific fire. The blaze was believed to have started in the sawdust of the icehouse in the back of Ferd Priess's hotel and tavern. It quickly spread due to the summer heat and brisk, sultry breezes. Building upon building burned to the ground while residents watched, forced to fend for themselves. There was only a small volunteer fire department with a scant two pieces

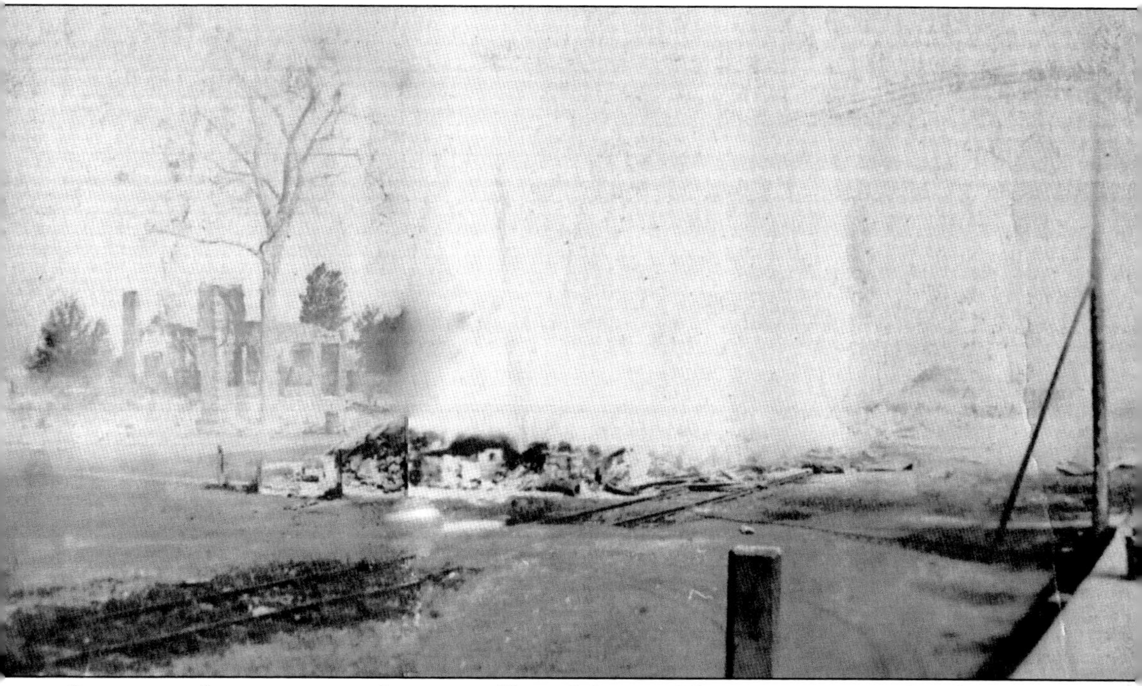

of equipment that were no match against a blaze of that size. This panorama was taken the next morning facing west with the Maether General Store on the left of the photograph. People were emerging to take stock of what was left of their town. The smoldering embers both east and west of the railroad tracks were all that remained of the vast majority of the small town. (Courtesy of Vernon Township.)

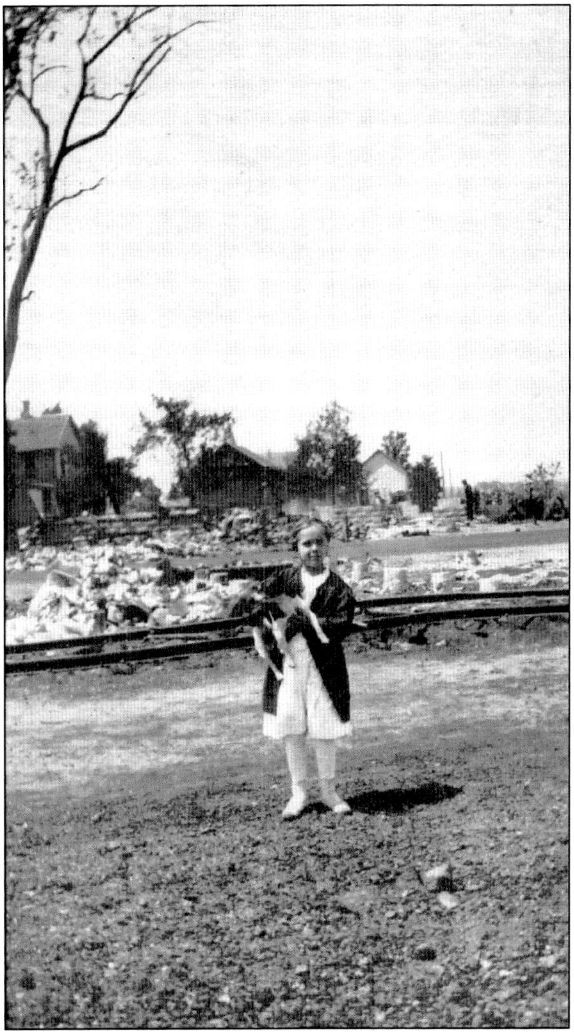

This girl poses with her dog the day after the conflagration. The nearby homes remarkably survived the night. The blaze was visible for miles and attracted hundreds of people to the site. It is amazing that no loss of life was noted on account of the inferno. (Courtesy of Vernon Township.)

The train depot is left standing in the distance. The fire and the tremendous damage it did to the development of Prairie View no doubt altered the course of the area's future. It took the town years to rebuild, and many businesses did not return, leaving one to wonder what may have been if the town was left to grow and the tragedy never occurred. (Courtesy of Vernon Township.)

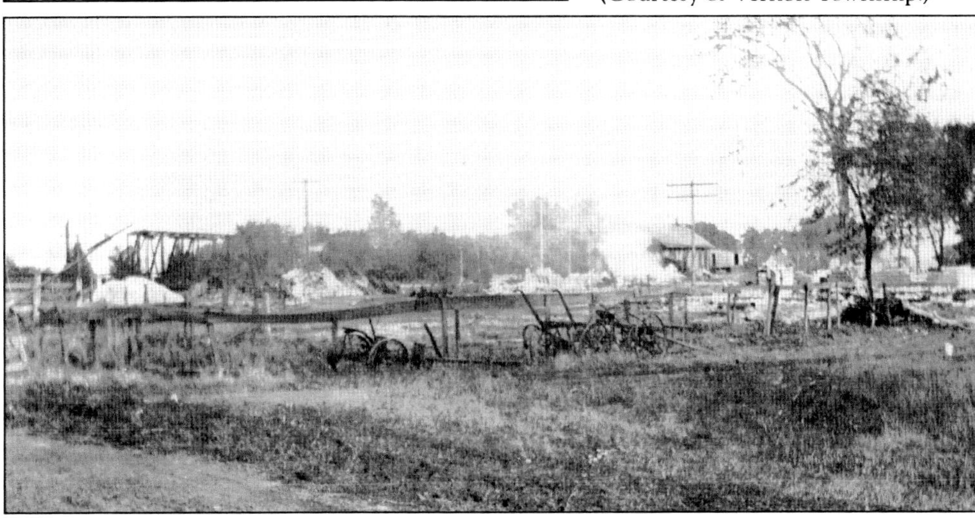

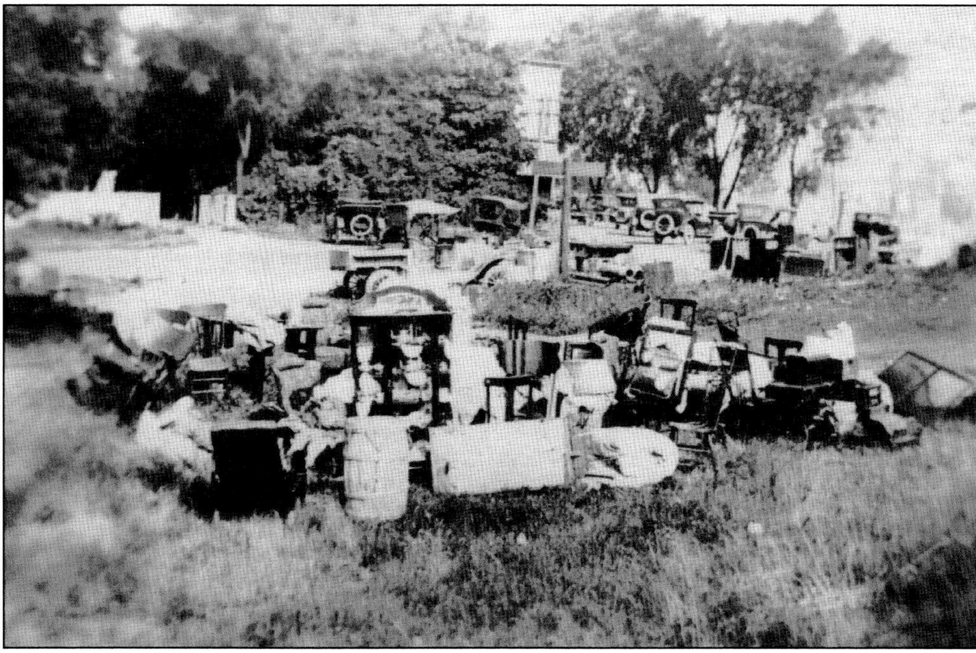

The morning after the catastrophe, piles of belongings lie in the grass that had been saved from the fire. Frightened residents hurriedly brought what goods they could carry out of their burning houses in order to salvage what they could. There were reports of other people rummaging through personal items and carrying them away.

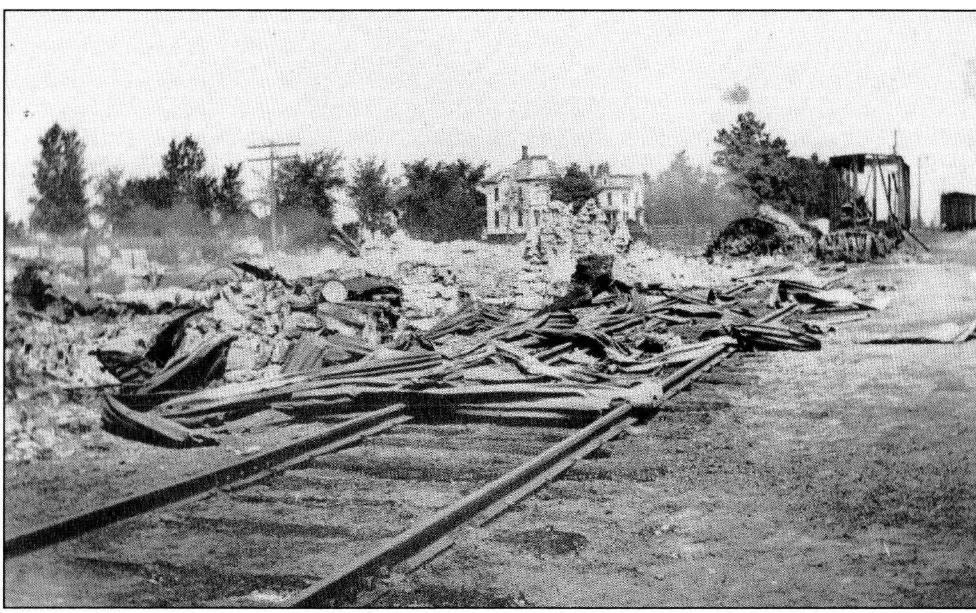

The fire was so intense that it twisted rails on the ground and destroyed two boxcars in the depot. The railroad was alerted about the fire during the night and sent an engine to the scene. The employees and some residents used water from the tender to save the depot from destruction. The frame of a burnt railcar is visible in the background. (Courtesy of Vernon Township.)

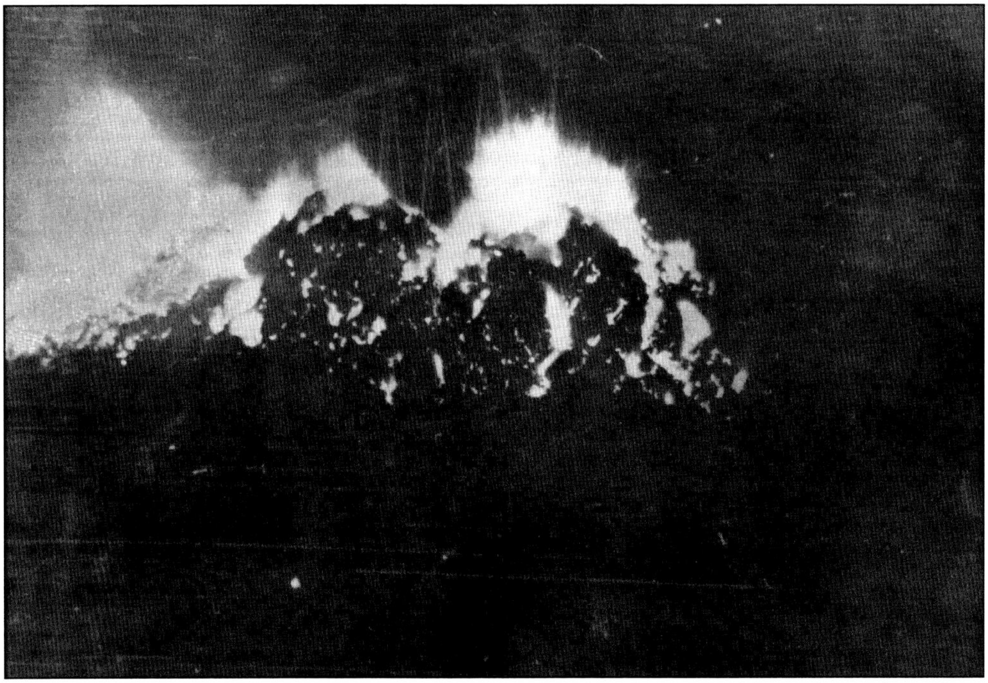

Two hundred tons of bituminous and anthracite coal were lost during the blaze. The coal seen here belonged to the S.L. Tripp Lumber Company and was located east of the railroad tracks; it would burn for days afterward. The fire jumped the tracks because of a high wind. All of the residences on the east side of the tracks were in constant danger of being engulfed by the flames.

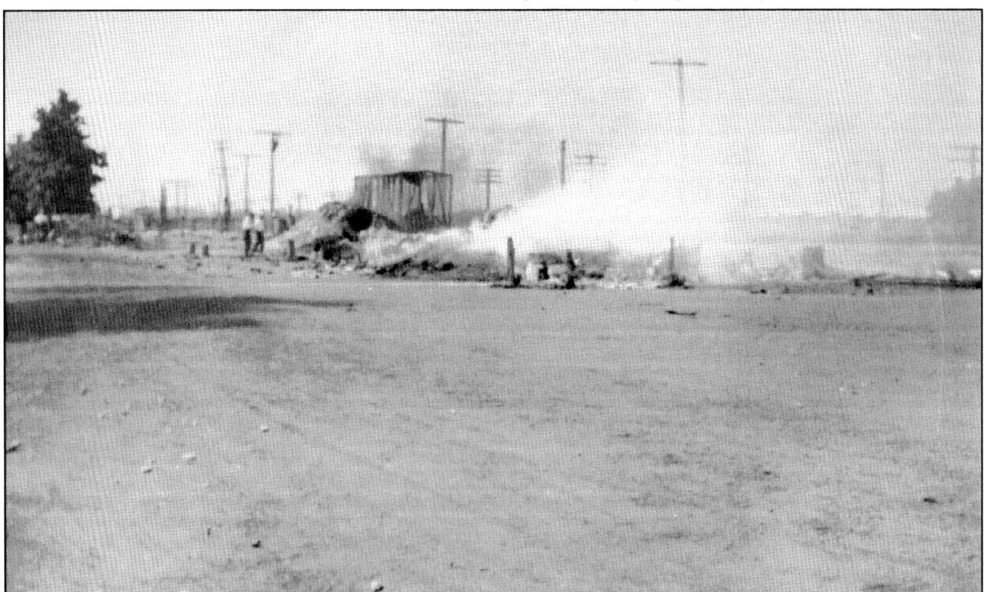

S.L. Tripp was fortunate to have carried insurance on his business and was able to get reimbursed for the losses endured that night. The remnants of his lumberyard and other buildings are pictured. Not everyone was so fortunate. Others, like Herman Albrecht, owner of the blacksmith shop, lost everything.

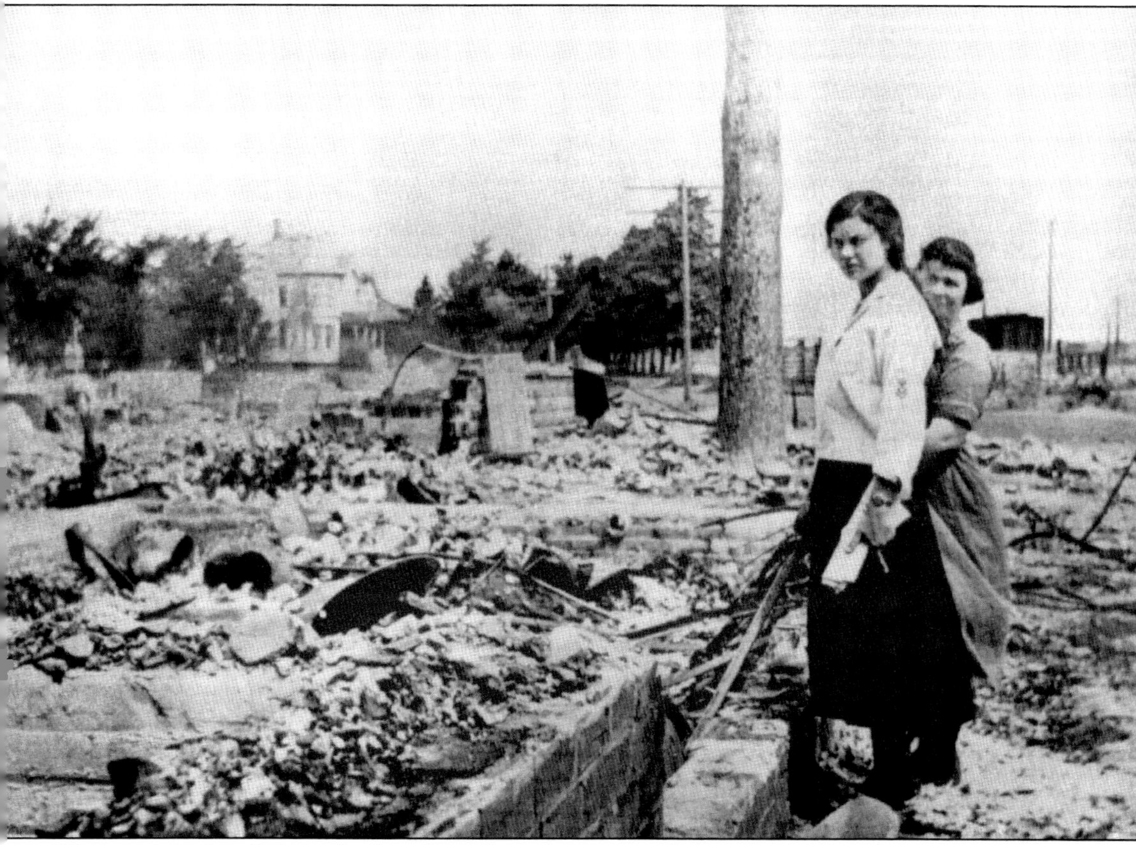

Florence Maether (left) and a friend stand amid the ruins that remained after the inferno. The only water available to fight the fire came from wells that belonged to the property owners. The volunteer fire department ran a hose from the Maethers' well to cool down the side of the building, which was smoking from the heat of the blaze. The sole reason the store did not perish was because the well did not run dry before the fire was extinguished. The only damage the business sustained was to the exterior of the structure, which was repainted afterward. The Brockman house is visible to the north in the top photograph. The fire destroyed a large number of buildings, including a blacksmith's shop, confectionery, farm implement shop, barbershop, stockyard sheds and pens belonging to the railroad, two hotels, a tavern, and S.L. Tripp Lumber Company's feed elevator and coal shed.

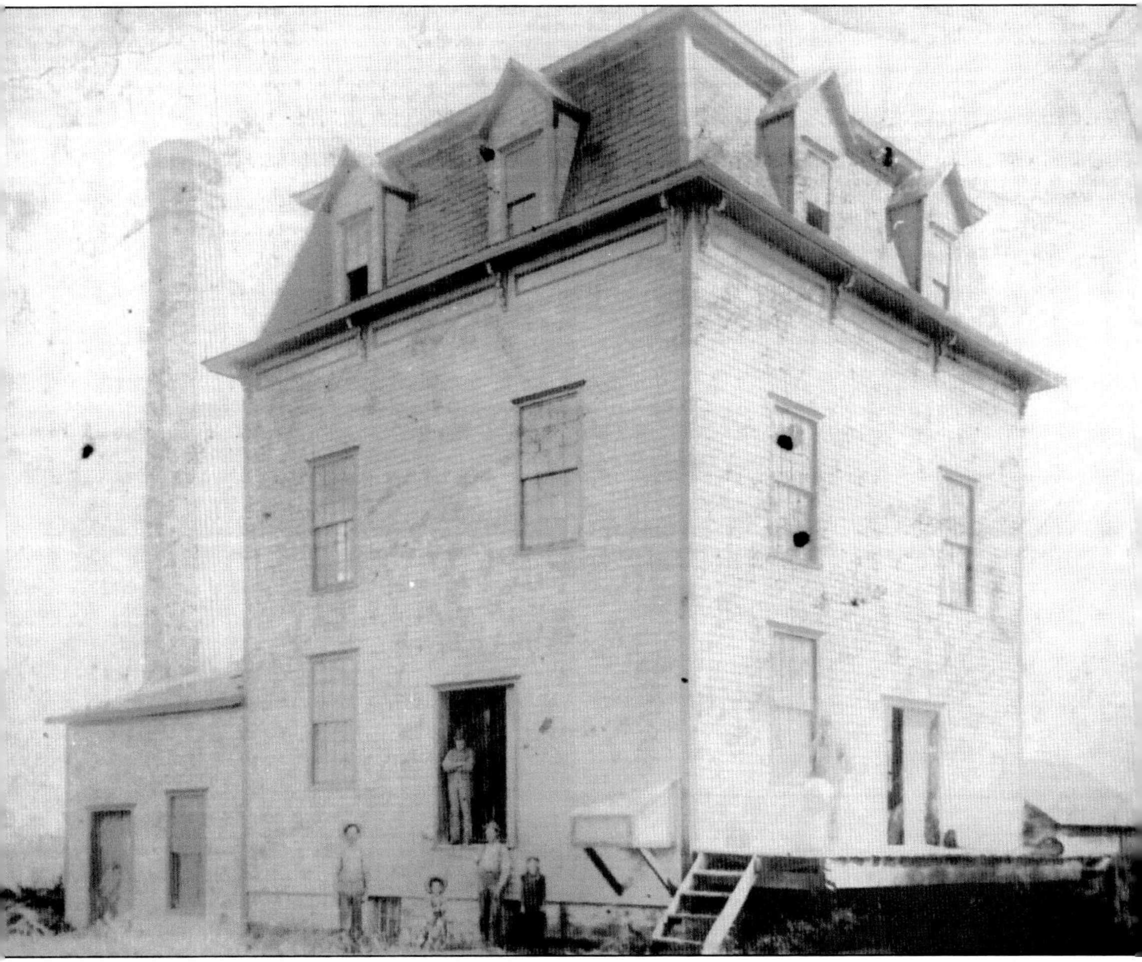

In 1888, brothers Silenus and Marion Webb Knedler bought an acre of land east of the new railroad tracks in Prairie View from Jabez Sprague for the amount of $1. They built a three-story gristmill, which would be vital to the community for nearly 100 years. The mill initially ground flour and animal feed, and then only feed after the Depression and the collapse of wheat markets. It was first powered by a steam engine whose boiler relied on coal and corncobs for fuel. At the time, the mill had a towering chimney built from 22,000 bricks. Longtime Knedler employee and fireman Sidney Loomis operated the boiler. This undated photograph has several members of the Knedler family in it. Pictured (from left to right), Silenus, Ted Knedler, Marion, and Ethyl Marjorie Knedler (Ted and Ethyl Marjorie were Marion's children) are all in the foreground while Sidney Loomis stands to the right on the porch with an unidentified man in the doorway. Silenus built his home north of the mill, and Marion had his south of it.

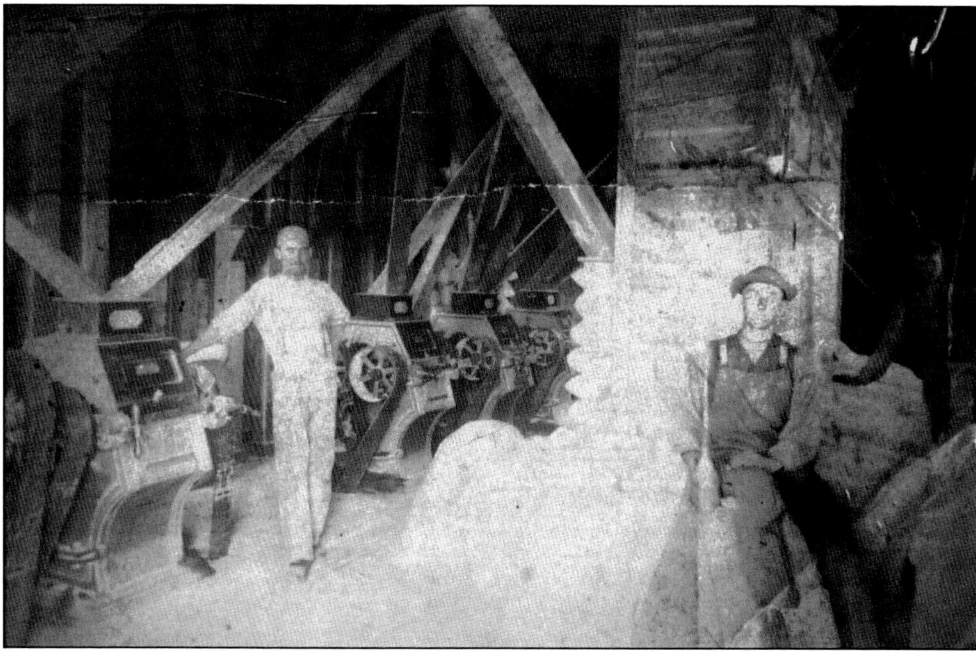

This interior photograph of the basement of the Knedler Mill shows the machinery that is belt-driven in the background. The belts lead to the first floor of the mill and run the equipment located there. Silenus Knedler is standing on the left and Marion Knedler is on the right of the photograph, and the other man is unidentified.

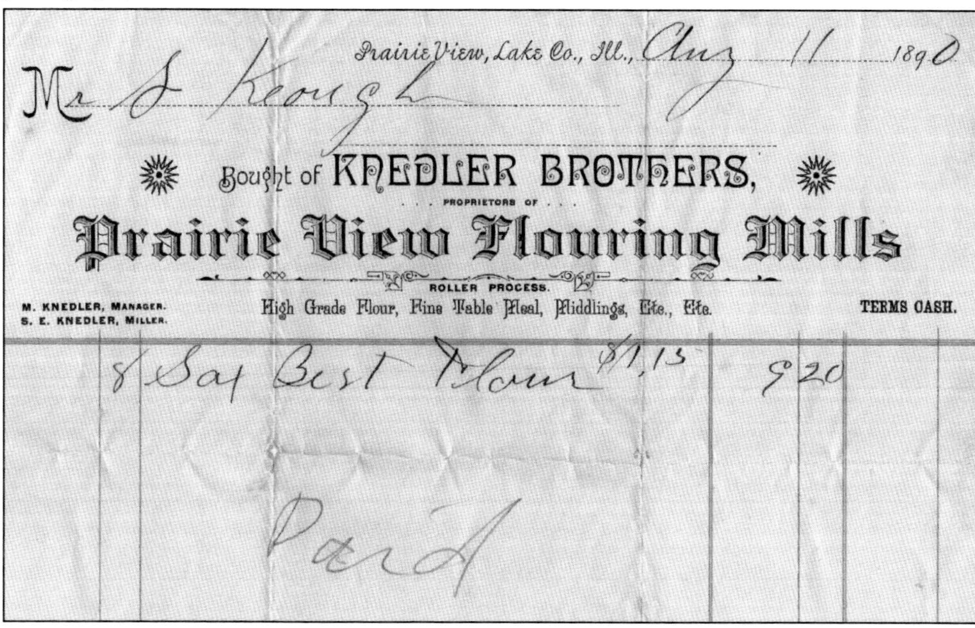

Prairie View, Lake Co., Ill., Aug 11 1890

Mr S Keough

Bought of KNEDLER BROTHERS,

PROPRIETORS OF

Prairie View Flouring Mills

ROLLER PROCESS.

M. KNEDLER, MANAGER.
S. E. KNEDLER, MILLER.

High Grade Flour, Fine Table Meal, Middlings, Etc., Etc.

TERMS CASH.

8 Sa Best Flour $1.15 9 20

Paid

This receipt is for flour ground from the Prairie View Flouring Mills a little more than a year after the mill had begun operation. The basic process of making flour involves crushing the grain between two rotating stones. The distance between the stones can be controlled in order to determine the grade of the flour desired. The closer the stones are to one another, the finer the flour. (Courtesy of Leona Elfering.)

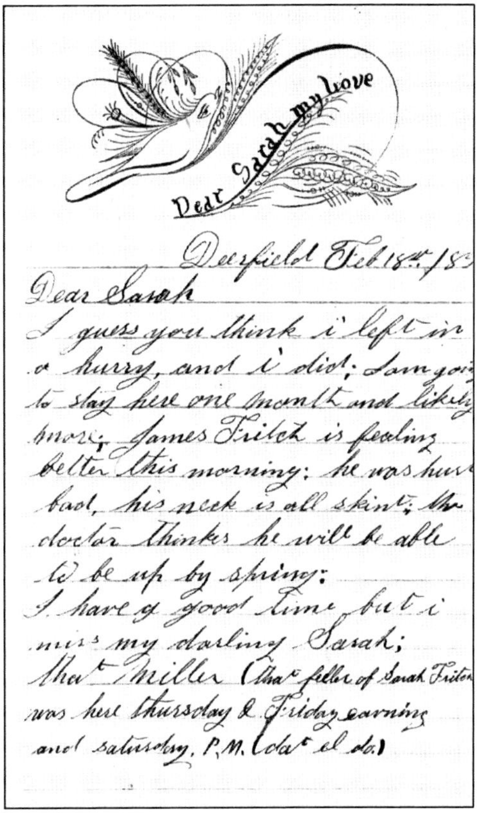
Dear Sarah my Love

Deerfield Feb 18th /83
Dear Sarah
I guess you think i left in
a hurry, and i did; I am going
to stay here one month and likely
more; James Fritch is fealing
better this morning; he was hurt
bad, his neck is all skint; the
doctor thinks he will be able
to be up by spring;
I have a good time but i
miss my darling Sarah;
That Miller (that feller of Sarah Fritch
was here thursday & Friday evening
and saturday, P.M. (dat el da)

This very ornate love letter from young Silenus Knedler to Sarah Ritzenthaler is dated February 18, 1883. Silenus was in Deerfield at the time. The letter refers to his cousin James Fritch, who worked at a mill in Deerfield, being injured. Sarah and Silenus ended up marrying in June 1886. The union produced three children, Jennie, Harold, and Ben. Sarah died after nine years of marriage in 1895.

Picnicking has long been a popular pastime, but at the beginning of the 20th century, men and women primarily socialized separately. This happy gathering included Amanda Elmira Knedler (center top) and her children Ethel Marjorie (middle left), Ted (front), niece Jennie Knedler Stahl (middle right), and two unidentified women.

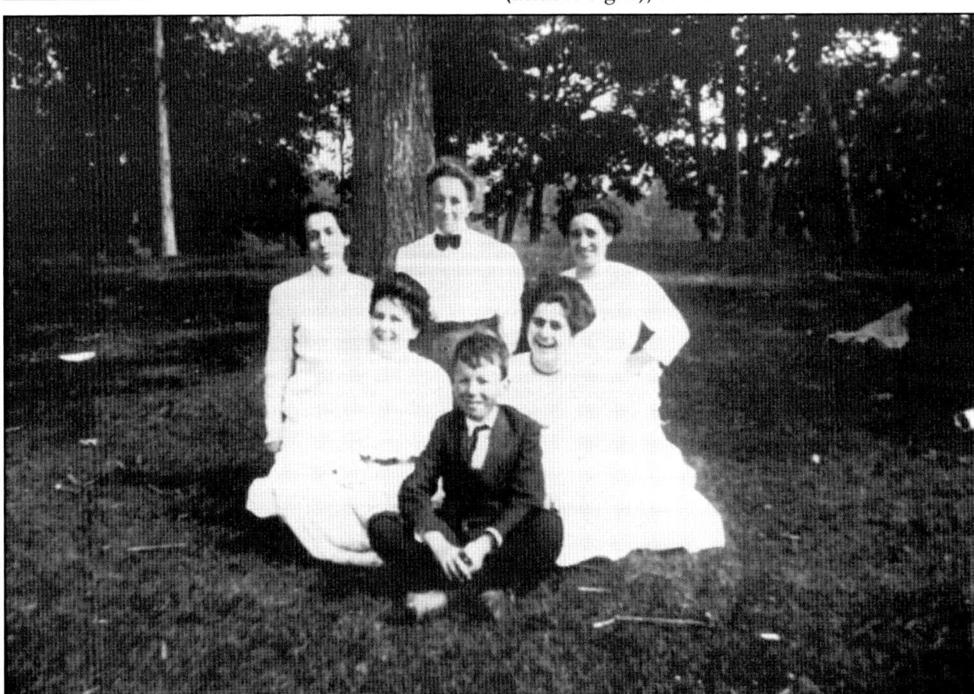

This portrait features four generations important to Marion Knedler. From left to right are Salome Gutzler (mother of Amanda Elmira Knedler), daughter Ethyl Marjorie Knedler Ray, wife Amanda Elmira Knedler, and grandson Vance Ray. Marion and Amanda Gutzler were married in 1889 and also had a son, Ted, who was killed at the age of 25.

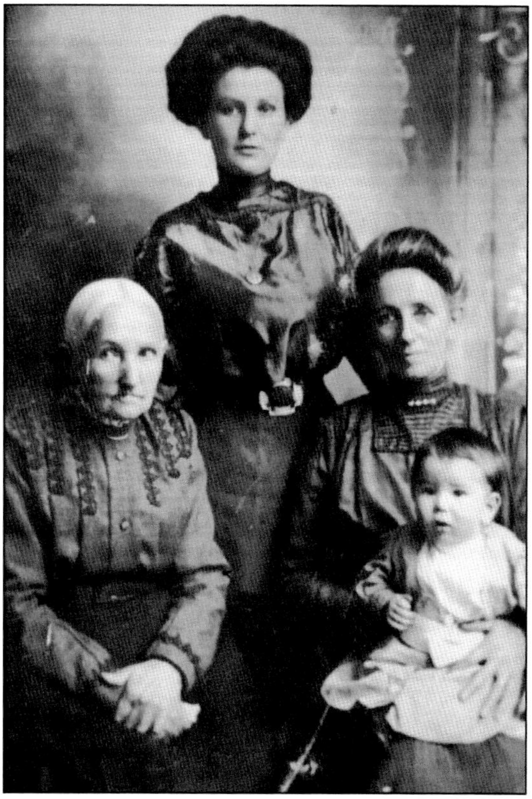

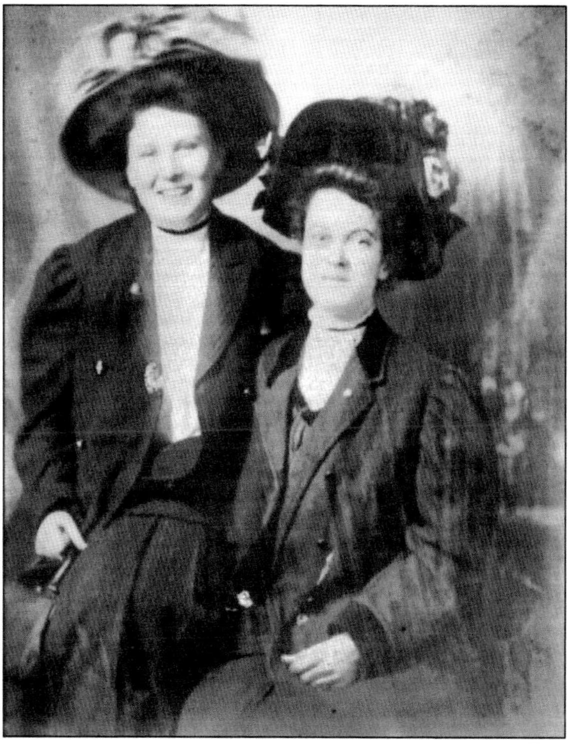

Ethel Marjorie Knedler Ray (left) and her dear friend Tillie Mitchell are the picture of fashionable young ladies in their stylish outfits. Wearing stiff collars with their hair piled high and adorned with broad-brimmed hats, the young women epitomized the "Gibson Girl" fashion trend of the period.

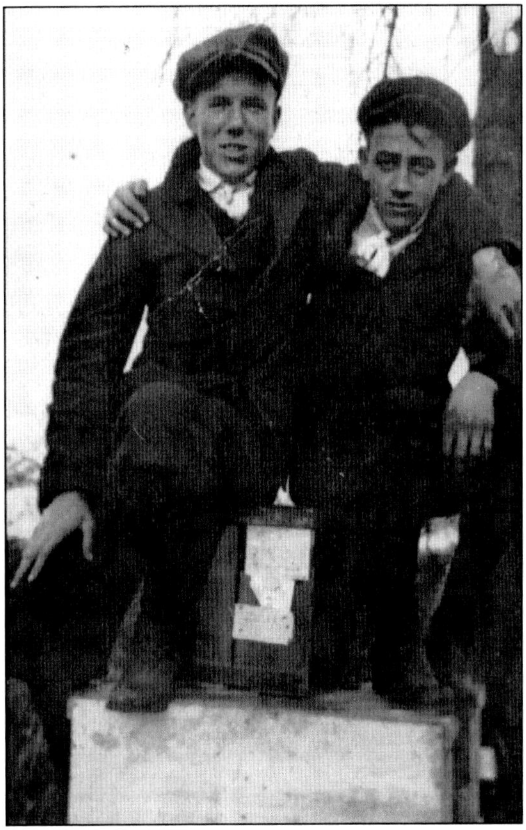

Ted Knedler (left), son of Marion, seen here with his first cousin Bill Knedler, son from Silenus's second marriage to Emma Frey, sit arm in arm for this photograph in a jaunty schoolboy pose. Ted was killed when he was just 25 years old, but the cause of death is unknown.

This photograph, taken in the springtime, shows Ted Knedler (far right) and his cousin Bill Knedler posing playfully for the camera while perched with unidentified friends over a small stream. While some trees are evident, the majority of the area remained flat, farmed fields.

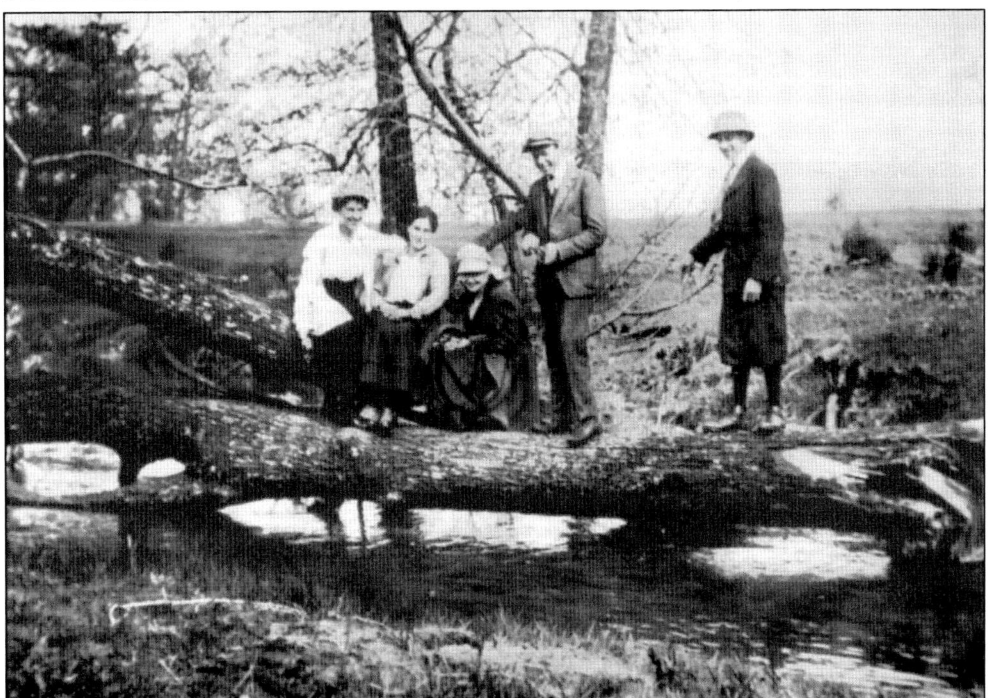

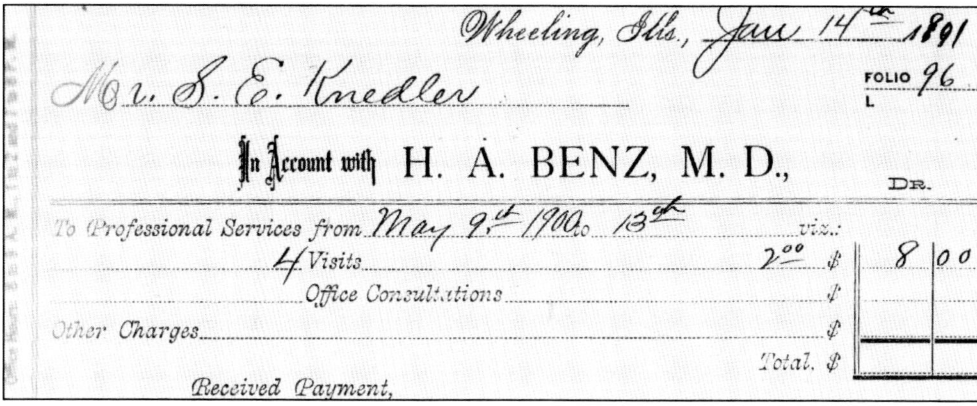

Wheeling, Ills., Jan 14th 1891

Mr. S. E. Knedler FOLIO 96 L

In Account with H. A. BENZ, M. D., DR.

To Professional Services from May 9th 1900 13th viz.:

4 Visits 2.00 $ 8 00

Office Consultations $

Other Charges $

Total. $

Received Payment,

Pictured is a bill to Silenus from Dr. H.A. Benz for four visits at a cost of $2 per visit. Doctor Benz was a physician and surgeon who was educated in Chicago at Rush Medical College. He brought his practice to Wheeling in 1890.

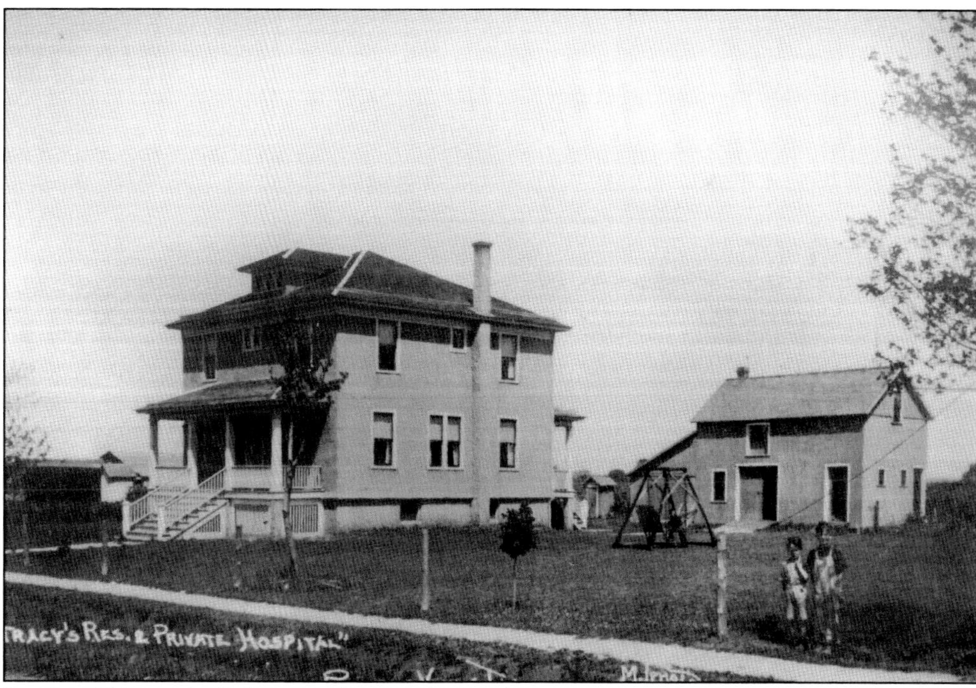

Dr. Evert E. Tracy had a home and private hospital on Easton Avenue. Doctor Tracy was educated in Albany, New York, and practiced for a time in Ohio before coming to Illinois. He was the resident physician for a time at the penitentiary in Joliet. He began his practice in Prairie View with his wife acting as nurse in 1906. Doctor Tracy died of an illness in 1913.

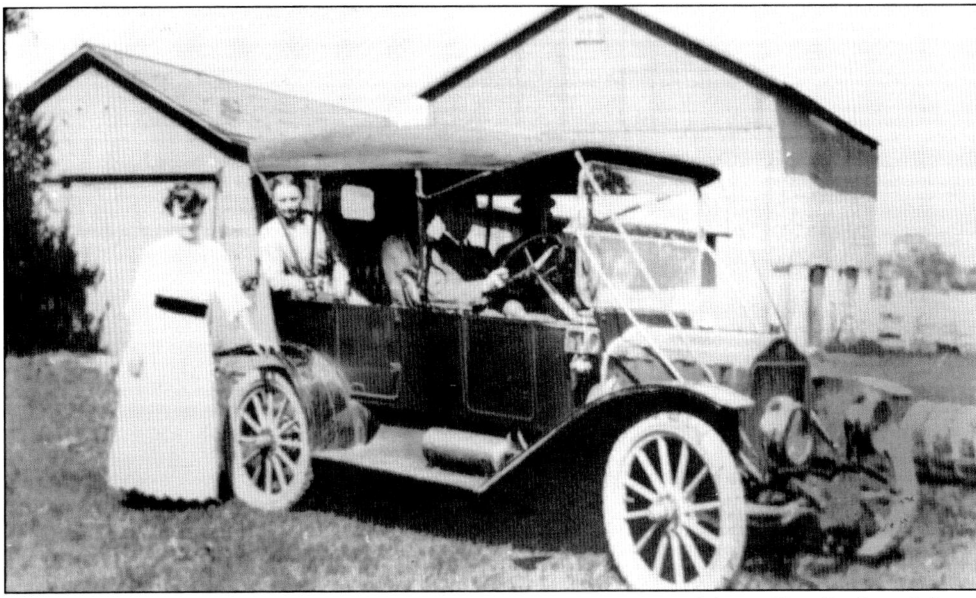

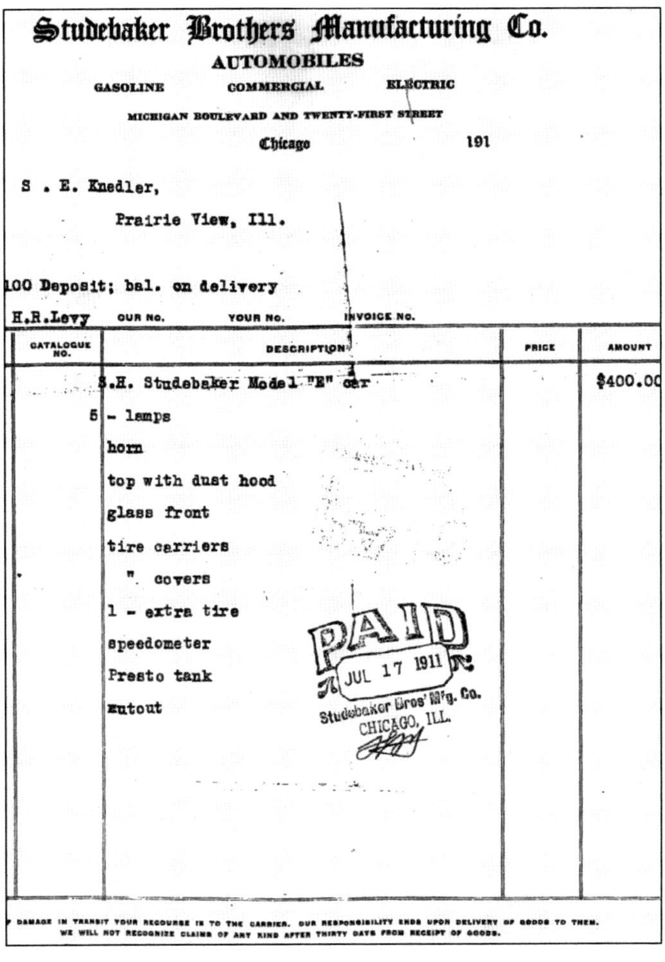

Studebaker Brothers Manufacturing Co.

AUTOMOBILES

GASOLINE COMMERCIAL ELECTRIC

MICHIGAN BOULEVARD AND TWENTY-FIRST STREET

Chicago 191

S . E. Knedler,

Prairie View, Ill.

100 Deposit; bal. on delivery

H.R.Levy OUR NO. YOUR NO. INVOICE NO.

CATALOGUE NO.	DESCRIPTION	PRICE	AMOUNT
	S.H. Studebaker Model "E" car		$400.00
5	- lamps		
	horn		
	top with dust hood		
	glass front		
	tire carriers		
	" covers		
	1 - extra tire		
	speedometer		
	Presto tank		
	cutout		

PAID JUL 17 1911 Studebaker Bros' M'f'g. Co. CHICAGO, ILL.

DAMAGE IN TRANSIT YOUR RECOURSE IS TO THE CARRIER. OUR RESPONSIBILITY ENDS UPON DELIVERY OF GOODS TO THEM. WE WILL NOT RECOGNIZE CLAIMS OF ANY KIND AFTER THIRTY DAYS FROM RECEIPT OF GOODS.

Silenus Knedler loved the automobile. The first car he owned was this 1911 Studebaker. He is pictured proudly behind the wheel of his car with his daughter and other family members. He ordered the car new from a Studebaker dealer in Chicago. The deposit was $100 with the balance of $400 upon delivery. Driving was a true adventure. Automobiles had to be put away in the winter, since roads were not plowed. Even during the rest of the year, cars often had to be pulled out by local farmers when they got stuck. The going rate was $1 to be pulled out. After Silenus got a car, his expenses were said to have soared.

A very popular Sunday school class began in Prairie View in 1903. So great was its popularity that a church congregation emerged from the program a year later. A church named Grace Evangelical was built and soon became the center of many families' lives. Social events as well as religious ones revolved around the church, and a popular band even formed by the very musically inclined congregation.

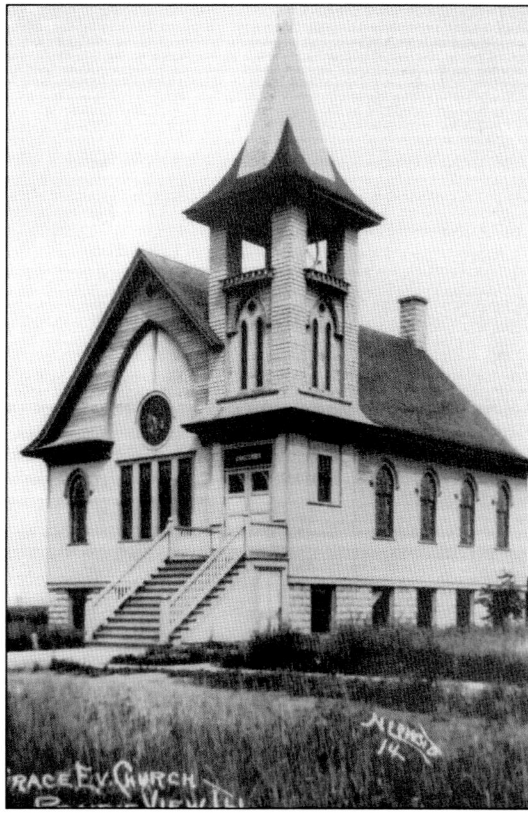

A darkened basement is the backdrop for this photograph taken during the construction of Grace Church. Foundation work is evident as seen by the large number of workers needed to do the backbreaking job. Marion Knedler is pictured in the last row on the far right with Silenus Knedler standing next to him.

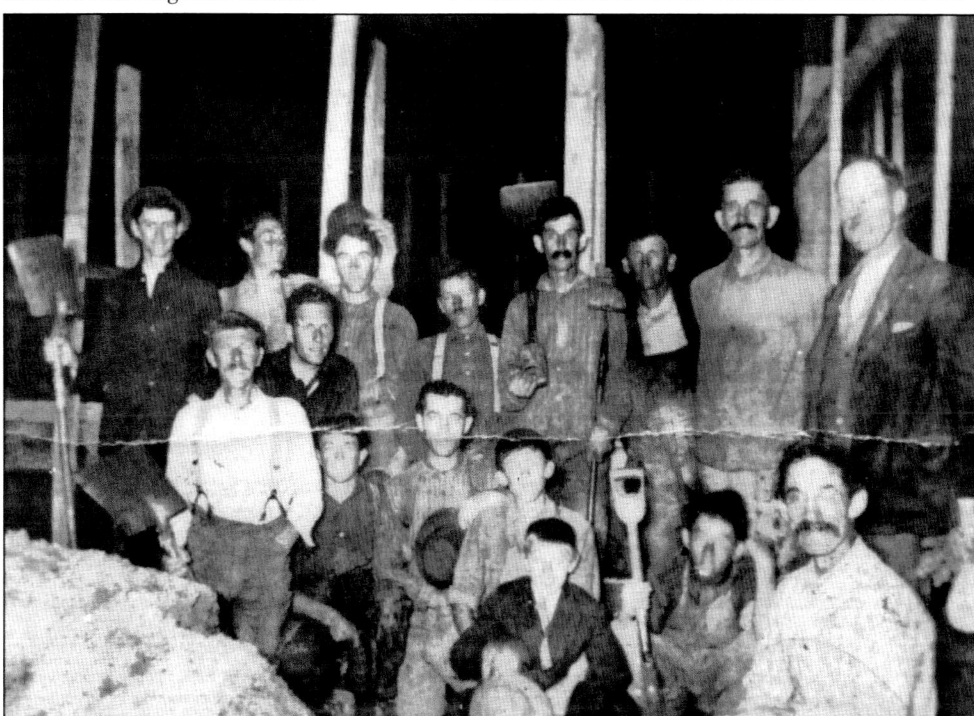

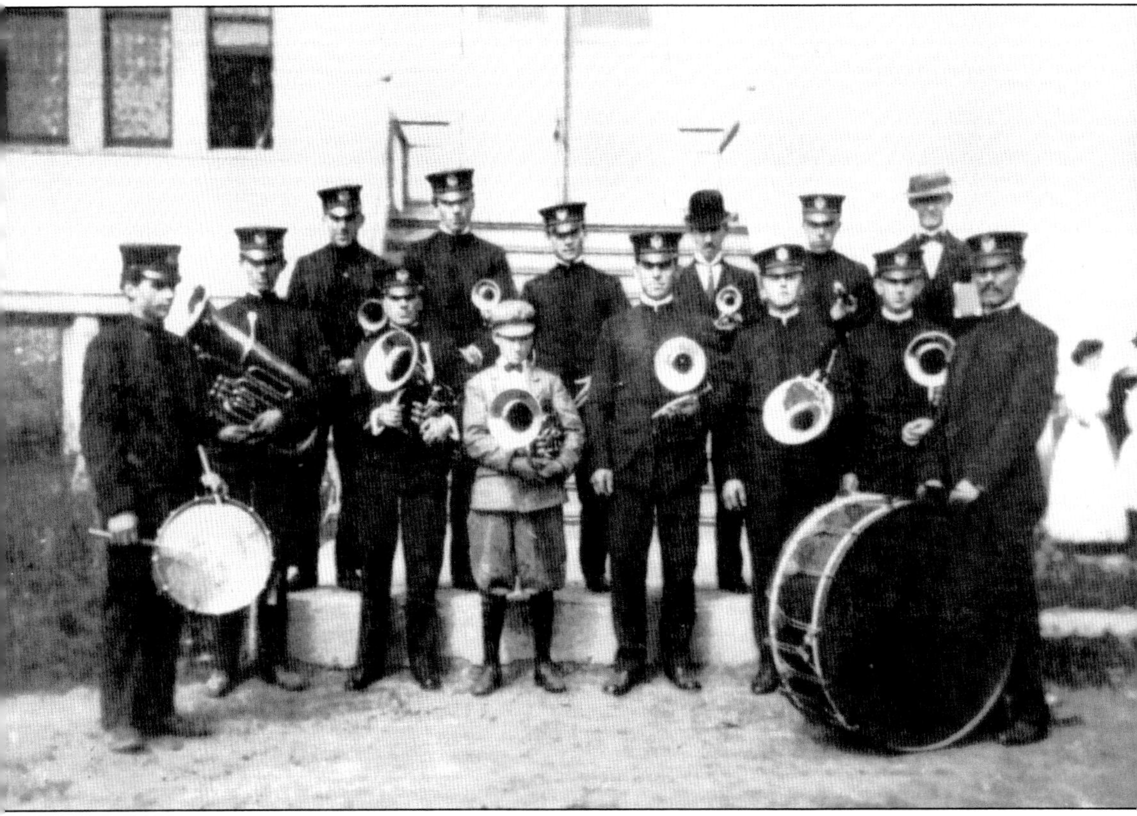

The Prairie View Band was comprised of musicians from the congregation at Grace Church as well as others from congregations in Deerfield and Highland Park. Lloyd Ritzenthaler led this popular band, seen on the steps of the church in this 1911 photograph. He is standing in front of the unidentified man wearing the bowler hat. Silenus played the bass drum and is pictured on the far right. Most of the social life in Prairie View revolved around the church and the band. The membership grew to 35 people at one point, and the group was so well regarded that it was invited to play on Chicago radio station WMBI.

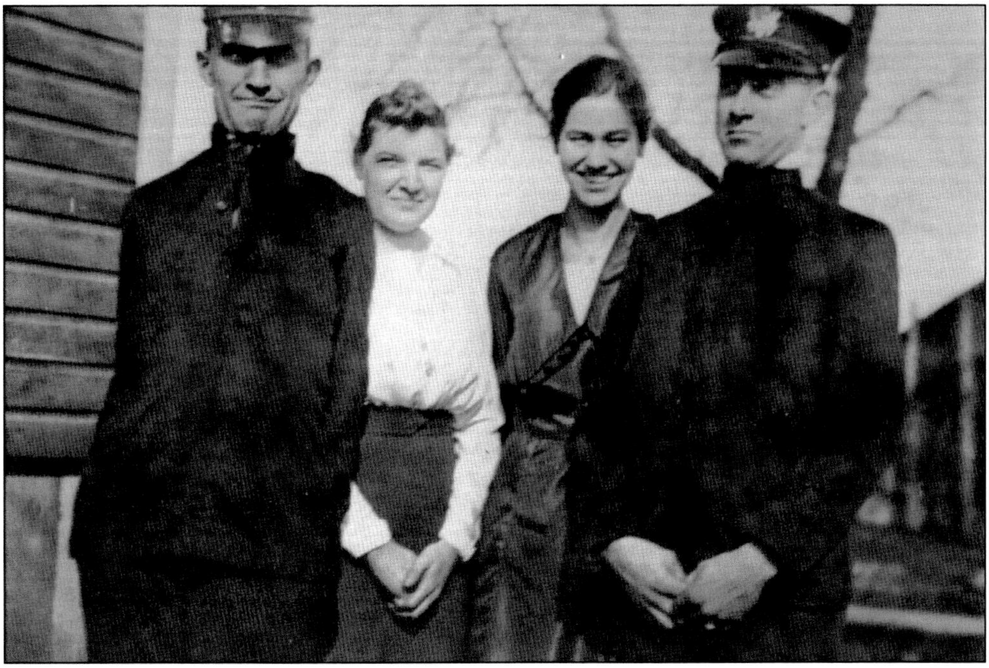

Uniformed Prairie View Band members Harry (left) and Bill Knedler are seen standing with Hattie Holtje (left) and Flossie Knedler. Harry is the son of Silenus from his first marriage to Sarah Ritzenthaler while Bill and Flossie are also Silenus' children from his second marriage to Emma Frey. Hattie Holtje would eventually become Harry's wife.

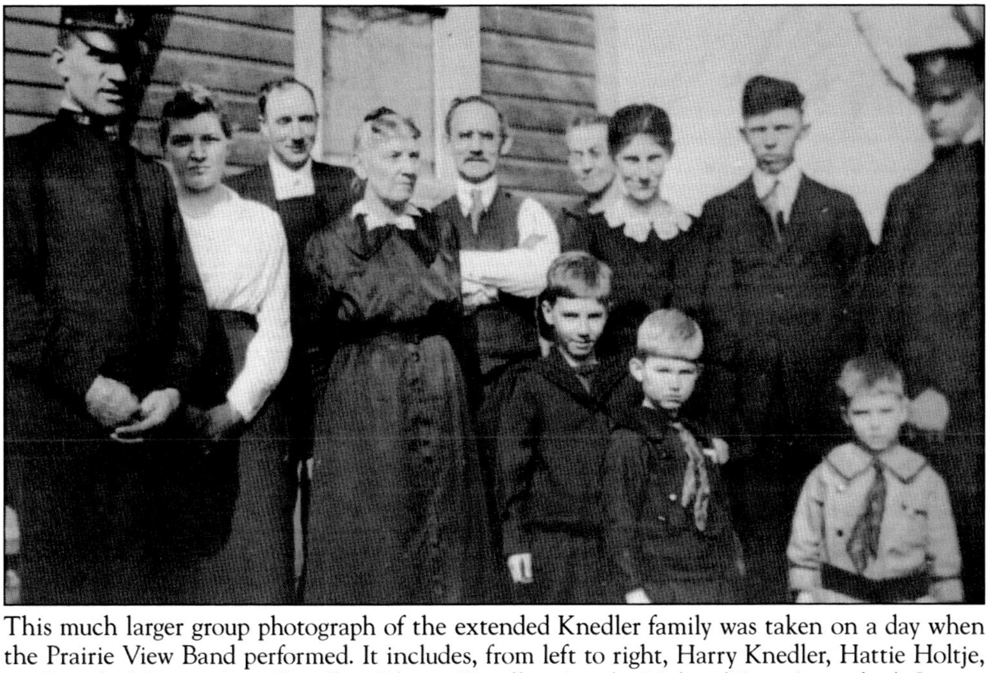

This much larger group photograph of the extended Knedler family was taken on a day when the Prairie View Band performed. It includes, from left to right, Harry Knedler, Hattie Holtje, unidentified, Emma Frey Knedler, Silenus Knedler, Amelia Holtje (Hattie's mother), Jennie Knedler Stahl, unidentified, and Bill Knedler. Three Knedler grandchildren, Don, Bob, and Harold Stahl, are in the foreground.

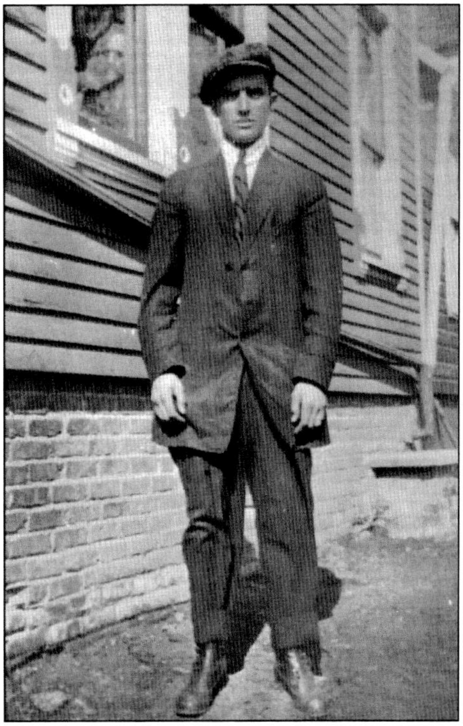

Lloyd Ritzenthaler was a man of many interests and a pillar of the community. He was a farmer, formed and conducted the Prairie View Band, was the postmaster from 1928 until 1933, and Vernon Township supervisor from 1944 until 1949.

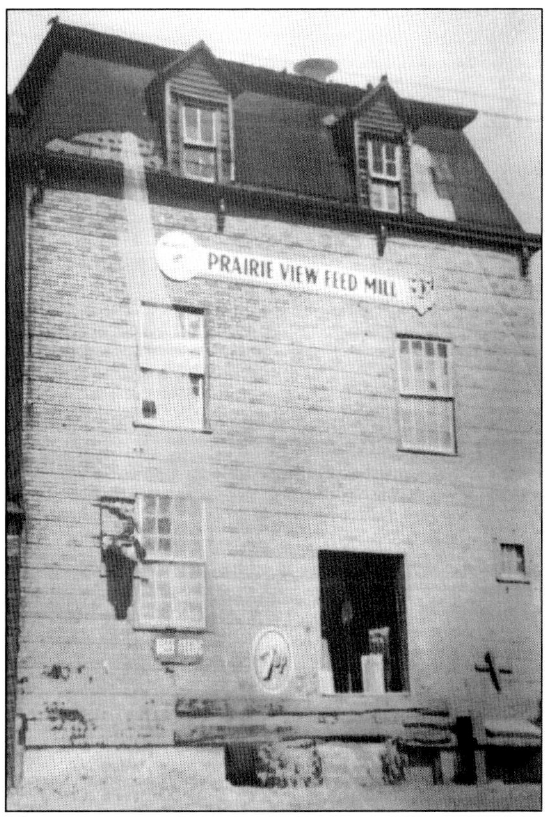

After Marion Knedler died in 1945, the mill was sold to Leonard Liepelt, who kept it running for the next 32 years before it was sold again to businessman Norman Ahrens. Before the building was converted to a restaurant, it was struck by lightning and burned down in 1978. The building was a favorite with artists, who have memorialized it over the years. (Courtesy of the Lincolnshire-Riverwoods Fire Protection District.)

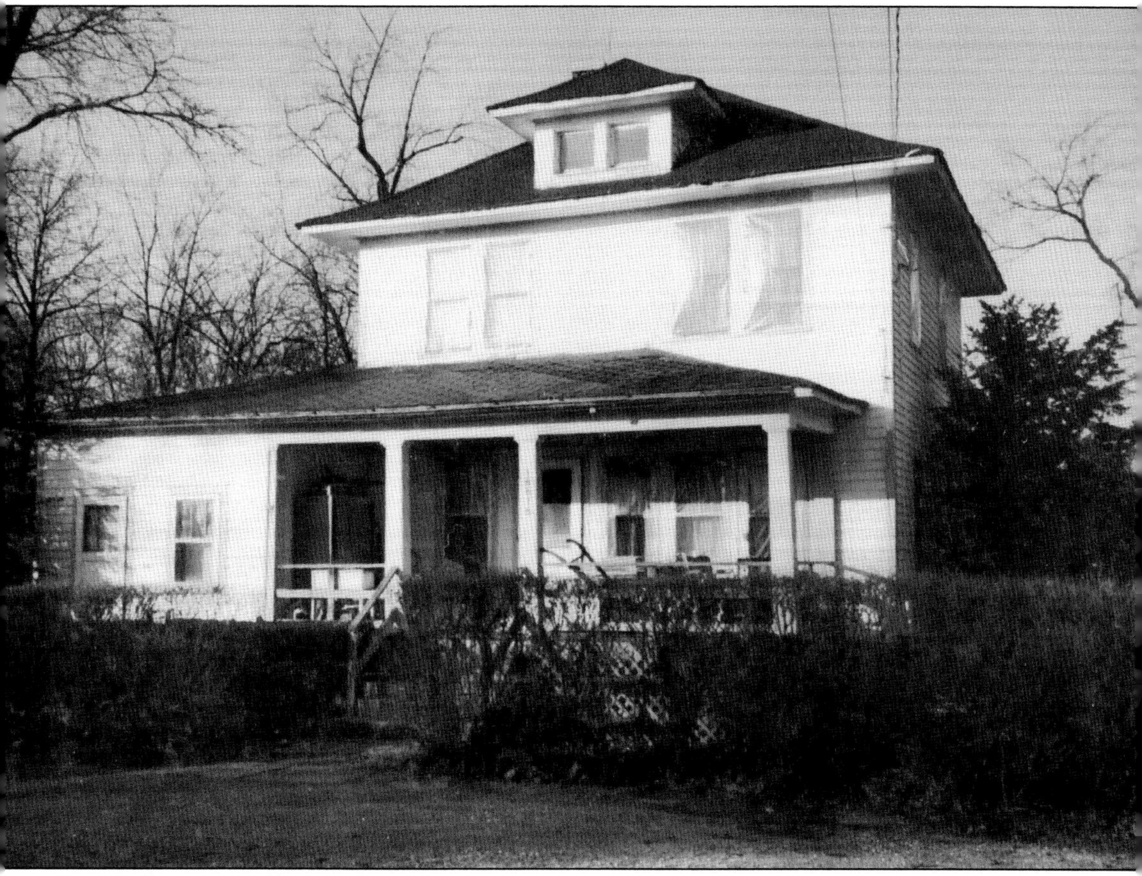

Long before a post office was built in Lincolnshire, there was one in Prairie View that served the area along with Half Day, Aptakisic, and Buffalo Grove. Back then, the position of postmaster was a political appointment. The post office would be located wherever the postmaster wished, even if it were a private residence. For example, the post office was located in a bedroom and porch of the Catherine and William Mason home from 1905 until 1928. One of the more unusual things that would be sent through the mail was baby chicks. Farmers would place orders in the spring, and they would arrive via train to the post office in the middle of the night. The peeping boxes would then be delivered by the carrier. Many a hurried driver would speed down the roads rushing the just-hatched baby birds to the expectant farmer, who was waiting with an incubator. Care and speed were of the utmost urgency, as the birds needed to be kept warm and delivered quickly since they had been shipped without receiving their first food or water.

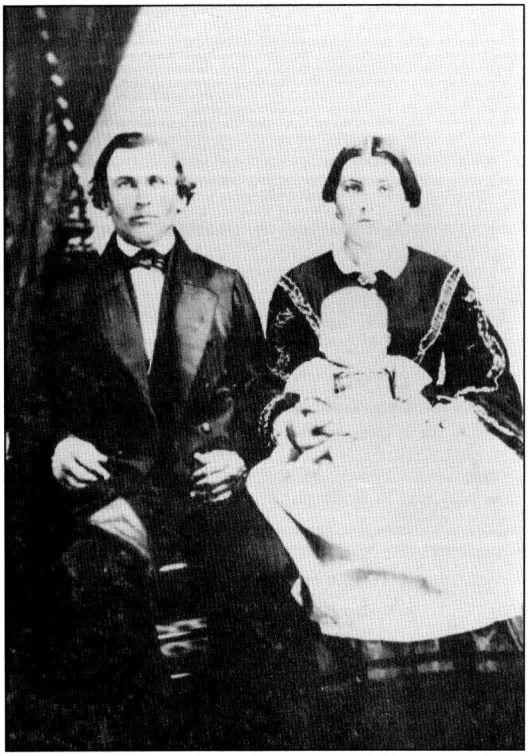

Frederick Brockman and his wife, Emmalina, moved to Prairie View in 1905 after he had retired from farming. They are pictured with one of their sons. They purchased land and a home from John Seely Gridley. The couple had three surviving sons, Herman, Ed, and William, and a daughter, Emma. There is a street in town that is named after Frederick Brockman.

Farm work was backbreaking and never finished, but there have been innovations over the years. All three Brockman brothers—Herman, William, and Ed—are shown working on one of their farms along with an unidentified man. The sawing of lumber used to be done exclusively at a sawmill until portable mills, like this one, were introduced and sold by companies like Sears or Montgomery Ward.

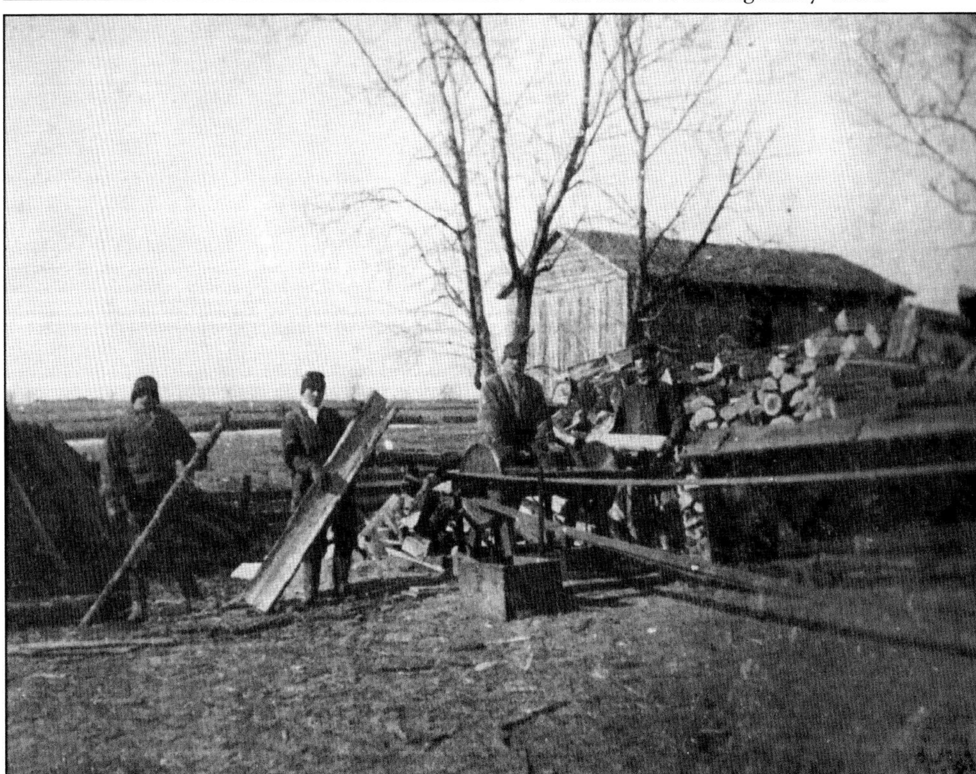

The name Brockman has been around Vernon Township for generations. William Brockman, son of Frederick and Emmalina, was also an area farmer. His first wife, Caroline Lemker, died when their young daughter, Leonora, was six months old. Leonora's unmarried aunt, rather than her bachelor father, raised her until he remarried in 1905 to Emma Keiler (pictured).

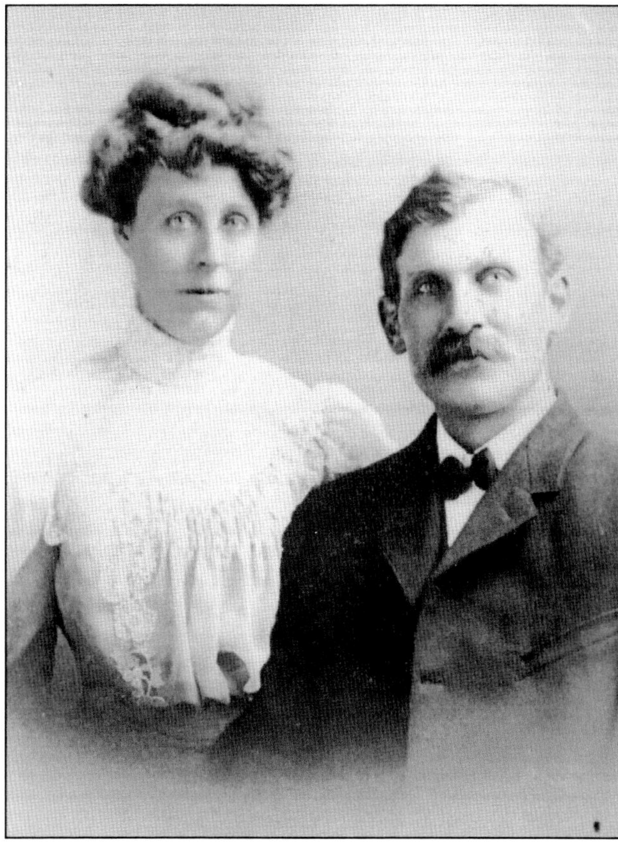

This family portrait was taken around 1915 with William, Emma, and Helen Brockman in front of their family car. William's second marriage to Emma produced another daughter, Helen. Many cars of the period had convertible roofs so that people could enjoy motoring in the outdoors. The family had to enjoy each other's company rather than music, since the car radio had not yet been invented.

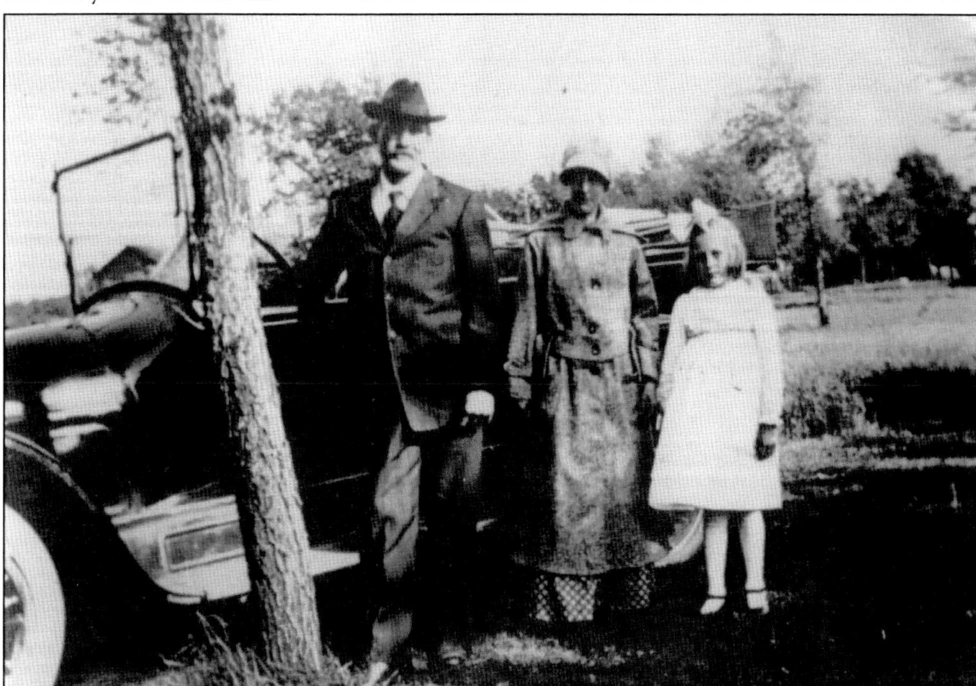

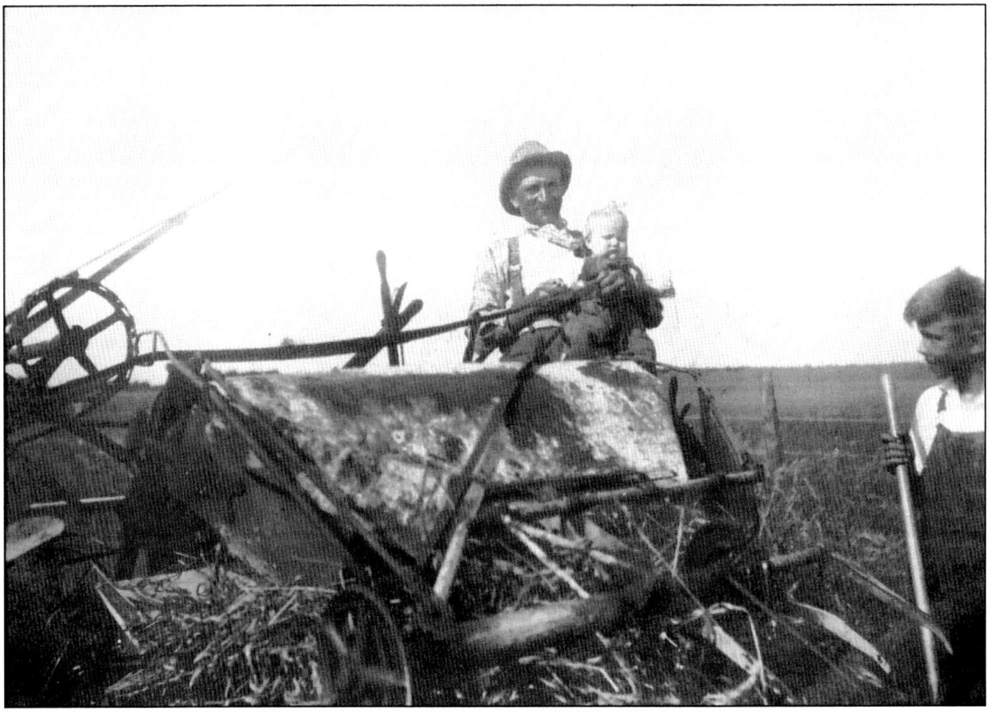

John Link was born in Prairie View to George and Susan Link. Farming was in his blood and was his passion; he enjoyed it his entire life. He bought and farmed land in Vernon Township beginning in 1912. It was left in the care of his daughter Mary Sue and her husband, Herb Didier, and is now known as Didier Farms. John is shown here holding his infant daughter in 1925. The farm has not just survived but thrived. It has become a treasured institution in an area that has been overtaken by development. (Courtesy of Mary Sue Didier.)

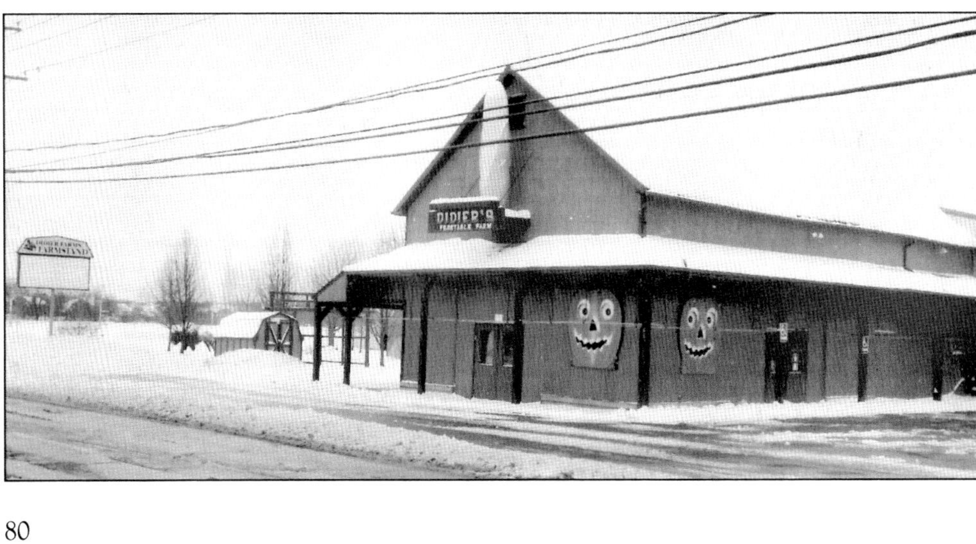

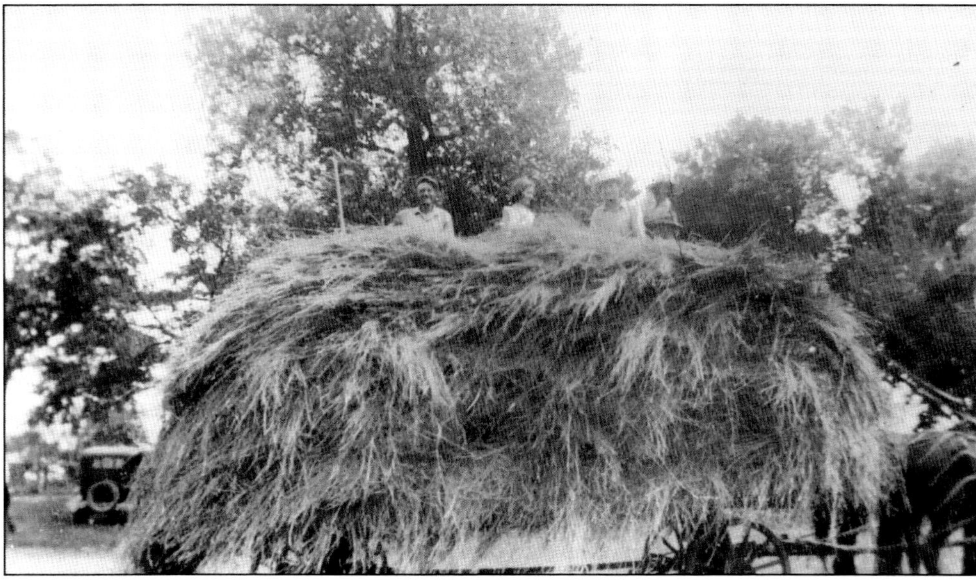

Threshing time was an exciting event around Vernon Township. A threshing ring was formed so work could be done cooperatively. Farmers joined together to thresh, or separate the seed from the straw to make hay. The ring would travel until all farmers in the ring had their crop harvested. The women of the families would get together and make large lunches for the men working in the fields. It was a time that brought families and neighbors together for a common cause and to also enjoy each other's company. Threshing time could continue for weeks. The top photograph shows John Link and his daughter Mary Sue (left) perched on top of a hay wagon after threshing had ended. At right sits Mary Sue Link (middle) surrounded by her cousins as threshing time began. (Photographs courtesy of Mary Sue Didier.)

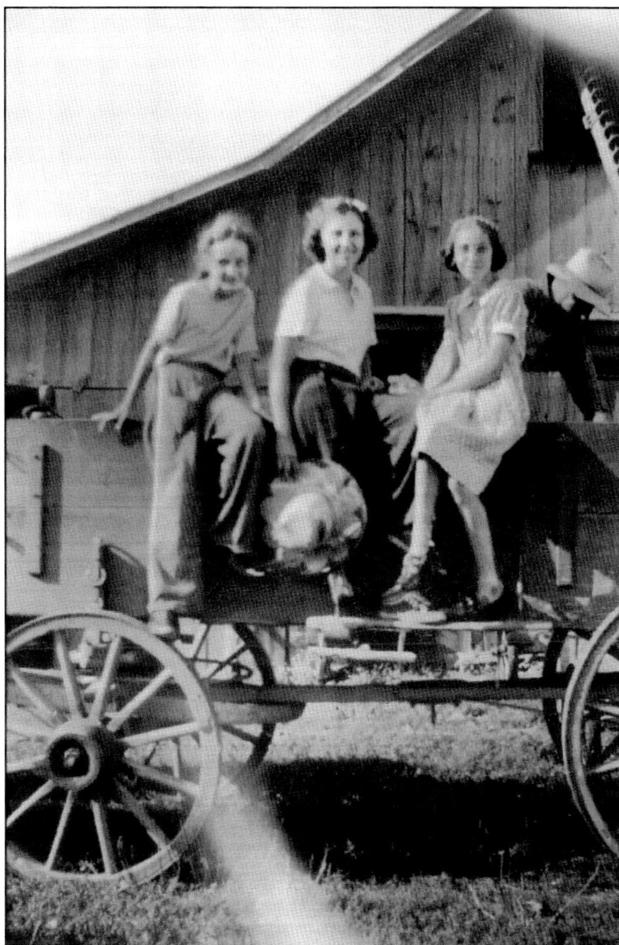

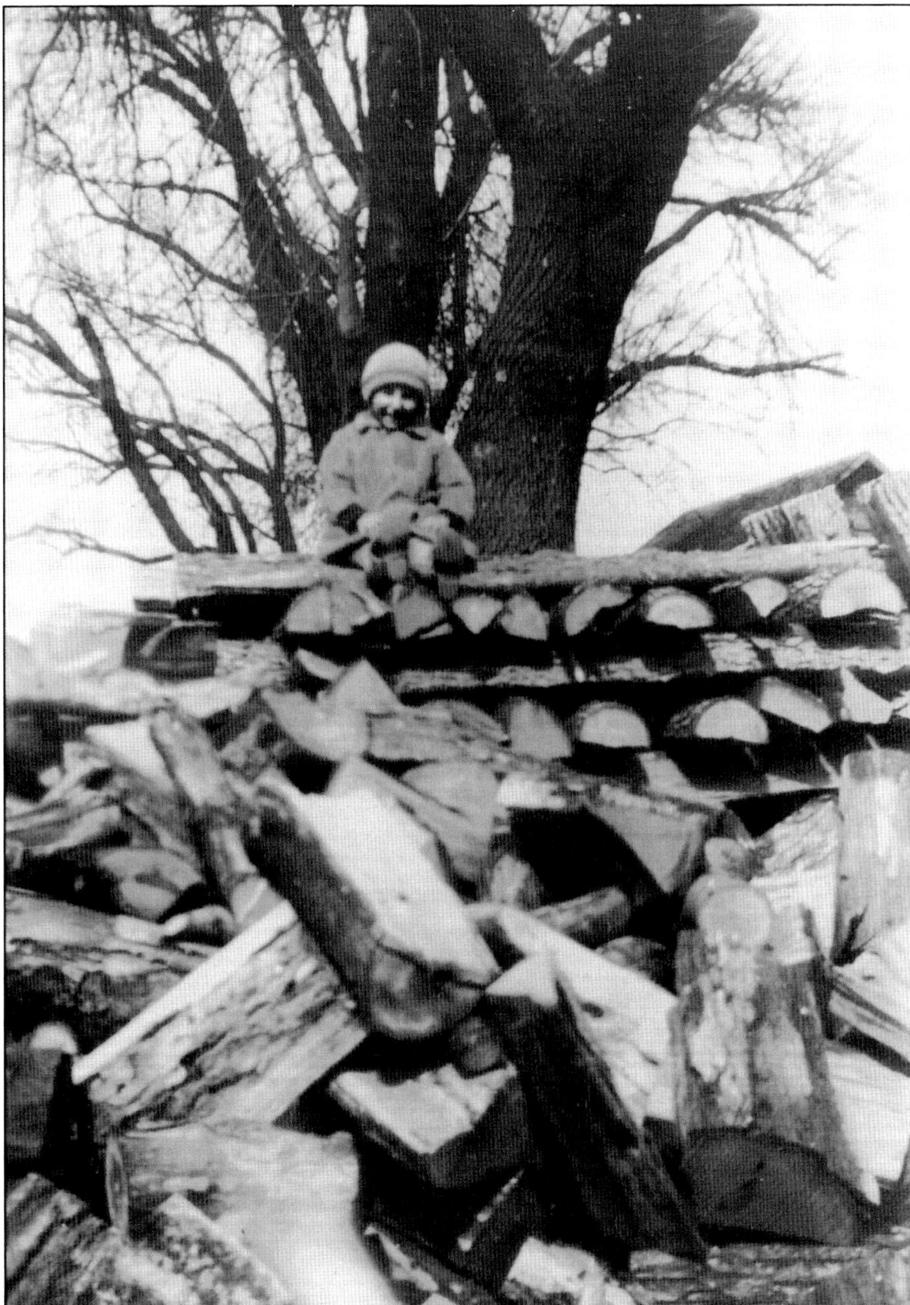

Mary Sue Link sits upon the family woodpile. Most local families owned woodlots on Elm Road or Riverwoods Road in addition to the property on which they lived. Many of the woodlots were landlocked and inaccessible by the road. When people cut trees from their lots, they would have to either drag the trees out to bring them to their wagons or split the wood on sight in order to transport it. People used wood for a variety of things, such as fuel for cooking, warmth for homes in the winter, and as raw materials for building supplies for homes and fencing. (Courtesy of Mary Sue Didier.)

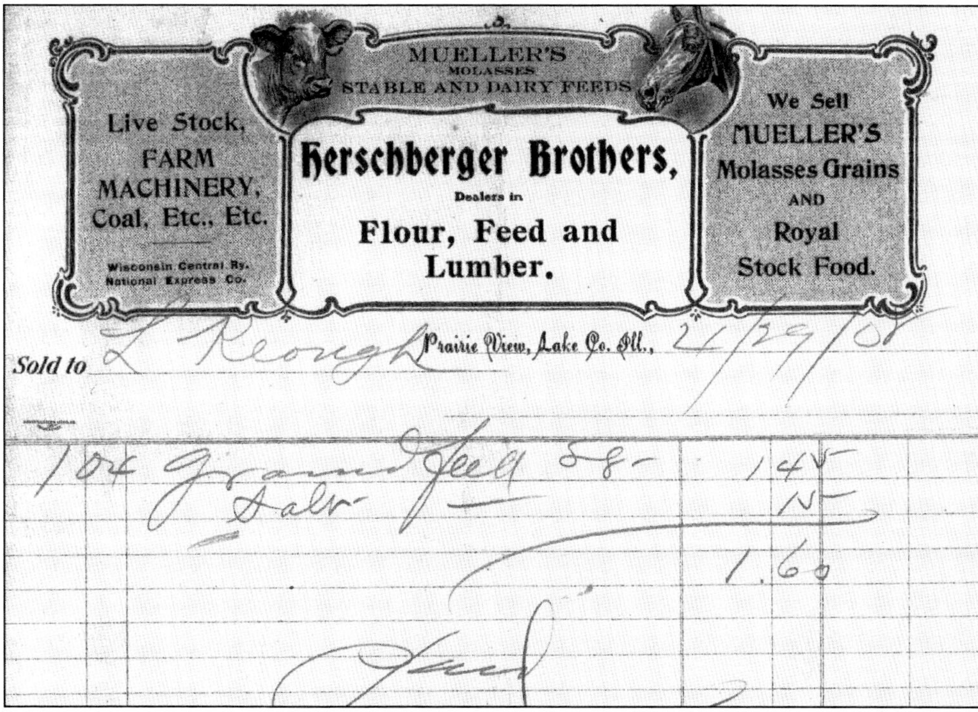
MUELLER'S
MOLASSES
STABLE AND DAIRY FEEDS

Live Stock,
FARM
MACHINERY,
Coal, Etc., Etc.

Wisconsin Central Ry.
National Express Co.

Herschberger Brothers,
Dealers in
Flour, Feed and
Lumber.

We Sell
MUELLER'S
Molasses Grains
AND
Royal
Stock Food.

Sold to L Keough Prairie View, Lake Co. Ill., 2/29/08

104	Grand Feed 58-		1.45
	Salt		.15
			1.60

Paid

This very decorative receipt from the Herschberger Brothers business is dated 1908. The family had several business dealings in town, including lumber, grain, and farm implements. Their business has been lost several times over the course of its history to fire but has always been rebuilt. Fire was a common occurrence in the days before the area had a full-time fire protection district. (Courtesy of Gertrude Moon.)

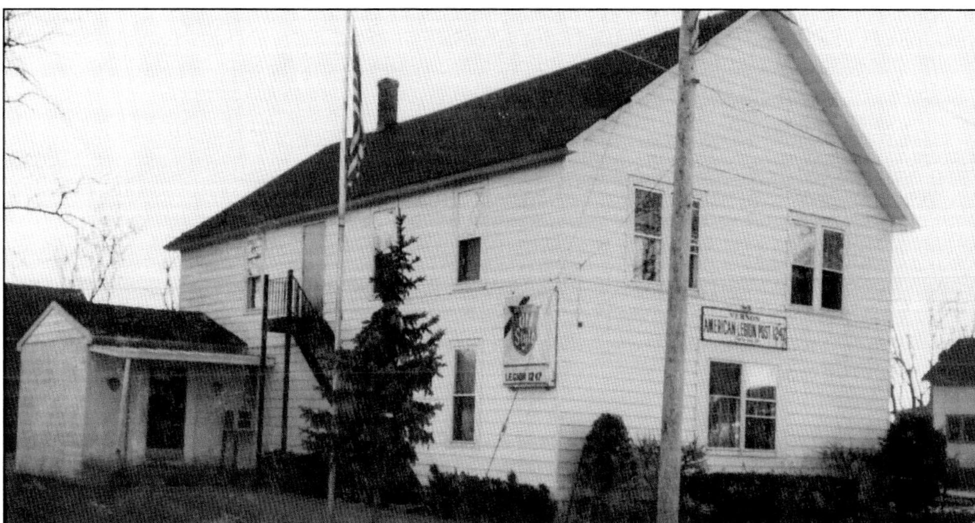

Herschberger Hall was a fixture of the landscape for years. It was built as Woodmen Hall and purchased by the Herschberger family, who had a successful farm implementation business. Over the years, the building has had many uses; it was used to store equipment and then for recreation. The 10-foot ceilings allowed a space for a basketball court and dance hall, and later, the American Legion used it.

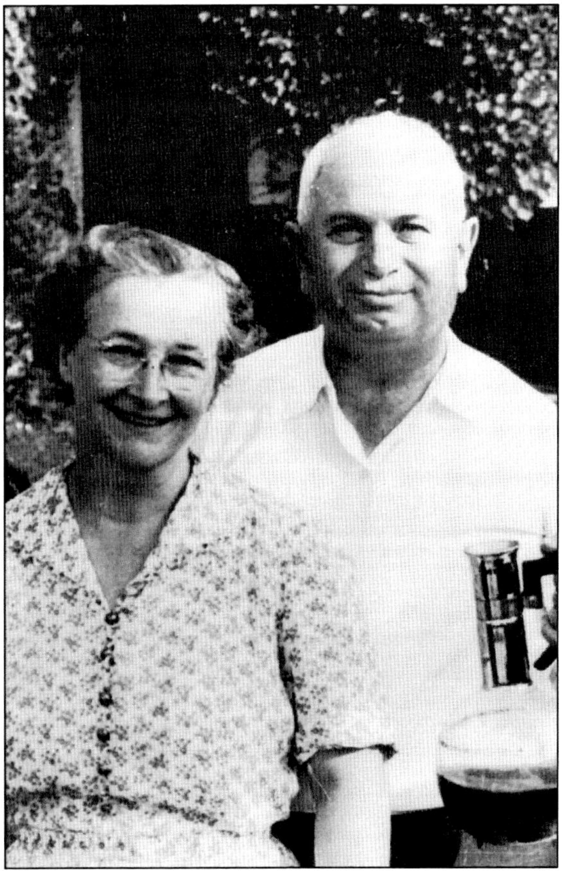

Charles Fiore was born Pascuale Fiori in Bari, Italy, in 1895 and came to the United States when he was 15 years old. He later changed his name to Charles, married Josephine Taliani, and built a thriving nursery and landscaping business in Prairie View. Among the many noteworthy deeds he was responsible for was the development of three different garden displays for the Century of Progress World's Fair held in Chicago during 1933 and 1934. He won outstanding garden both years. Fiore and his nursery supplied trees for world's fairs all over North America, the White House, and the Bah'ai Temple in Evanston as well as for such notable people as Philip Armour, Charles Schweppe, John T. Pirie, and Frank Lloyd Wright. Perhaps the best measure of the man is the fact that he had his largest workforce during the height of the Depression, hiring some even for a half-day's work so that their families would have some source of income during that difficult time. (Left photograph courtesy of Loretta Foss; below, courtesy of author.)

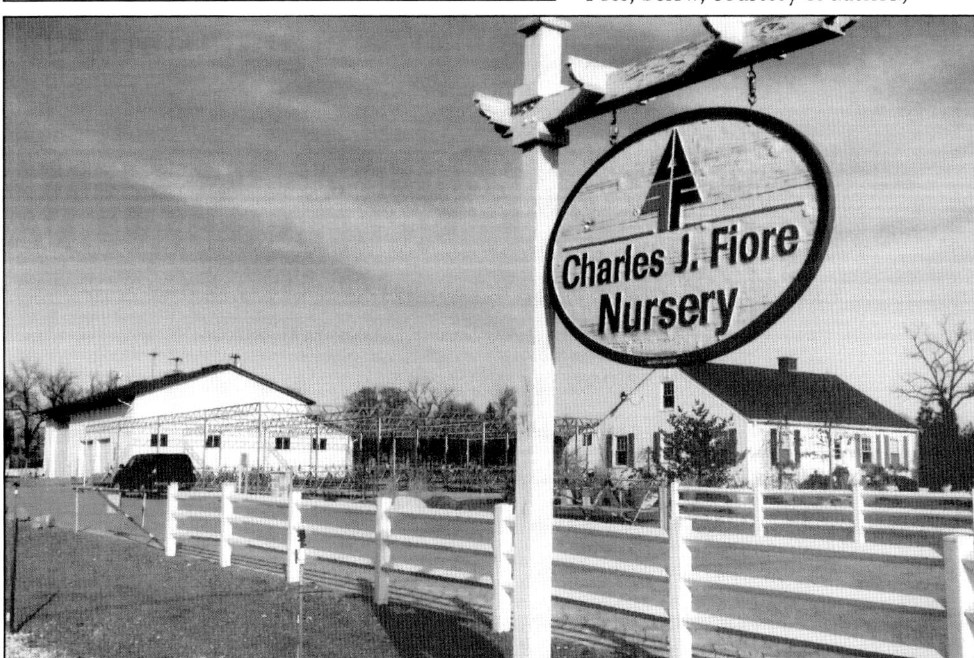

Three

Birth of a New Village

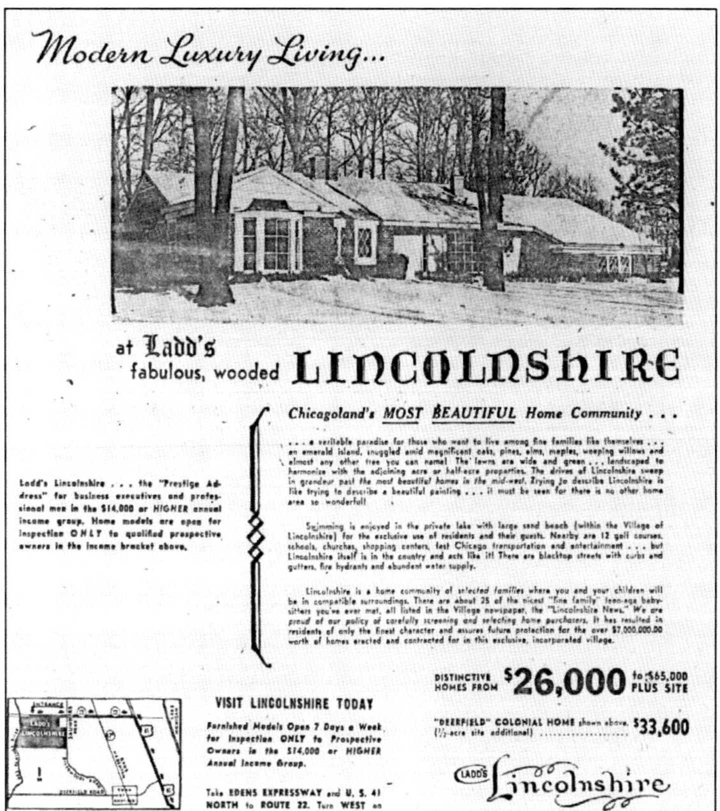

Families looking to get out of the hustle and bustle of the city and find a more genteel way of life had to look no further than Ladd's Lincolnshire. Conveniently located near major roadways and the brand-new Illinois Tollway, the area had much to offer. The new village would take its name from the development that beckoned to residents. (Courtesy of the Village of Lincolnshire.)

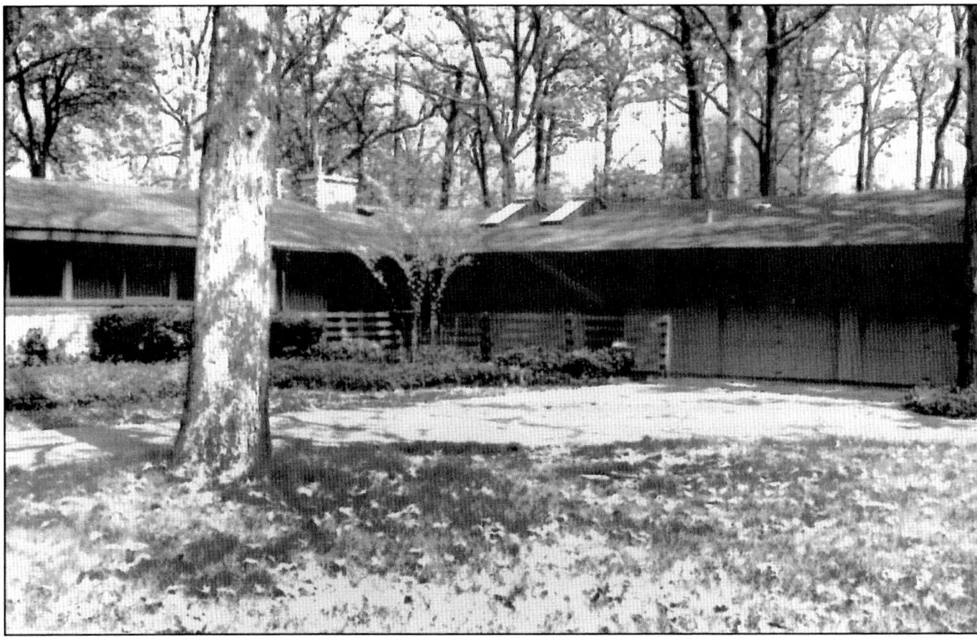

The homes, which were designed by Don Scholz, were unique and revolutionary for the time because they were prefabricated. The finished sides arrived by truck and were assembled on top of a pre-poured slab of concrete that had the ductwork, electrical wiring, and pipes already roughed in. Construction of the structure took about three days to complete once all the parts were in place. (Courtesy of the Village of Lincolnshire.)

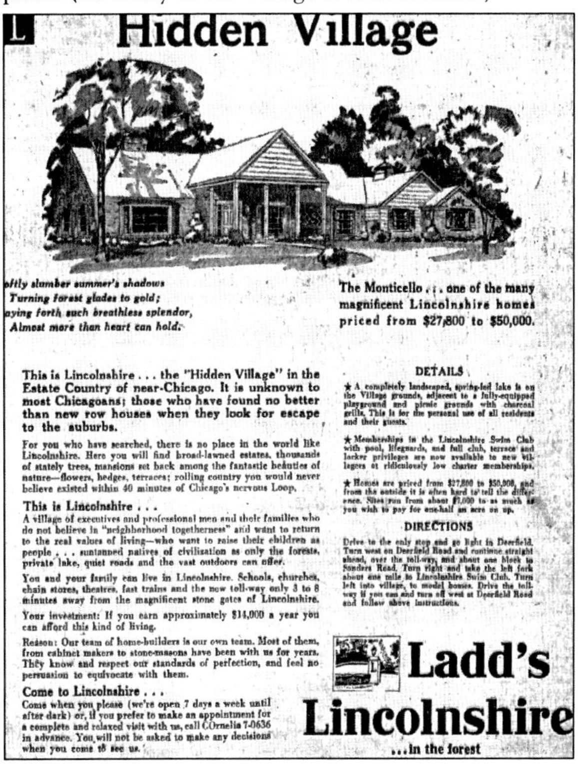

Roger Ladd was a developer who purchased land on Riverwoods Road from businessman Louis Leverone to create a subdivision called Ladd's Lincolnshire. Leverone was the president of the Automatic Canteen Company as well as majority stockholder in the Lustron Company, which manufactured metal siding on porcelainized steel. After Ladd's subdivision was built, Leverone built his own subdivision in Stonegate Circle with prefabricated Lustron homes. (Courtesy of the Village of Lincolnshire.)

The residents of Ladd's Lincolnshire subdivision formed a property owner's organization called the Cambridge Forest Association, named after a major street in the development. It was soon apparent that the growing area needed to incorporate in order to provide adequate police protection and other municipal services. On August 5, 1957, the Village of Lincolnshire was created. (Courtesy of the Village of Lincolnshire.)

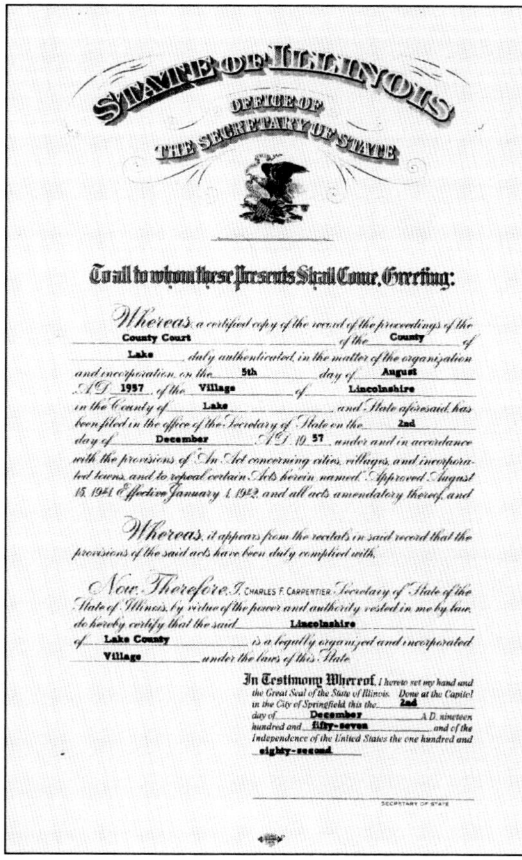

STATE OF ILLINOIS
OFFICE OF
THE SECRETARY OF STATE

To all to whom these Presents Shall Come, Greeting:

Whereas, a certified copy of the record of the proceedings of the County Court of the County of Lake duly authenticated, in the matter of the organization and incorporation, on the 5th day of August A.D. 1957, of the Village of Lincolnshire in the County of Lake and State aforesaid, has been filed in the office of the Secretary of State on the 2nd day of December A.D. 19 57, under and in accordance with the provisions of "An Act concerning cities, villages, and incorporated towns, and to repeal certain Acts herein named." Approved August 15, 1941, Effective January 1, 1942, and all acts amendatory thereof, and

Whereas, it appears from the recitals in said record that the provisions of the said acts have been duly complied with,

Now, Therefore, I, CHARLES F. CARPENTIER, Secretary of State of the State of Illinois, by virtue of the power and authority vested in me by law, do hereby certify that the said Lincolnshire of Lake County is a legally organized and incorporated Village under the laws of this State.

In Testimony Whereof, I hereto set my hand and the Great Seal of the State of Illinois. Done at the Capitol in the City of Springfield, this the 2nd day of December A.D. nineteen hundred and fifty-seven and of the Independence of the United States the one hundred and eighty-second

SECRETARY OF STATE

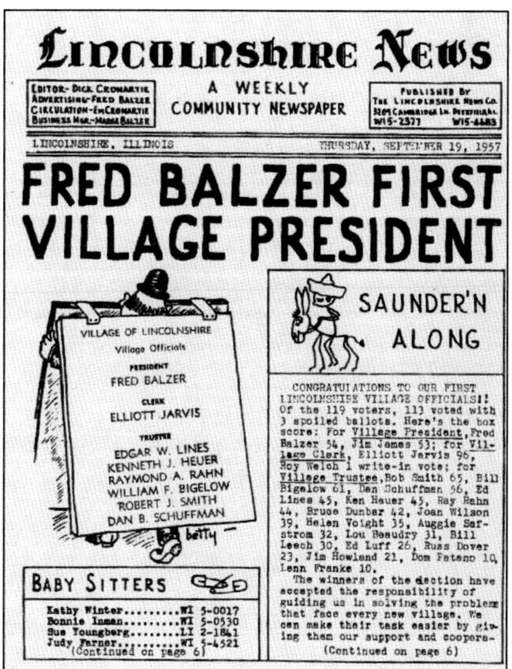

Lincolnshire News

EDITOR- DICK CROMARTIE
ADVERTISING- FRED BALZER
CIRCULATION- EM CROMARTIE
BUSINESS MGR.- MARGE BALZER

A WEEKLY COMMUNITY NEWSPAPER

PUBLISHED BY
THE LINCOLNSHIRE NEWS CO.
3209 CAMBRIDGE LN. DEERFIELD, ILL.
WI5-2377 WI5-6683

LINCOLNSHIRE, ILLINOIS — THURSDAY, SEPTEMBER 19, 1957

FRED BALZER FIRST VILLAGE PRESIDENT

SAUNDER'N ALONG

CONGRATULATIONS TO OUR FIRST LINCOLNSHIRE VILLAGE OFFICIALS!! Of the 119 voters, 113 voted with 3 spoiled ballots. Here's the box score: For Village President, Fred Balzer 54, Jim James 53; for Village Clerk, Elliott Jarvis 96, Roy Welch 1 write-in vote; for Village Trustee, Bob Smith 65, Bill Bigelow 61, Dan Schuffman 56, Ed Lines 45, Ken Heuer 45, Ray Rahn 44, Bruce Dunbar 42, Joan Wilson 39, Helen Voight 35, Auggie Safstrom 32, Lou Beaudry 31, Bill Leech 30, Ed Luff 26, Russ Dover 23, Jim Howland 21, Dom Fateno 10, Lenn Franke 10.

The winners of the election have accepted the responsibility of guiding us in solving the problems that face every new village. We can make their task easier by giving them our support and coopera-

(Continued on page 6)

BABY SITTERS

Kathy Winter..........WI 5-0017
Bonnie Inman..........WI 5-0530
Sue Youngberg.........LI 2-1841
Judy Farner...........WI 5-4521

(Continued on page 6)

The headline for the *Lincolnshire News* announced that Lincolnshire had its first mayor, Fred Balzer. Proving the old adage that every vote counts, Balzer was elected to the office by one vote. He went on to serve the village as mayor for the next 18 years. (Courtesy of the Village of Lincolnshire.)

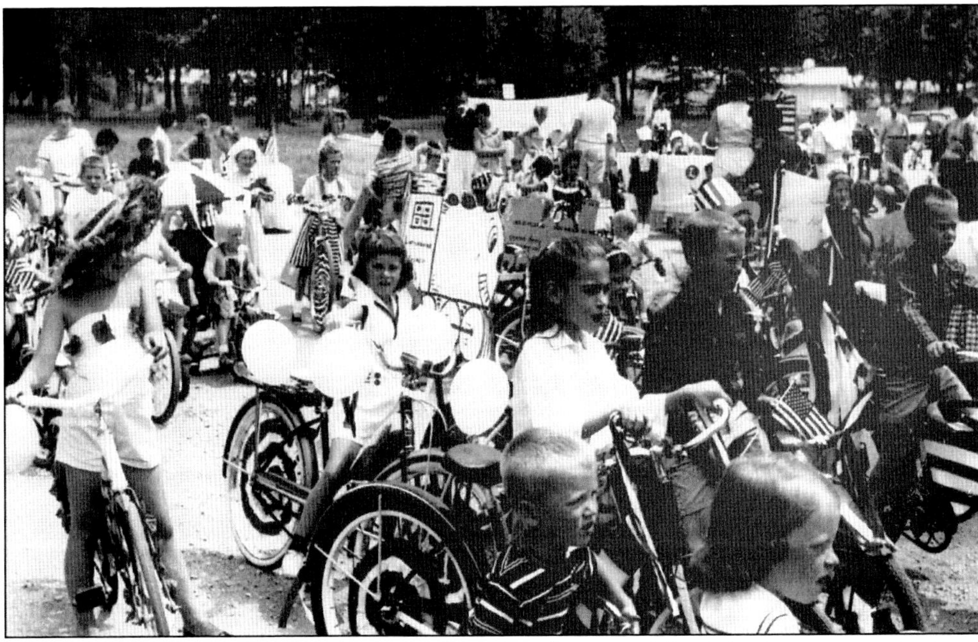

Nothing could be more American than celebrating the nation's birthday by participating in an old-fashioned Fourth of July parade. Dozens of children lined up for a chance to be in the 1958 Independence Day parade in Lincolnshire. With their bicycles festooned with colorful red, white, and blue steamers, the children are just waiting for the word to go racing down the street when the parade begins. The two young ladies below are enjoying themselves as they ride along the lanes of the village, decorated with their streamers and balloons in the gala annual event. It is an activity that proudly continues along the streets of Lincolnshire today. (Both, courtesy of the Village of Lincolnshire.)

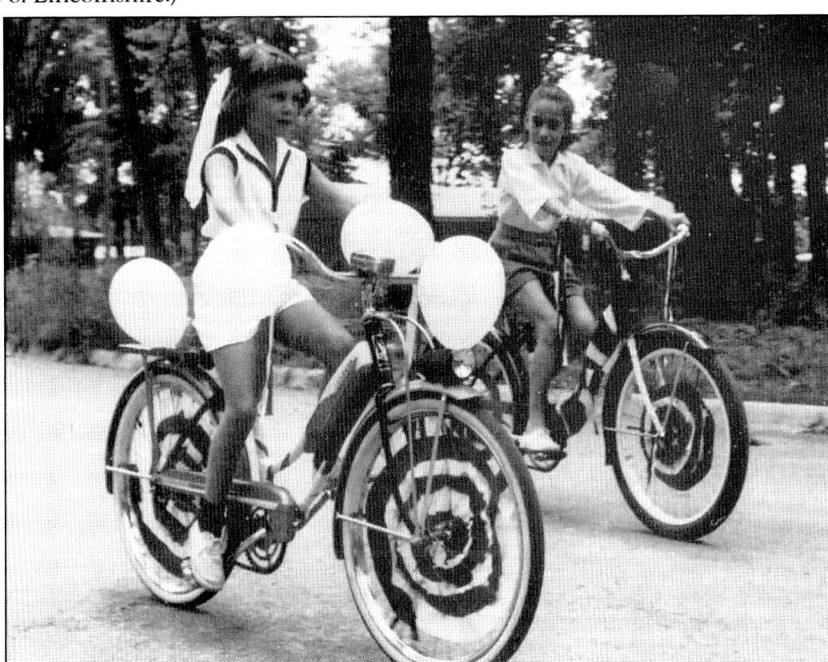

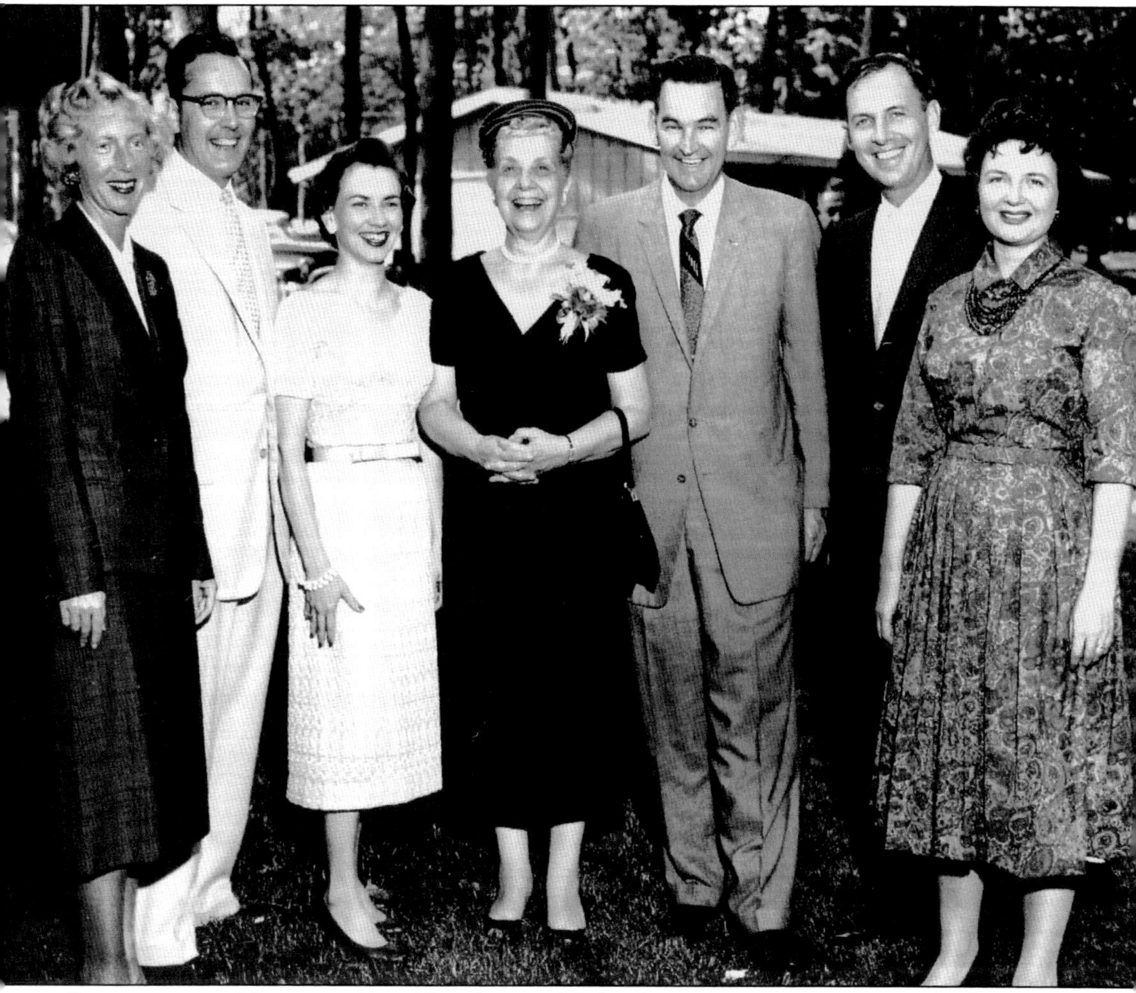

Congresswoman Marguerite Stitt Church visited Lake County's newest incorporated village in September 1958. The congresswoman was elected to the district and represented the North Shore after her husband, Ralph Church—who had been serving in that capacity—died suddenly. She was a staunch supporter of the Peace Corps and both women's and civil rights legislation in her distinguished career. While serving as the ranking Republican member on the Foreign Economic Policy subcommittee in 1959, she logged 40,000 miles to 17 different countries. She was famously dedicated to the constituents in her district, replying to an average of 600 letters a week. She is surrounded by local residents and elected officials in this photograph. People present were, from left to right, Em Cromartie, Bruce Guelich, Betty Guelich, Marguerite Church, Dick Cromartie (editor of the *Lincolnshire News*), Mayor Fred Balzer, and Marge Balzer. (Courtesy of the Village of Lincolnshire.)

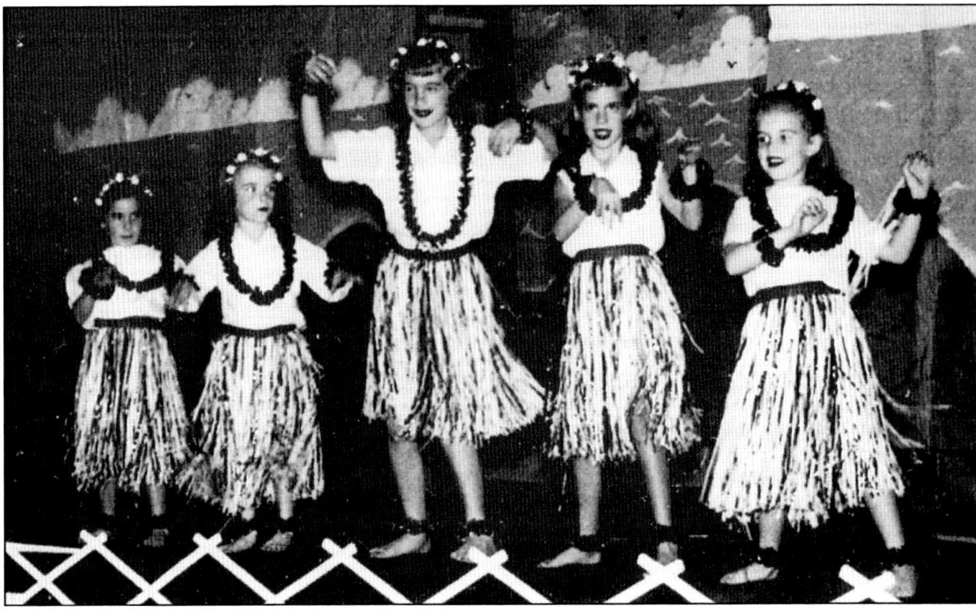

The Half Day School Community Club Show theme in November 1958 was "Around the World in Half-a-Daze" and was performed to standing room only crowds for two consecutive nights. The event was a festive affair with both students and parents performing acts to delighted throngs. The evenings had an international theme. At that time, exotic Hawaii was a United States territory and there was debate in the news about it becoming the newest state in the union. The children above entertained with a hula number, swaying in time to the music. Students dancing above are, from left to right, Patty Beaudry, Nancy Alston, Starr Cromartie, Kim Nelson, and Dianne Balzer. The fathers' performance of the "Hawaiian War Chant" followed the girls. They are, from left to right, Clyde Nelson, Lou Beaudry, Dick Cromartie, and Fred Balzer. (Both, courtesy of the Village of Lincolnshire.)

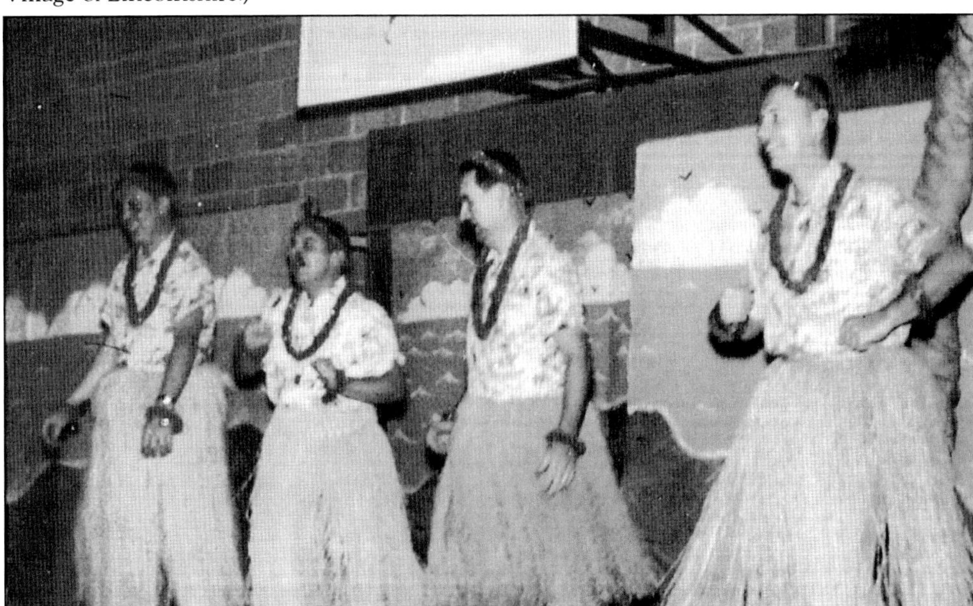

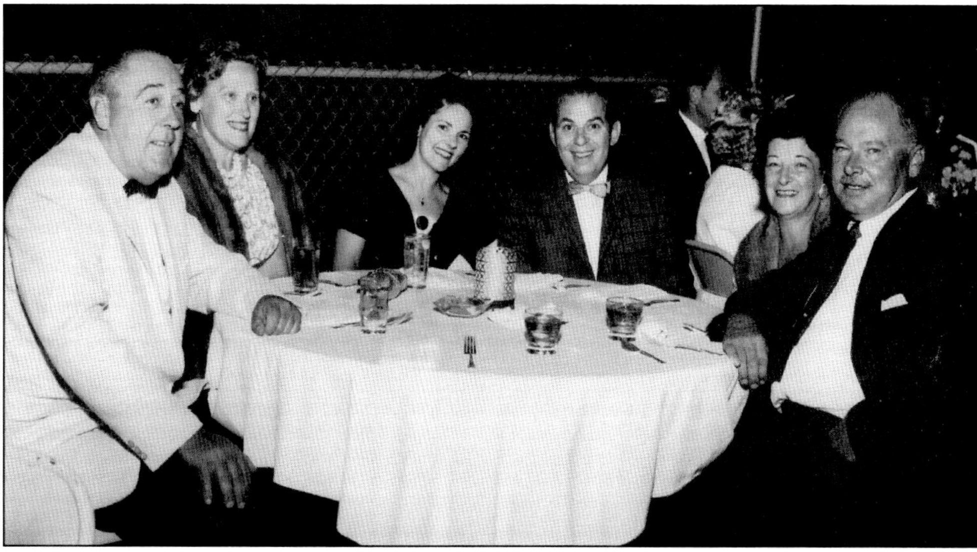

The Lincolnshire Swim Club was created so that residents of the new community could have a safe and supervised location for swimming and instruction. The club officially opened in May but was celebrated during a formal dinner dance on July 25, 1959. Attendees pictured are, from left to right, Ken Heuer, Della Heuer, Dot Beaudry, Lou Beaudry, Ella Miller, and Charlie Miller. (Courtesy of the Village of Lincolnshire.)

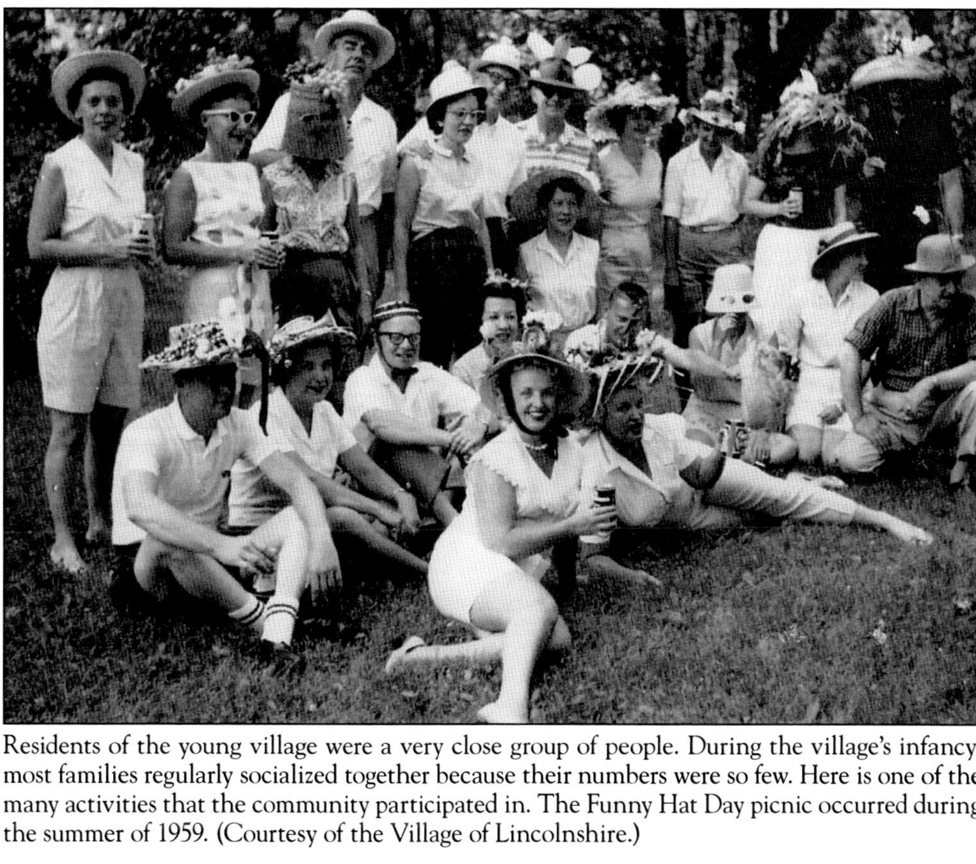

Residents of the young village were a very close group of people. During the village's infancy, most families regularly socialized together because their numbers were so few. Here is one of the many activities that the community participated in. The Funny Hat Day picnic occurred during the summer of 1959. (Courtesy of the Village of Lincolnshire.)

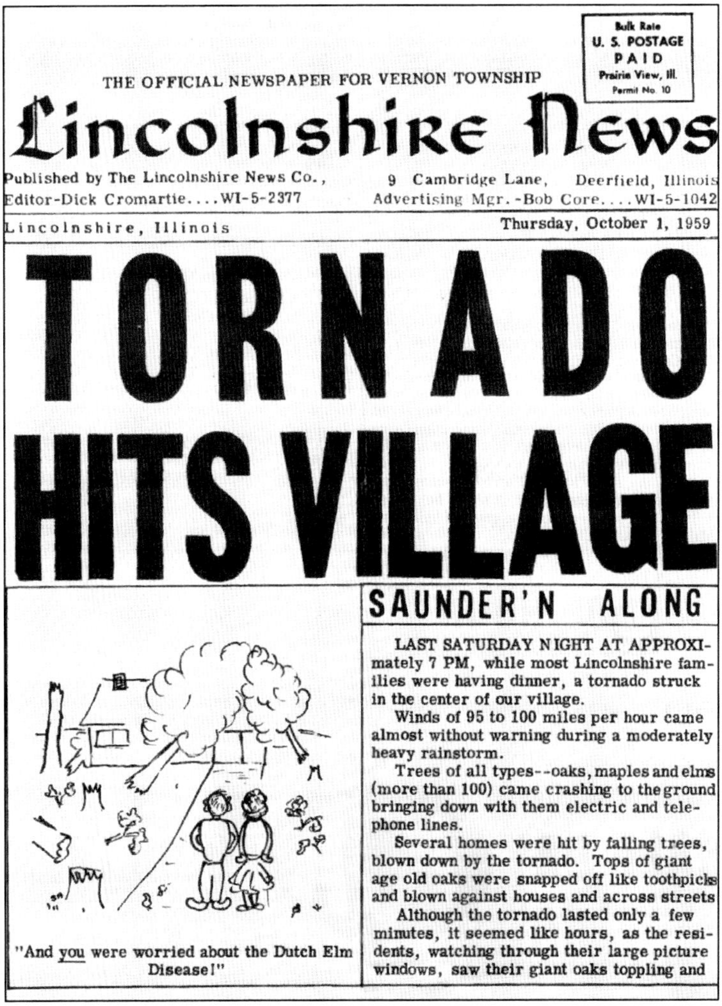

Bulk Rate
U. S. POSTAGE
PAID
Prairie View, Ill.
Permit No. 10

THE OFFICIAL NEWSPAPER FOR VERNON TOWNSHIP

Lincolnshire News

Published by The Lincolnshire News Co., 9 Cambridge Lane, Deerfield, Illinois
Editor-Dick Cromartie....WI-5-2377 Advertising Mgr.-Bob Core....WI-5-1042

Lincolnshire, Illinois Thursday, October 1, 1959

TORNADO HITS VILLAGE

"And you were worried about the Dutch Elm Disease!"

SAUNDER'N ALONG

LAST SATURDAY NIGHT AT APPROXImately 7 PM, while most Lincolnshire families were having dinner, a tornado struck in the center of our village.

Winds of 95 to 100 miles per hour came almost without warning during a moderately heavy rainstorm.

Trees of all types--oaks, maples and elms (more than 100) came crashing to the ground bringing down with them electric and telephone lines.

Several homes were hit by falling trees, blown down by the tornado. Tops of giant age old oaks were snapped off like toothpicks and blown against houses and across streets.

Although the tornado lasted only a few minutes, it seemed like hours, as the residents, watching through their large picture windows, saw their giant oaks toppling and

On the evening of Saturday, September 26, 1959, a tornado struck Lincolnshire. The twister arrived in the early evening during a rainstorm without much advance notice. There was heavy damage to the village, and many people lost trees and shrubs on their property. Several homes were severely damaged by falling fragments of trees; more than 100 of all varieties were lost to the weather. The *Lincolnshire News* reported that the damage to the village was extensive, but luckily, no life was lost during the ordeal, which only lasted for a few minutes. The community quickly came together to help one another. (Both, courtesy of the Village of Lincolnshire.)

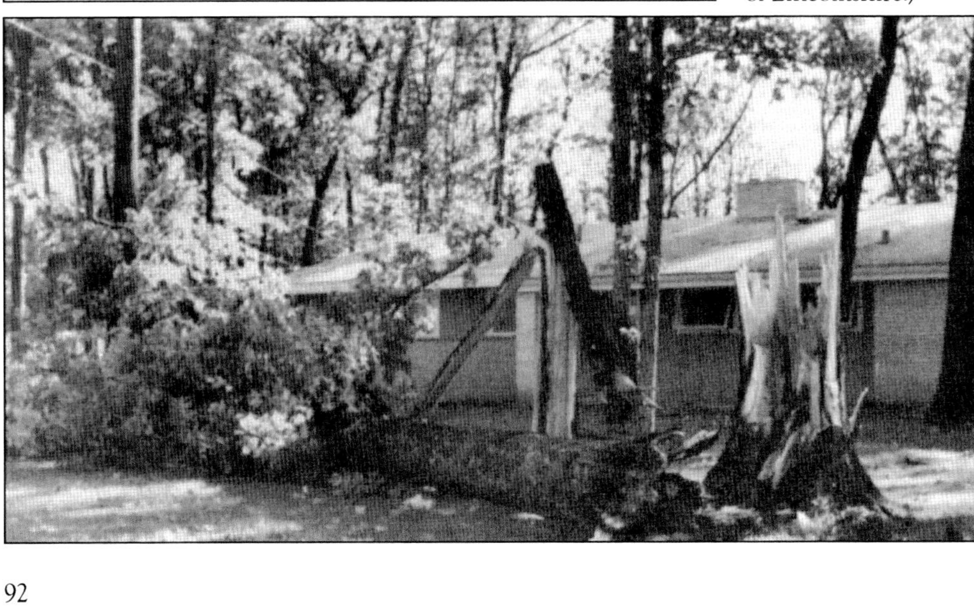

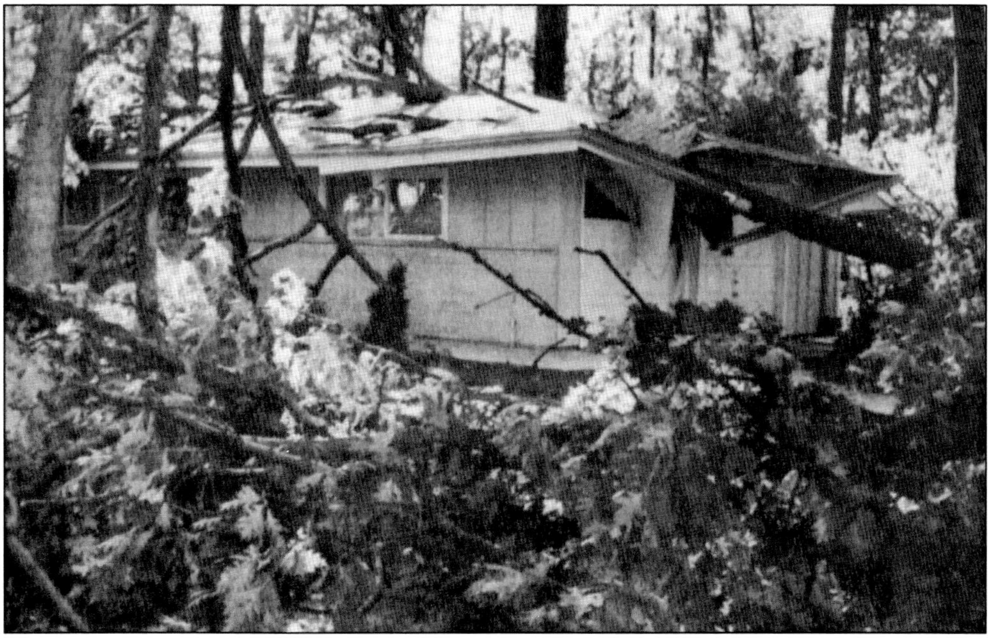

The tornado caused damage to roofs, automobiles, and windows. The electrical and telephone lines were damaged in the storm by all of the falling trees. Neighbors pulled together and began the tedious work of clearing the roads. Both adults and teens alike joined in common cause and started to remove the debris so that emergency vehicles could get through if needed. The volunteer Vernon Fire Department also arrived and finished the job of making the streets passable again. This would only be the first test of the strength and resiliency of the community. Floods and blizzards were also surmounted in the years to come by mutual cooperation and fortitude. (Both, courtesy of the Village of Lincolnshire.)

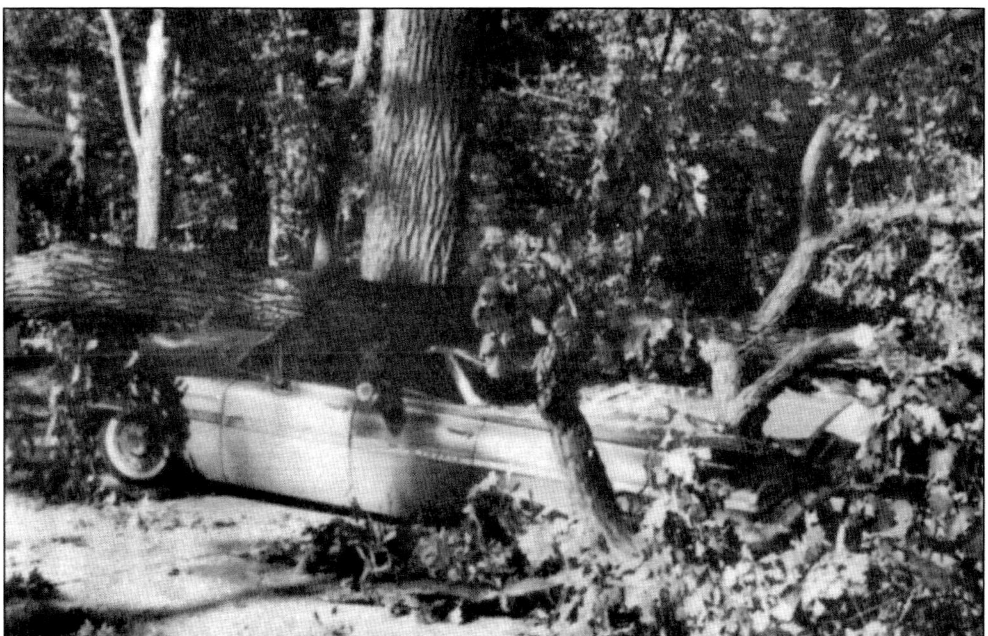

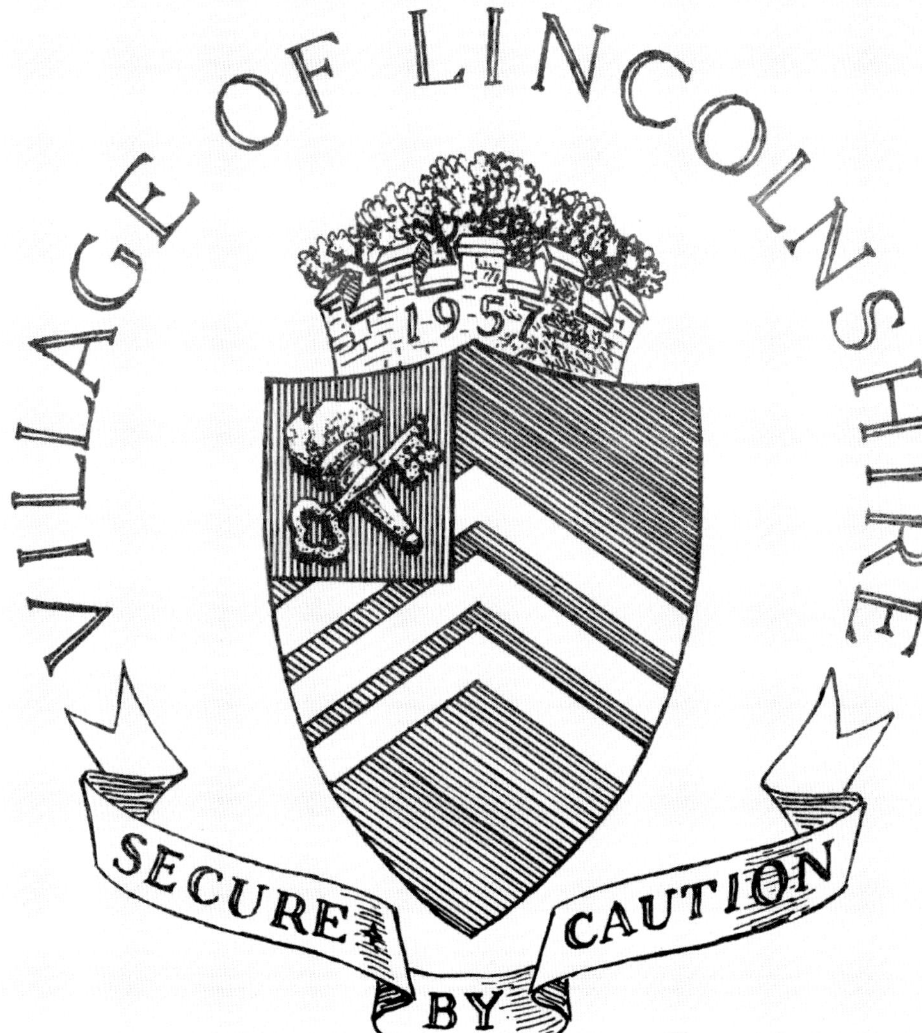

The meaning of the Village of Lincolnshire Coat of Arms is not widely known in the community. The design was first proposed by the First Citizens Committee in 1958. The emblem consists of items that either represent the area or the ideals that are to be strived for. The heraldic style is a nod to the English name of Lincolnshire. The three chevron bars suggest a community of homes. The motto "Secure by Caution" expresses the idea that citizens should secure their individual rights by being cautious in leadership. The flaming torch is recognized as a badge of leadership, lighting the way of community spirit. The key symbolizes the ownership of individual homes. The circular masonry wall stands for sovereignty with the year of the village's incorporation on it. The crown-like shape also is emblematic of regality. The importance of trees is demonstrated by their placement in the masonry wall. (Courtesy of the Village of Lincolnshire.)

One of the Lake County Forest Preserve District's first acquisitions was Wright Woods. It was named to honor the county's first settler; however, he actually settled in the Ryerson Conservation Area. The combination of maples and oaks here are a reminder that this place was not affected by the prairie fires that once swept eastward, destroying all in their wake. The preserve was dedicated in September 1965. (Courtesy of Vernon Township.)

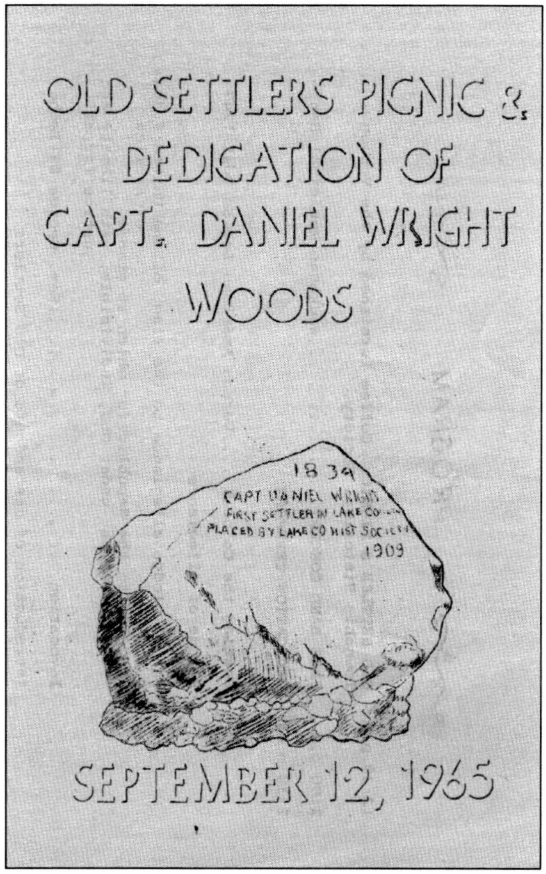

In 1909, the Lake County Historical Society placed this boulder commemorating Wright's settlement in Lake County on his former land, located near the intersection of Aptakisic Road and Milwaukee Avenue. It was moved to the Ryerson Conservation Area since it was becoming a danger with people stopping on the busy highway to see it. Confusion arose when the year 1834 was inscribed on it instead of 1833. (Courtesy of the author.)

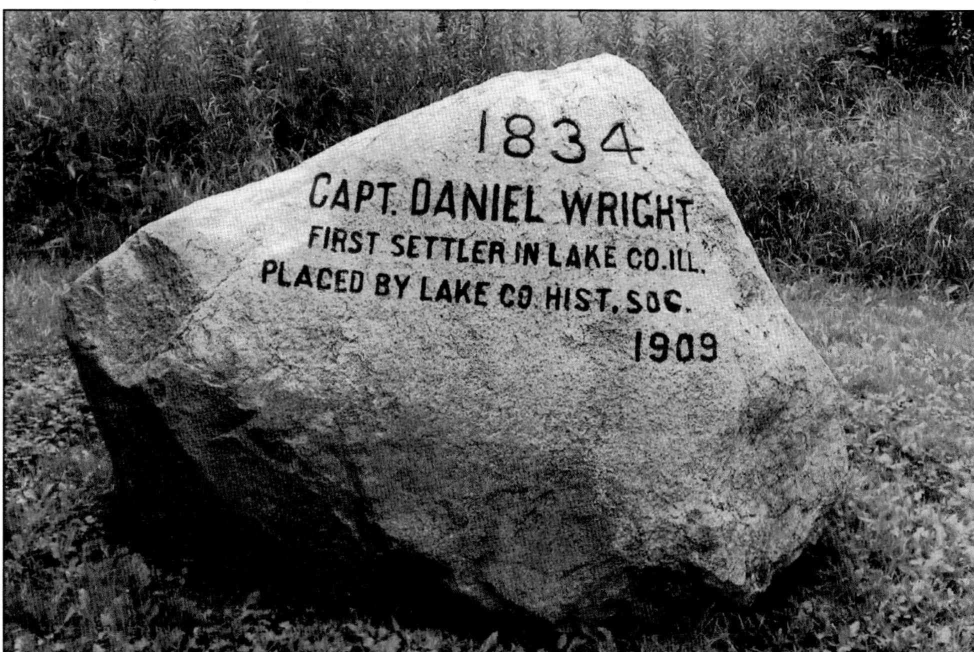

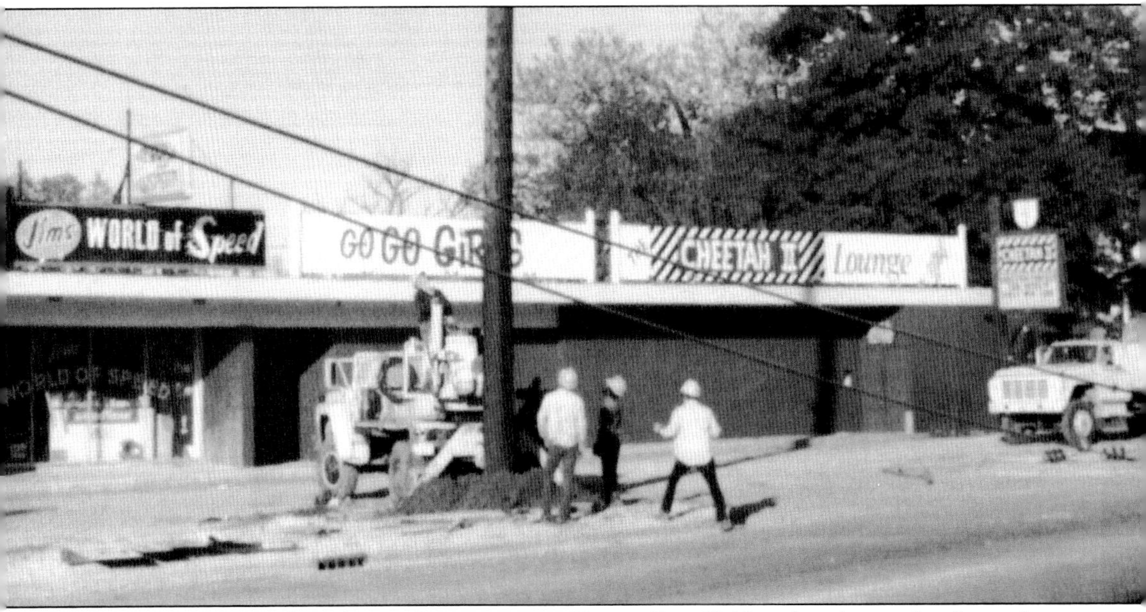

The shopping mall on the southwest corner of Route 45 and Milwaukee Avenue has housed many different businesses over the years. Two businesses that have left lasting impressions on people who grew up in the area were the Cheetah II Lounge and Jim's World of Speed. The Cheetah II and its dancers have long since been gone from the area, but it was an infamous spot where organized crime tried to get a foothold in Lake County. Jim's World of Speed was an automotive speed shop that sold all manner of high-performance accessories for different makes and models. They were a frequent advertiser at the local drive-in theaters. (Courtesy of the Lincolnshire-Riverwoods Fire Protection District.)

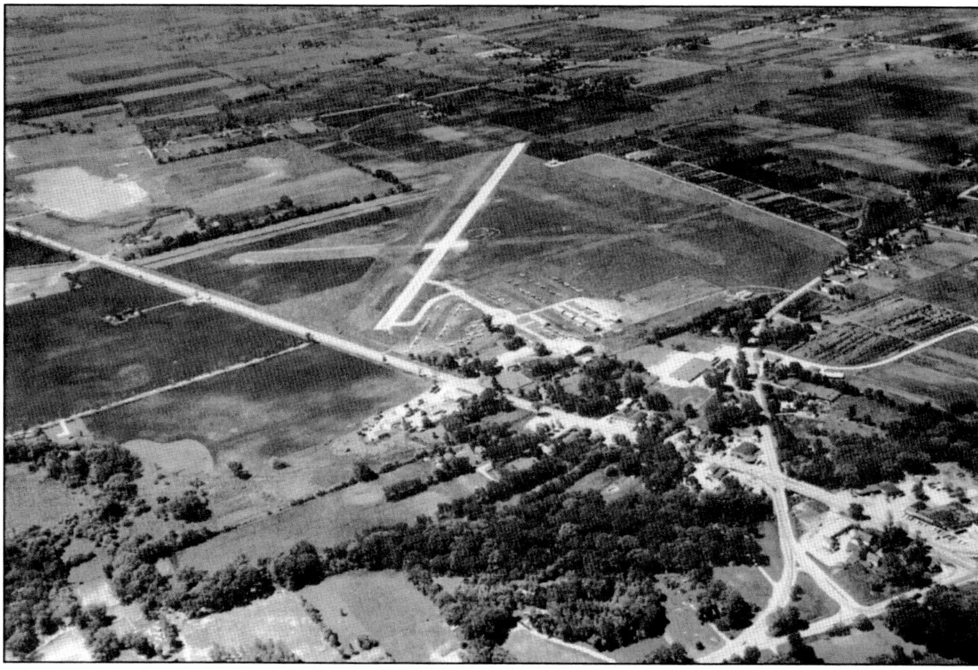

The Chicagoland Airport was previously located within the village's borders. The airport was located near the southwest corner of Route 22 and Milwaukee Avenue. It is now the Lincolnshire Corporate Center. It was owned and operated by Jack Schelter. Military trainers were housed there during World War II for the Glenview Naval Air Station. This view shows the roads before the Route 22 bypass was built. (Courtesy of Fred Kruger.)

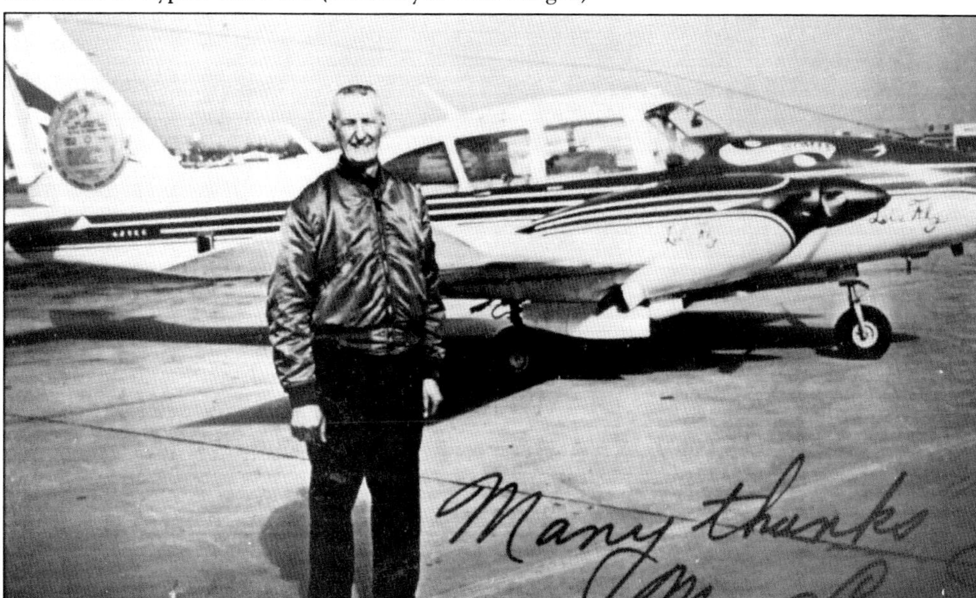

Famous aviator Max Conrad, known as the flying grandfather, flew into the Chicagoland Airport during his record-breaking feat for the longest sustained flight in a single-engine aircraft with one filling. The airport was used mainly for civil aviation but was put up for sale in 1971 and eventually sold for development.

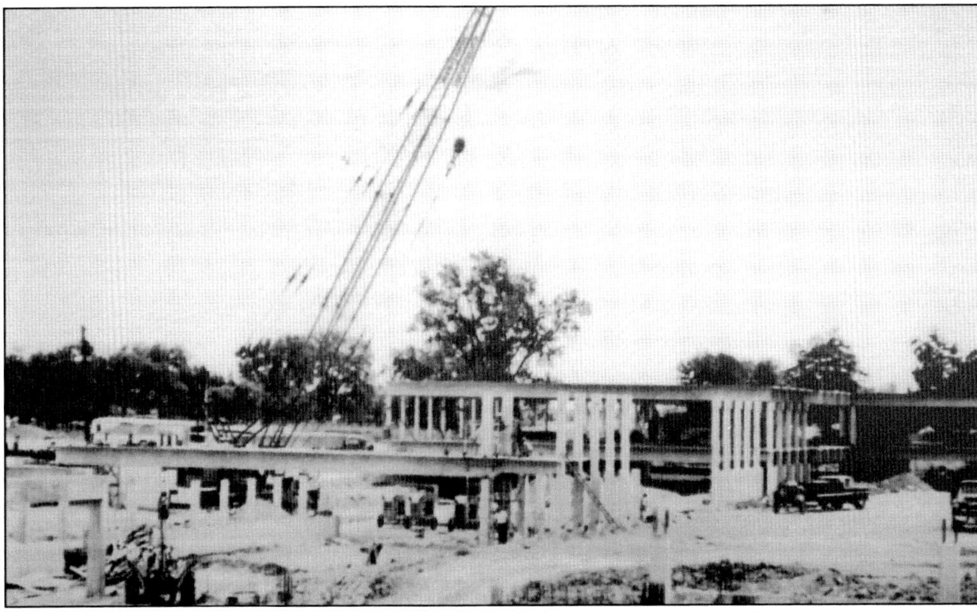

Vernon Township originally was a non–high school district area. In 1926, a secondary school called Ela-Vernon Township High School was built in Lake Zurich, and students from Half Day, Prairie View, and Lincolnshire schools attended there along with those from neighboring Lake Zurich. A second school, which was to be called Ela-Vernon East, had started construction in 1964 when the western portion seceded from the school district. The school was completed and classes began in 1965 with 467 students and 34 teachers. The process of choosing a name was underway at the time of Adlai E. Stevenson's sudden death. The school was named to honor the great statesman from this area. Early construction and aerial photographs show the evolution of the campus. (Above, courtesy of Adlai E. Stevenson High School.)

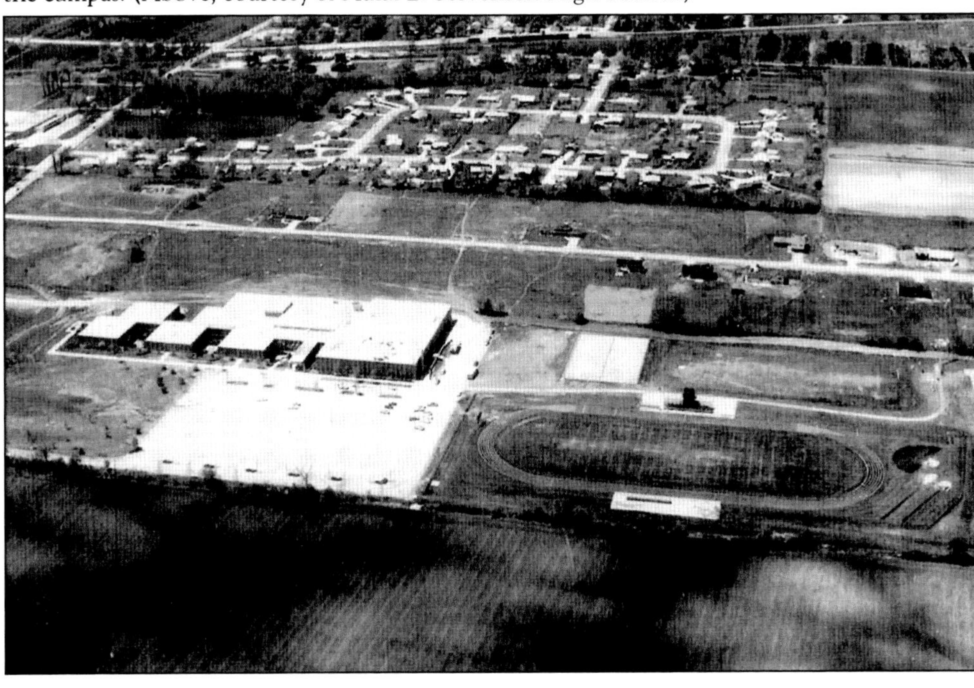

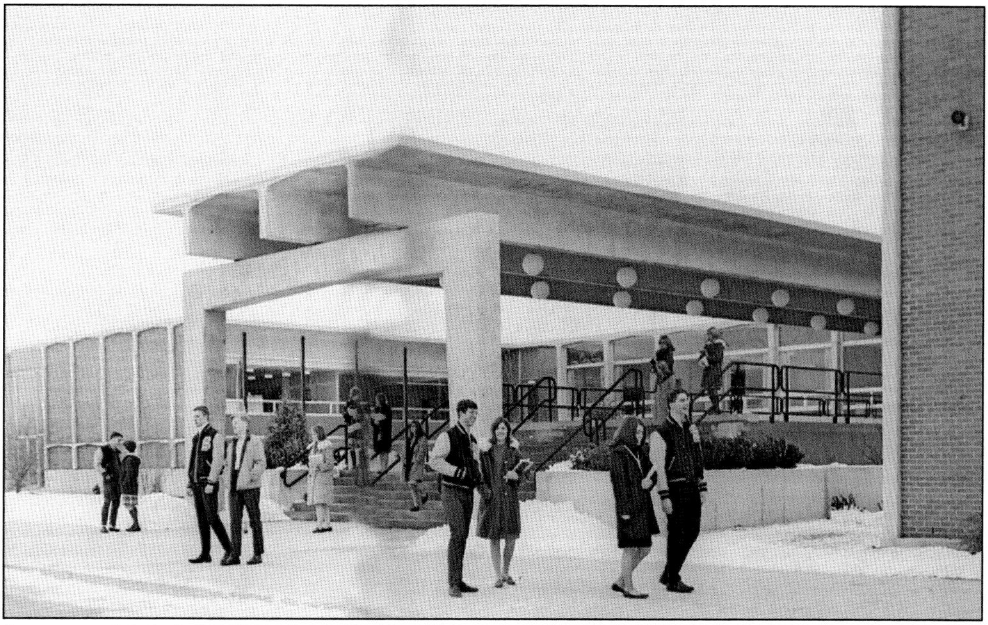

Stevenson High School continued to grow and increase in student population. The practice of oral exams was a short-lived experiment that saw each student interviewed and questioned by three faculty members concerning their proficiency in academics. By 1969, the graduating class was more than 100 students, and new residents continued to move into the district as development in the area continued. (Courtesy of Adlai E. Stevenson High School.)

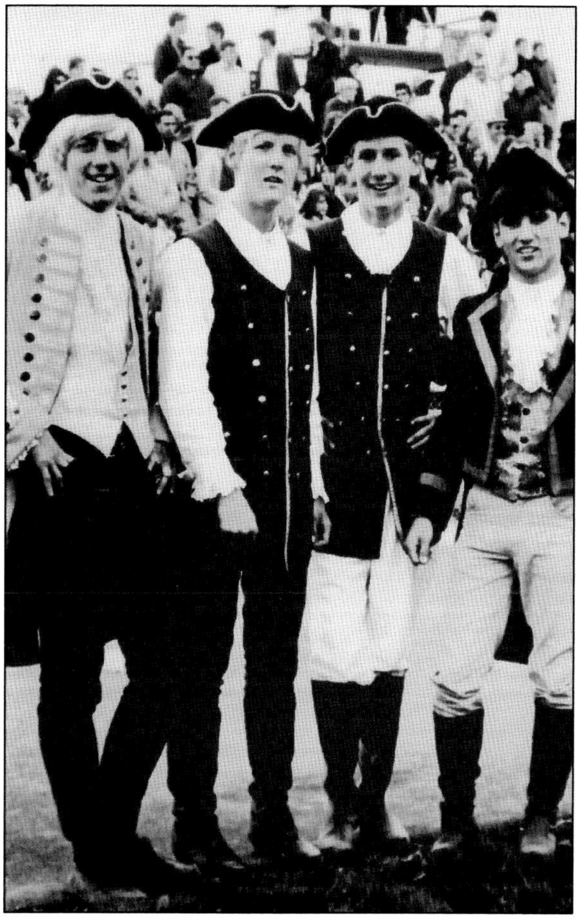

Themes that run throughout the high school's publications and mascots directly relate back to its namesake life and legacy. The mascot is the Patriot, the newspaper is the *Statesman*, the yearbook is the *Ambassador*, and the student newspaper is the *Wit*. The Stevenson High School Color Guard appears in its patriotic waistcoats and tri-corner hats at a home football game. (Courtesy of Adlai E. Stevenson High School.)

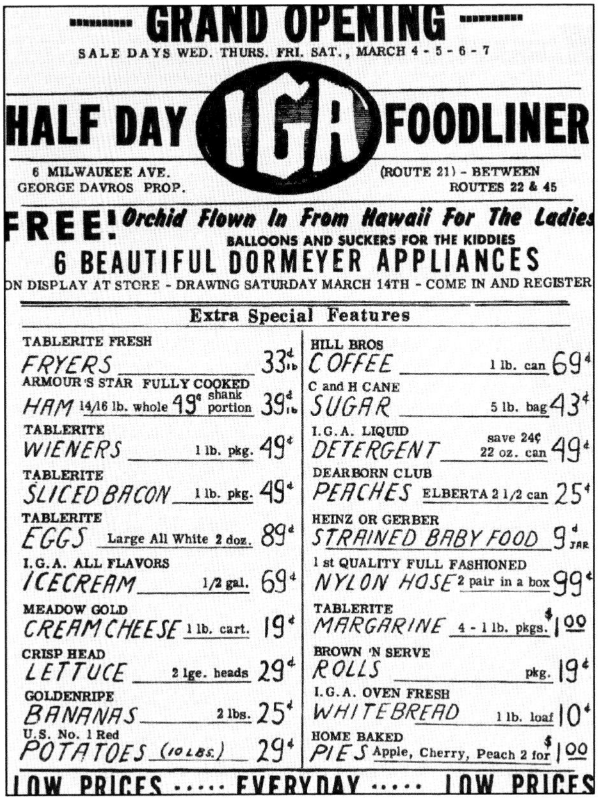

At one time, Lincolnshire did have a grocery store. The grocery was located between Route 45 and Olde Half Day Road on the west side of the road. The store opened on March 4, 1959, and carried the IGA moniker. IGA stood for Independent Grocers Alliance and was a franchise store rather than part of a national chain. The brand prided itself because their stores were located in smaller communities rather than large, urban environments. Another choice for fresh vegetables for local residents was the Leikam Farm Stand, which was also on the west side of Milwaukee Avenue but farther north. (Both, courtesy of the Village of Lincolnshire.)

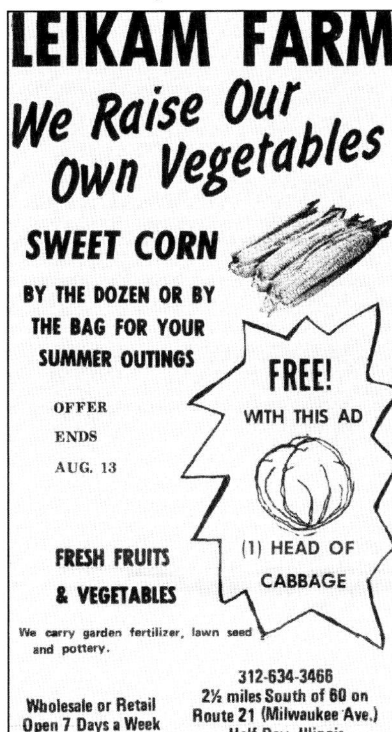

Four

Today's Lincolnshire and Vernon Township

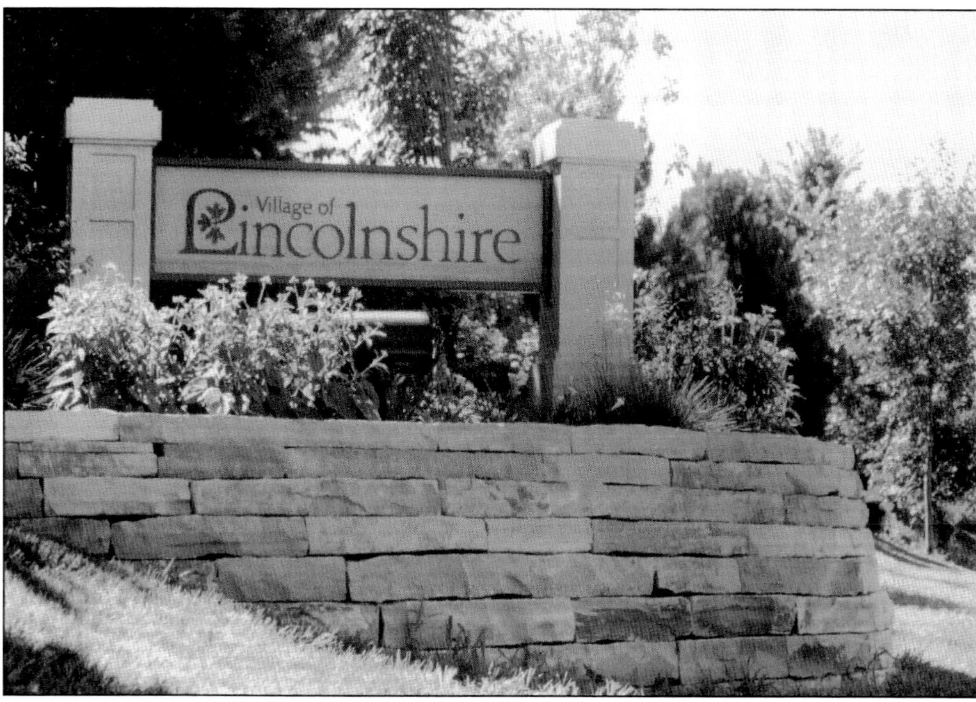

The Village of Lincolnshire has grown from a population of little more than 200 at incorporation to more than 6,000 residents today. The growth in Northern Illinois is even more astounding. With a current population of over 700,000 residents, Daniel Wright would have never foreseen the population boom that first day he stepped foot in what was to become Lake County. (Courtesy of the Village of Lincolnshire.)

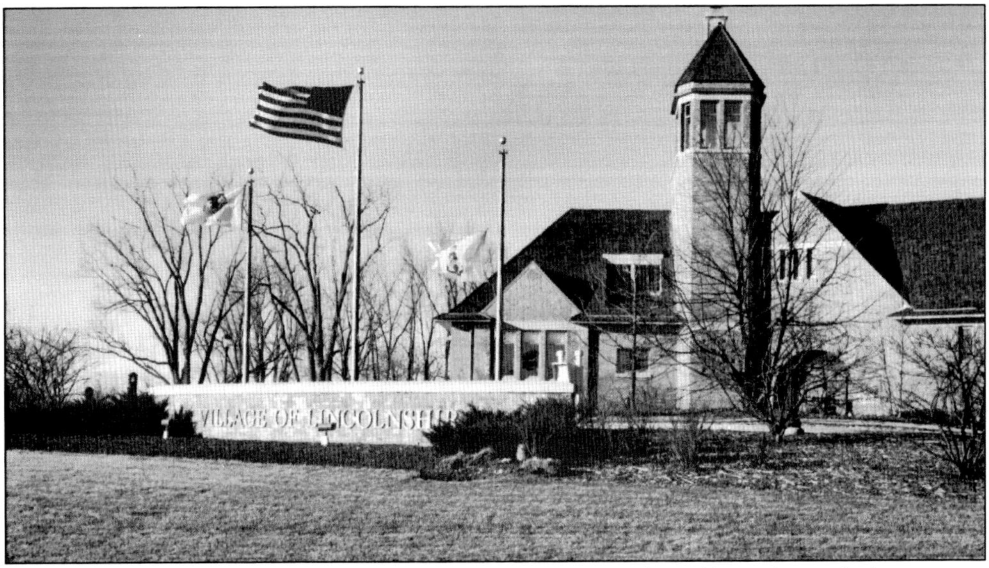

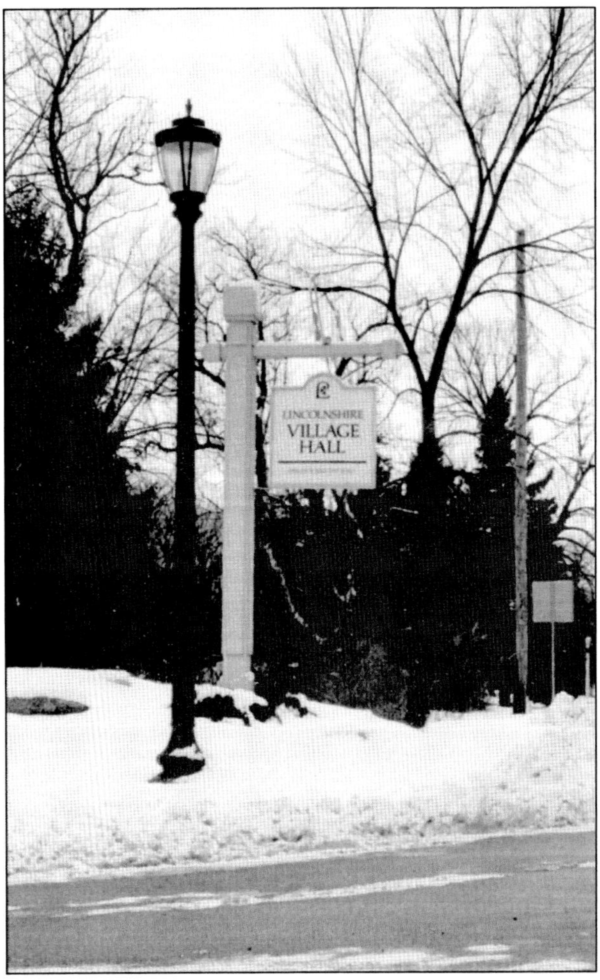

The Village of Lincolnshire built a new village hall in 1993 at the intersection of Routes 22 and 45. The beautiful structure houses village offices and is the location of the police department. Initially, the village's offices were run from the home of the very first elected officials. Over the years, the offices have moved and at one time were also located in the same building as Half Day School on Olde Half Day Road. The mayor and six trustees are elected to serve while a village manager carries out the daily functions of running the village. (Both, courtesy of the Village of Lincolnshire.)

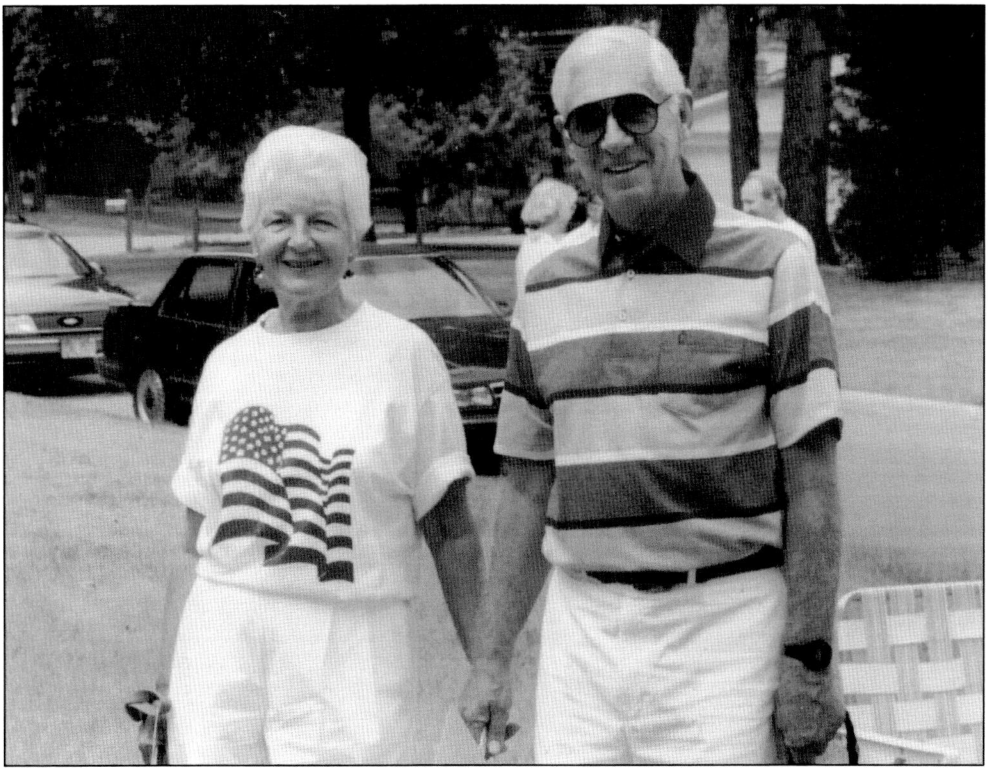

Fred Balzer was Lincolnshire's first mayor, retiring from the position in 1975. He and his wife, Marge, were the first to have purchased in what was to become the new community. He was responsible for much of the initial growth and direction of the village. With a degree in mechanical engineering, Balzer was involved in the heating and air-conditioning business. Marge was the director of admissions and public relations at Lake Forest Academy and later at Woodlands Academy. Both Fred and Marge were dedicated to their community and served it faithfully for many years. Balzer Park (below) is named in their honor. (Above, courtesy of Alice Moody; below, courtesy of the Village of Lincolnshire.)

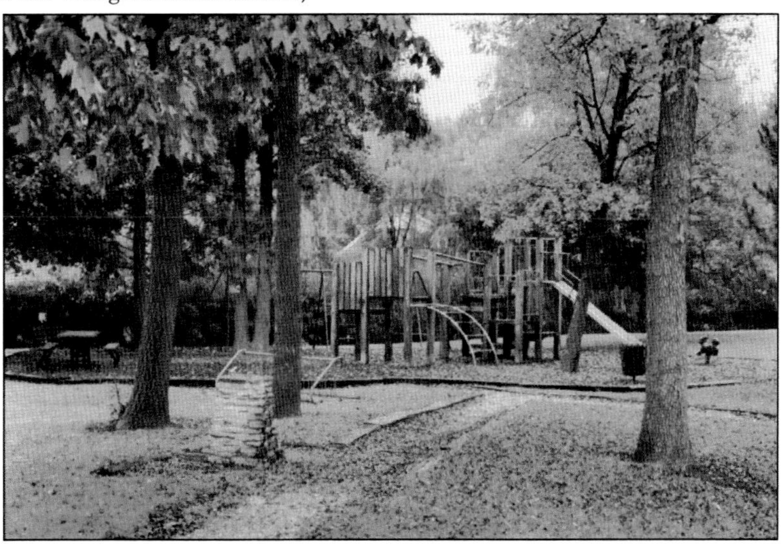

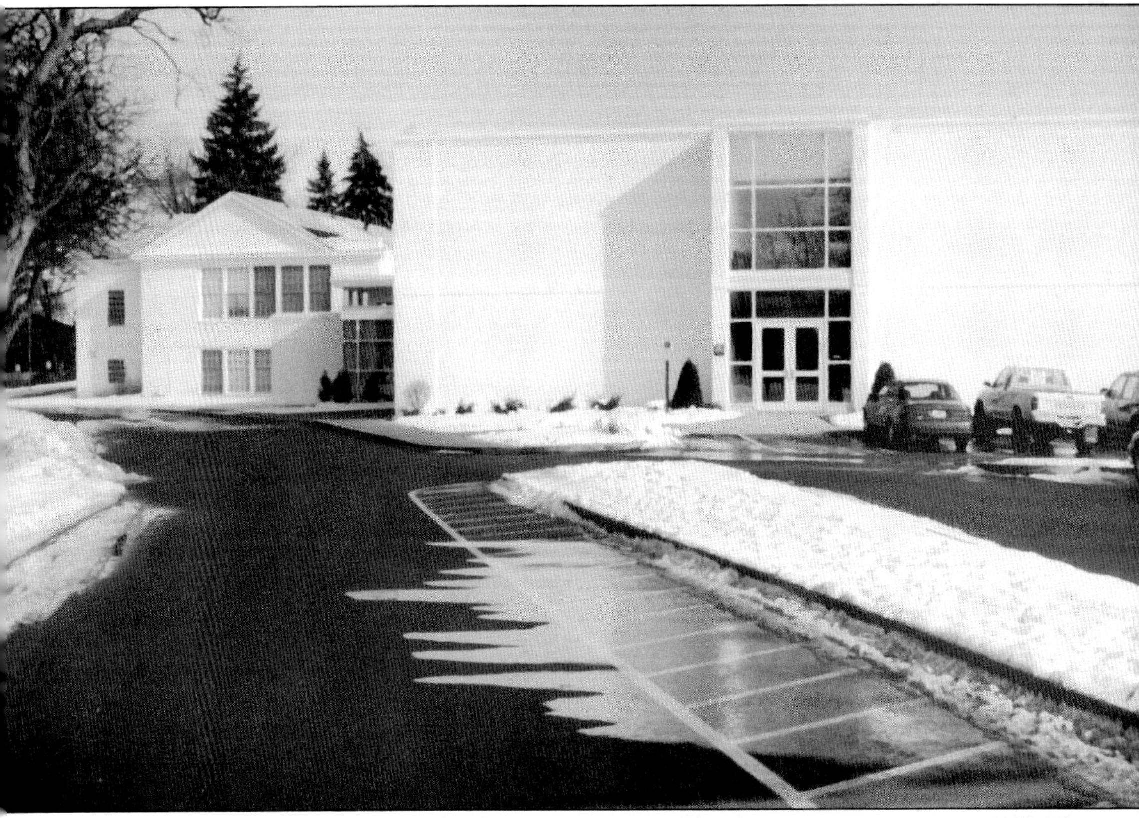

Half Day School is the oldest school in District 103 and has been in operation since 1839. The original frame building was replaced by a brick structure in 1938, and modern amenities like indoor plumbing and a furnace were added, replacing the outhouse and pot-bellied stove. Children would have to place their lunches by the stove, or they would often freeze in the cold during the winter. The school has since been enlarged several times, although the same brick building remains part of the current school. The school was closed in the 1980s because of shifting enrollment and leased to another school district from Vernon Hills for a short time before being used again in District 103. The school's mascot is a hawk and currently has third- and fourth-graders. (Courtesy of the Village of Lincolnshire.)

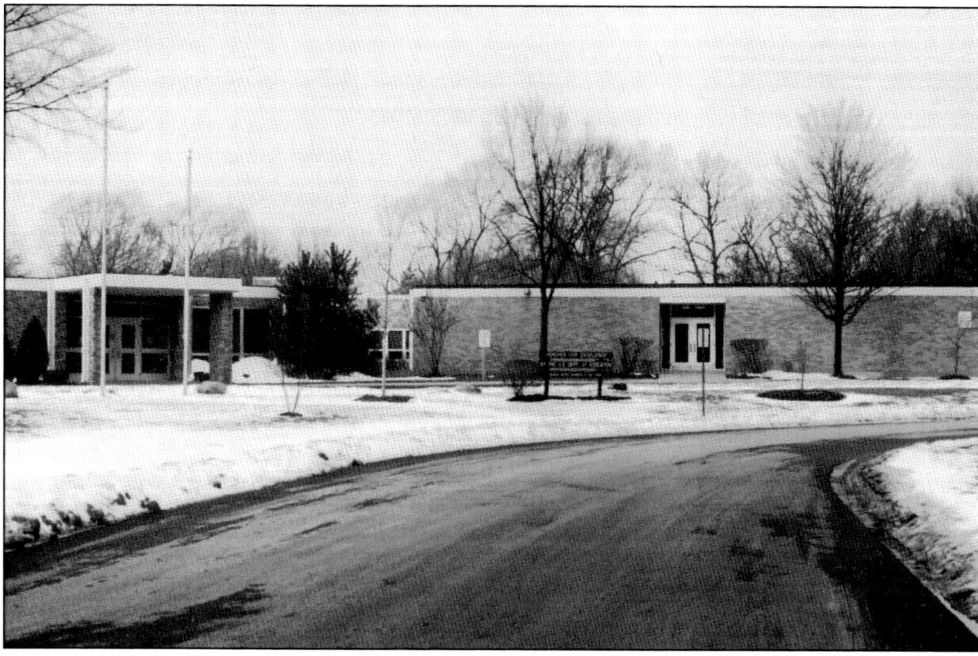

Laura B. Sprague Elementary School opened in 1964 and is named after the first teacher in Lake County. The mascot is a wildcat. Recently, it was discovered that Laura B. Sprague was a descendant of Richard Warren, one of the original passengers on the Mayflower in 1620. The school celebrates its namesake with Laura B. Sprague Day annually. (Courtesy of the Village of Lincolnshire.)

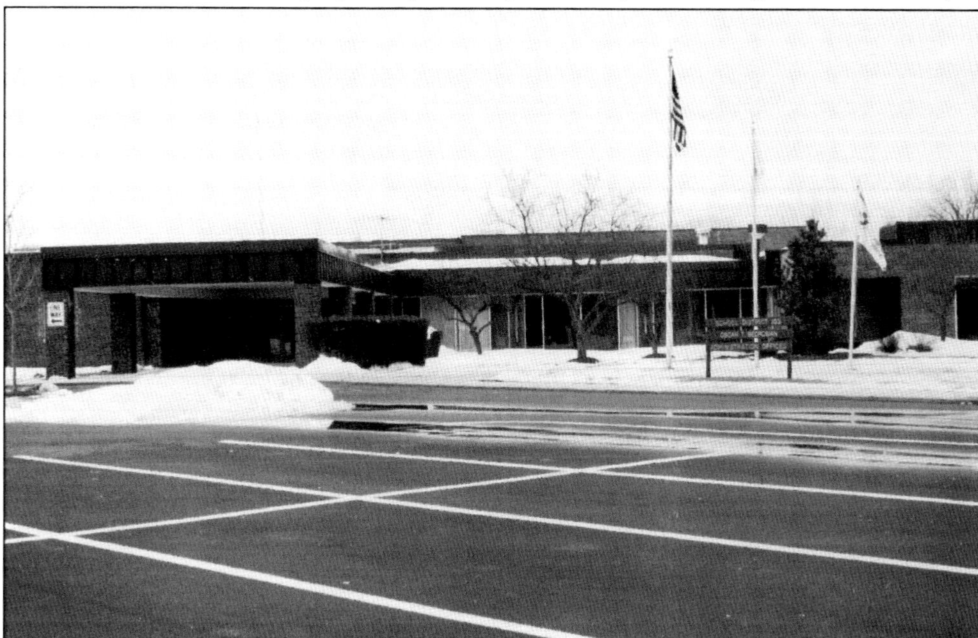

Daniel Wright Middle School, located on Riverwoods Road, is named after the first settler in the county. The school opened in 1971 and has the Trojan for a mascot. It is the newest school in the district and in the past has been reconfigured to allow grades five through eight to attend the facility. (Courtesy of the Village of Lincolnshire.)

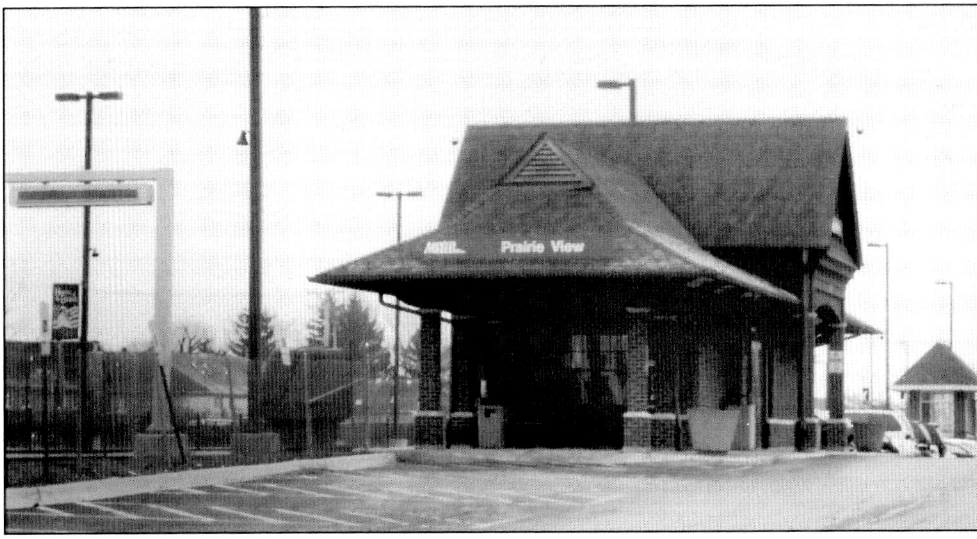

Metra reinstated regular train service to Prairie View in 1996. The North Central Service began stopping there going both northbound and southbound. Using the refurbished Wisconsin Central Lines, the new route leads from Antioch to Union Station in Chicago. A new parking area was created near the depot, and downtown began to be revitalized. Metra ridership continues to climb as does hope for an economic comeback for the railroad town of Prairie View. (Courtesy of the author.)

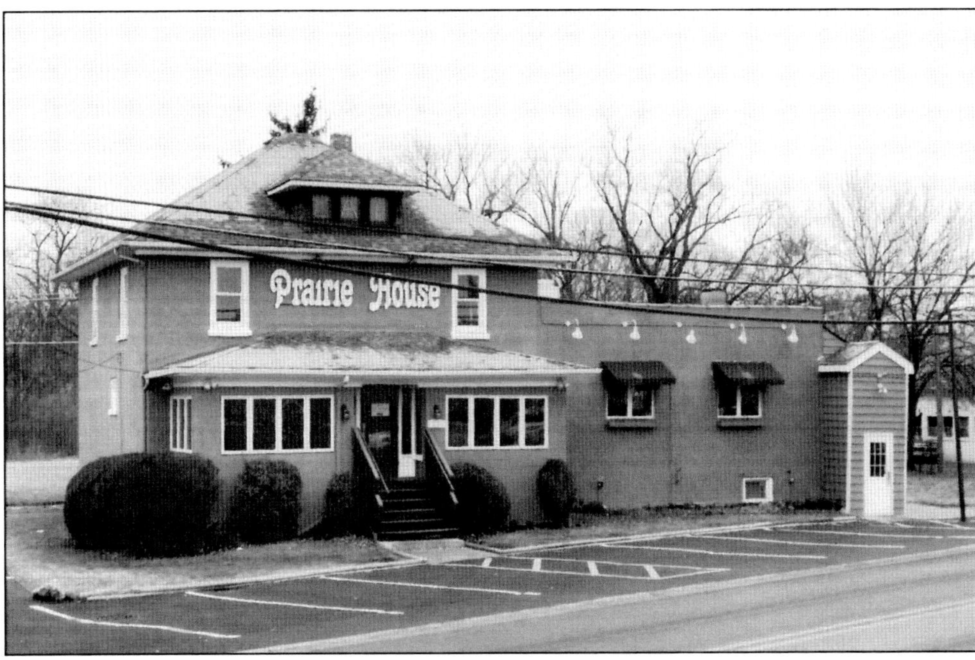

Sitting across Main Street facing the new station is what used to be known as Priess's Tavern. Originally destroyed in the great fire of 1920, Fred Priess rebuilt the establishment from its ashes. Now called the Prairie House, it is an establishment not too unlike the original building on the property. It is a testament that the human spirit can and will go on after it has faced adversity. (Courtesy of the author.)

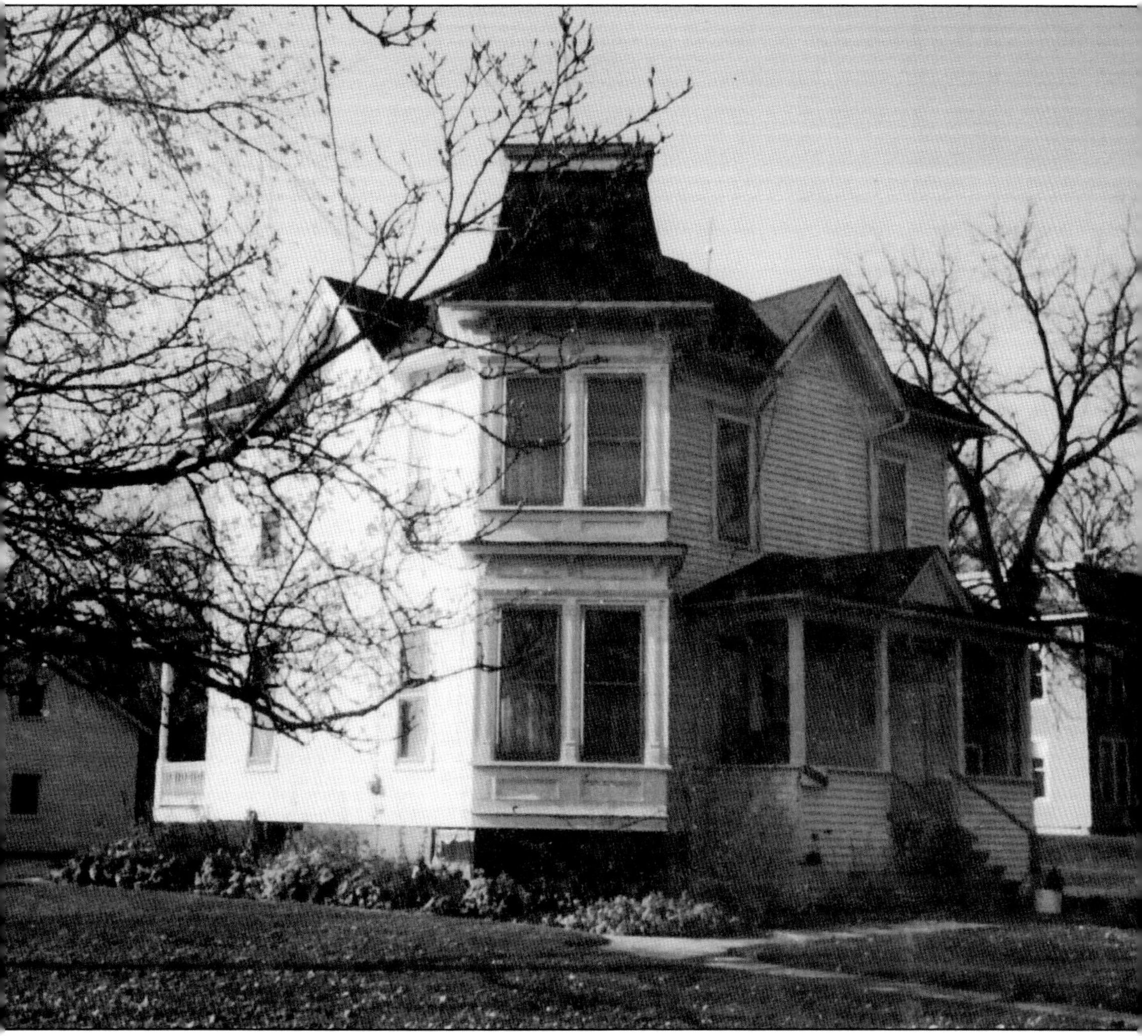

The Brockman family home, seen above, had a brush with fame in 1982. The home was used in a made-for-television episode of American Playhouse that was directed by Joanne Woodward. Woodward, an Emmy- and Academy Award–winning actress, was also the wife of legendary actor Paul Newman. The outside of the home was used as the setting for scenes in the film, as was the Vernon Cemetery. Some local residents got parts as extras in a few of the scenes. The extended Brockman family got to meet both Woodward and her famous husband, who had come along with her as moral support in her directorial effort.

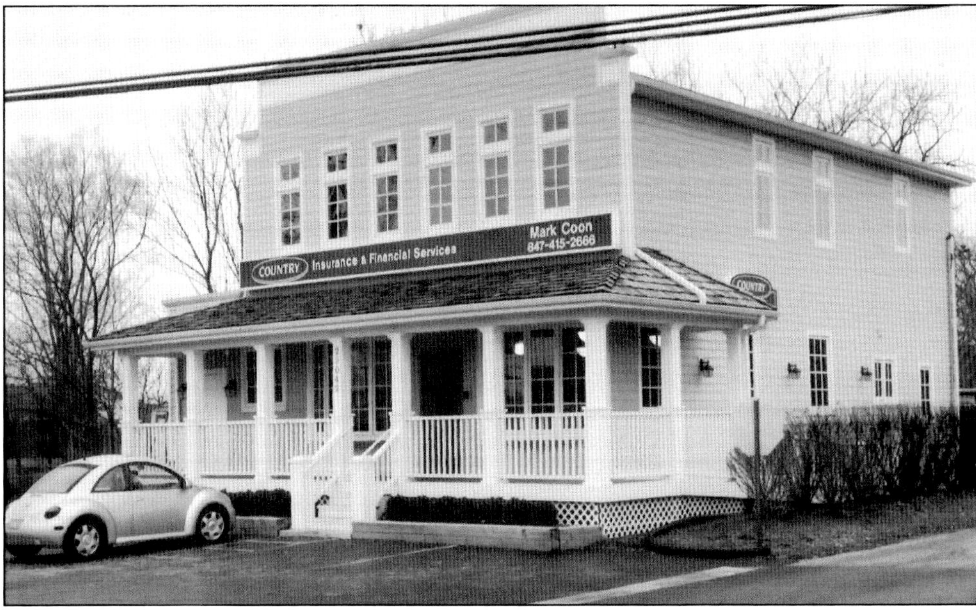

Many buildings from long ago remain in Prairie View. The Maether General Store was sold by Florence Stoerp after her husband, Frank, died in 1947. It was purchased by Aaron and Bernice Fell of Waukegan, who operated it as a general store and then as a thrift shop from 1952. The name changed from the Prairie View Thrift Shop to the White Elephant Shop. It changed hands again and is now a different business. The small building that was the post office for many years spent some of the recent past in disrepair but is now being used as a music shop. (Both, courtesy of the author.)

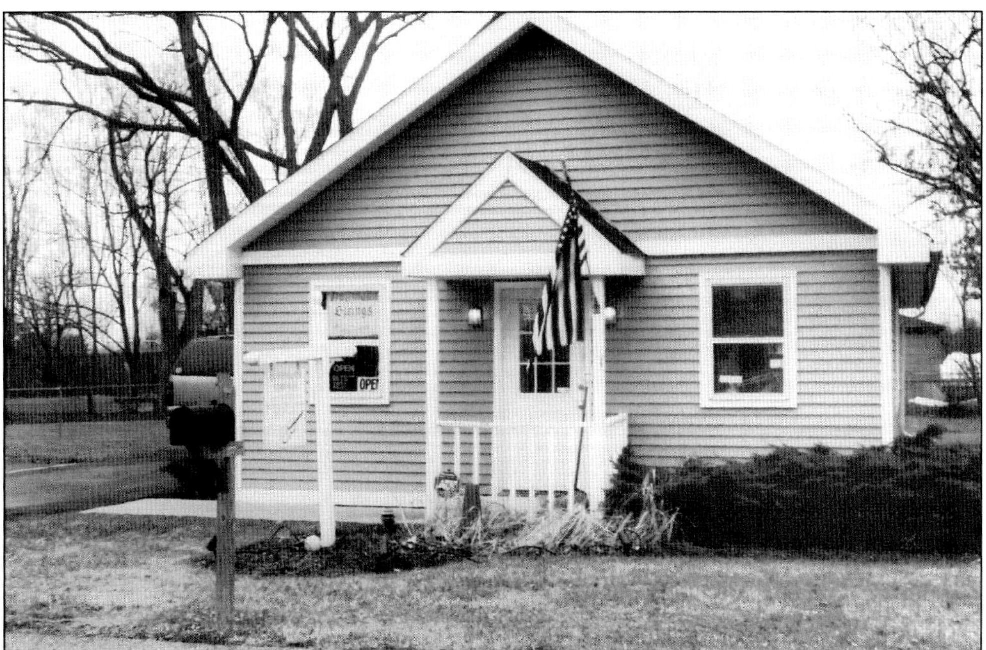

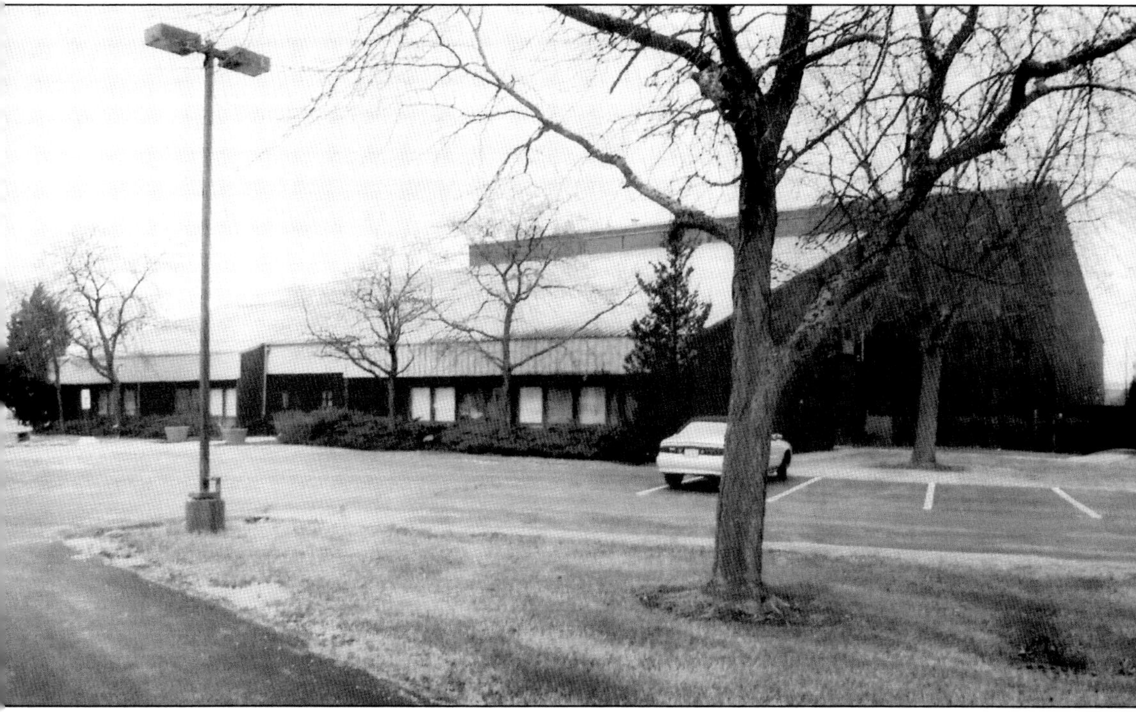

Vernon Township currently has its offices on Main Street. The township offers a wide array of services for residents. The duties of the township officials have evolved with the times, but the intent is still the same, which is to make Vernon Township a better place to live. The township offers a food pantry for those who need a helping hand, senior services, snow removal, road maintenance, and job counseling, just to name a few. The township has also taken over the responsibility of caring for the Vernon Cemetery and the Diamond Lake Cemetery, which also lies within the township's boundaries. It has become the caretakers to the past, in a sense. The means and methods may have changed over the course of the years, but a genuine sense of community and neighborliness remains in the area. (Courtesy of the author.)

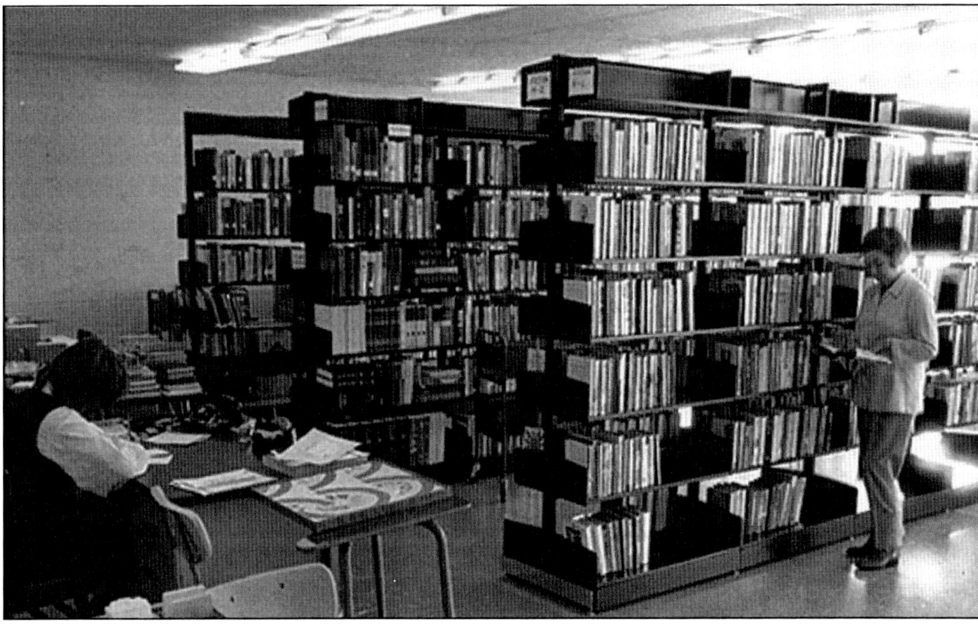

With no public library nearby, residents were forced to use libraries in other communities, the closest ones being in Libertyville, Lake Zurich, Lake Forest, and Wheeling. A group of forward-thinking citizens saw the need for a local library, and the Vernon Area Public Library was born. It began as a single room located in Stevenson High School.

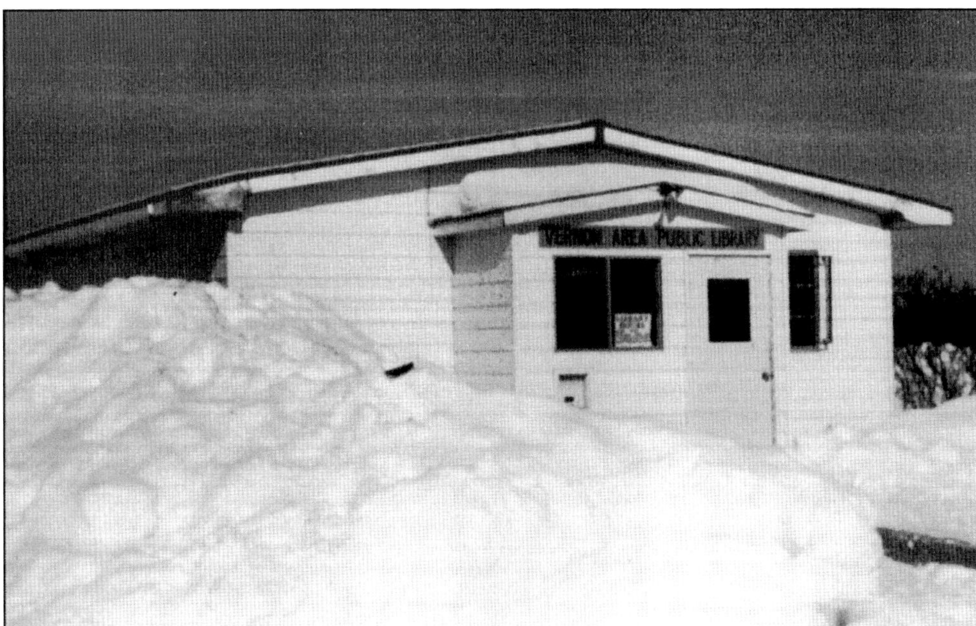

The district was formed with help from many local individuals and politicians. Help was also needed in order to take advantage of funds available from the government that were intended to help provide library services for those in underserved areas. The library grew and moved from the single room to a small location on the grounds of Adlai E. Stevenson High School, often referred to as the "Little Library on the Prairie."

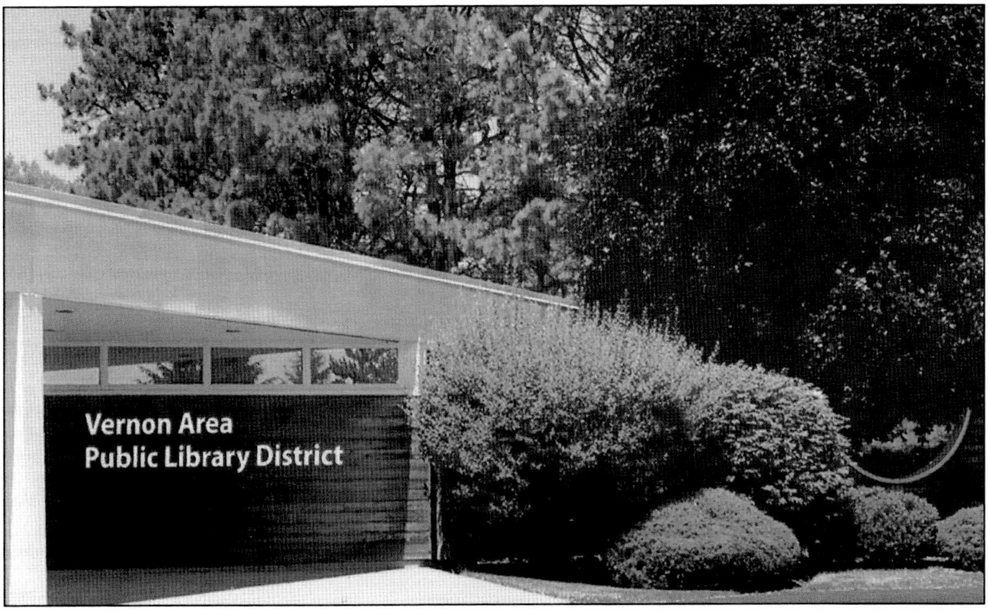

A referendum was passed and a new, larger building opened for the library on Indian Creek Road in 1974. The building had a separate adult and children's area, a meeting room, and room for a children's story time. As time wore on and the development in Lincolnshire and Vernon Township bloomed, the community outgrew the building on Indian Creek.

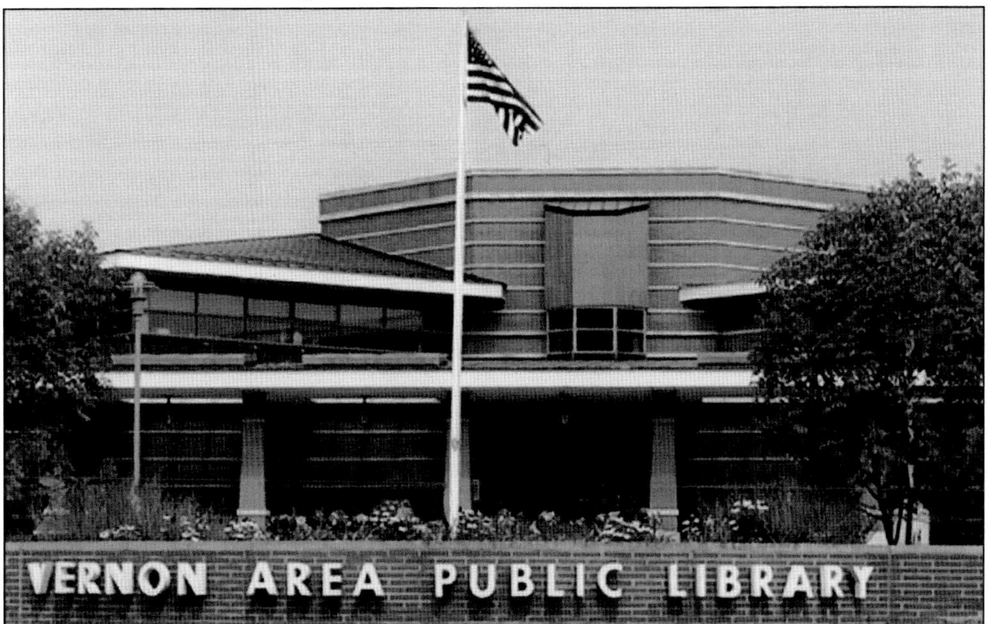

The library's present facility opened to the public amid much fanfare. Tours were given to the many community members who came to the library's grand opening on September 15, 1993. The building, which is 50,000 square feet, meets the needs of the library district, which has grown to include 44,000 people. A wide range of materials, both print and electronic, and many different services are now offered. They include visiting area nursing homes, retirement communities, and the homebound.

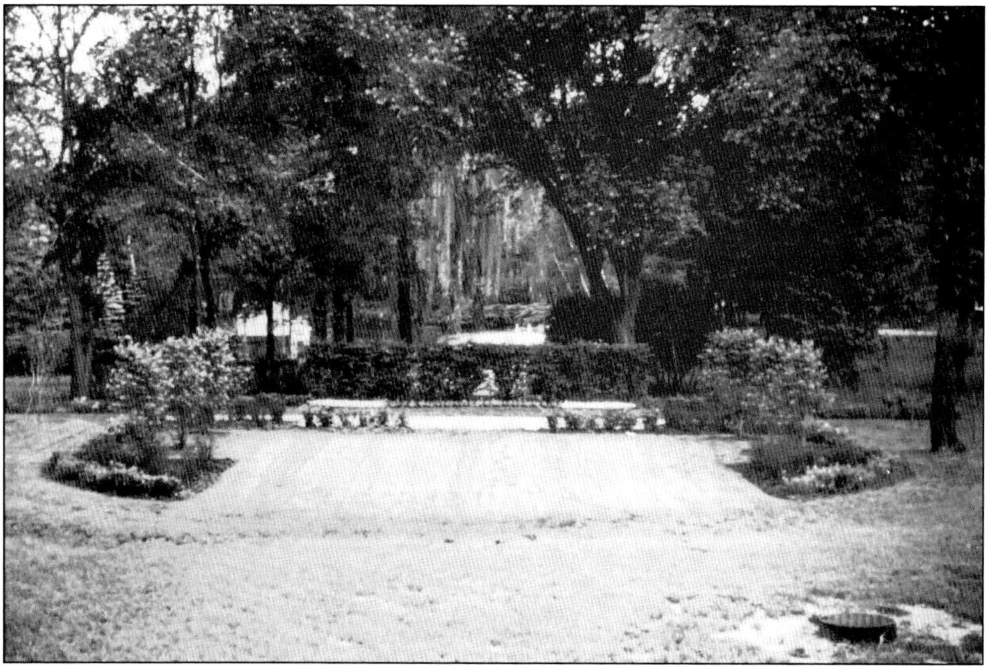

The Lincolnshire Garden Club has been in existence since 1958. The organization consists of residents interested in horticulture. Their goal is to beautify Lincolnshire, and the organization has won many awards. The formal garden at Spring Lake won first prize in the Civic Improvement Contest, which is sponsored by the Garden Club of Illinois. The garden is pictured above. They often donate time and plants to a wide array of causes. The club also raises funds for different charitable causes, such as the Ryerson Forest Preserve and Lincolnshire's Riverside Foundation, a facility that provides residential support and developmental training services to adults with developmental disabilities. Since 1974, the club has given over $186,000 worth of donations of one type or another to various organizations. Below, two members are in action planting bushes at Spring Lake Park. (Both, courtesy of the Lincolnshire Garden Club.)

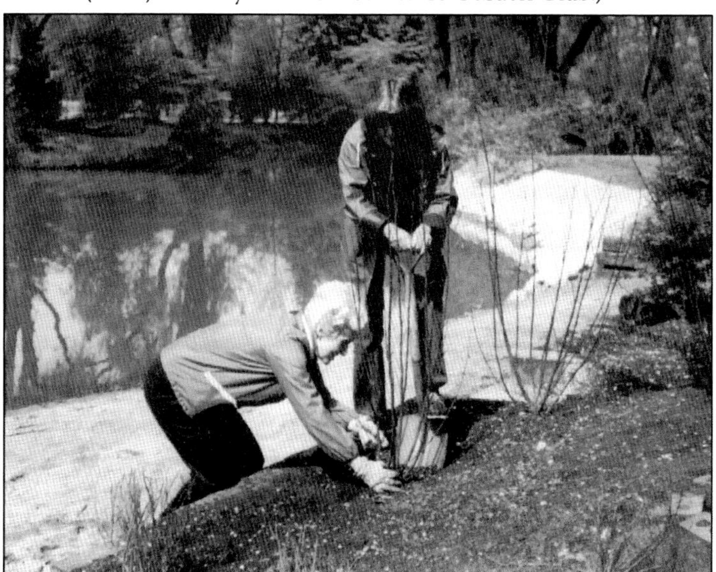

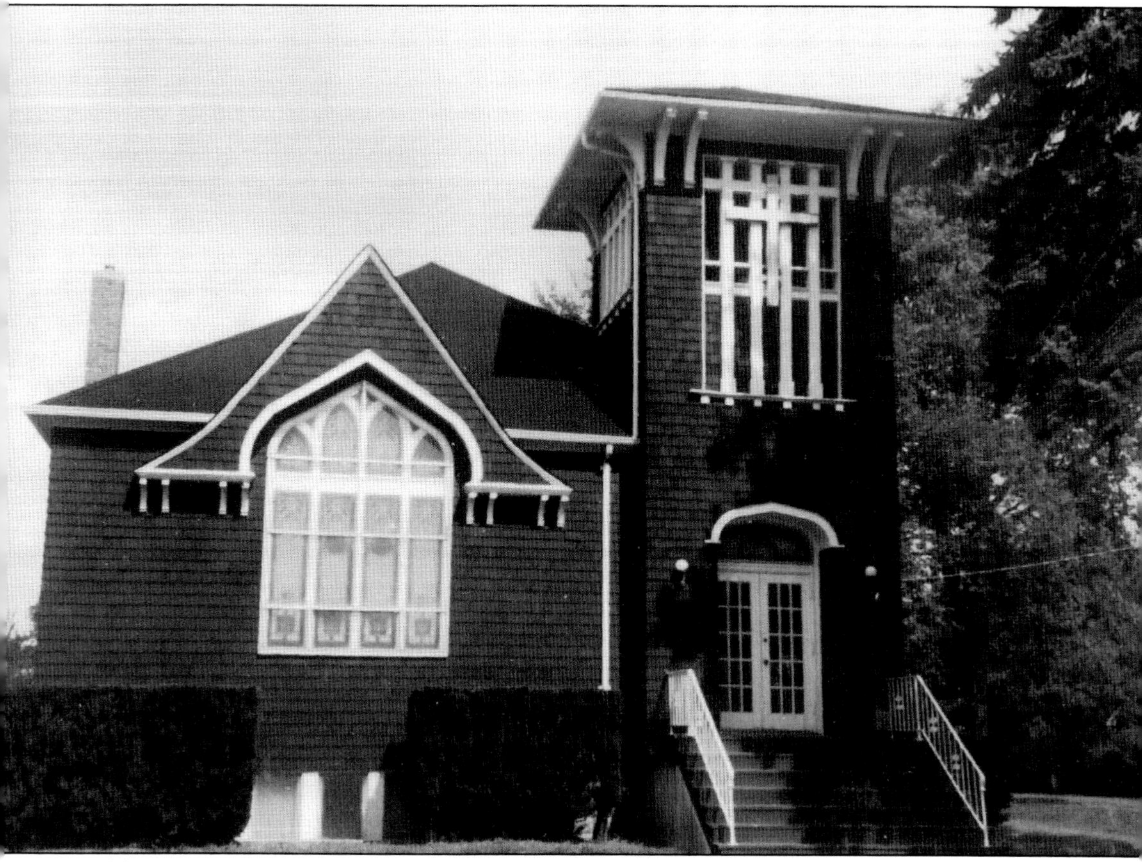

Washburn Congregational Church's attendance has dwindled in the last decade so much that there were fewer than a dozen members left in the congregation. Whether that was because of the lack of a full-time pastor, an aging population, changing times, or any combination of things, the United Church of Christ decided to close the doors on the church. A decommissioning service was held in October 2011, and the congregation was symbolically closed. Those in attendance reflected back on what an important role Washburn had played in the community and in each of their lives. The future of the church and annex buildings are uncertain, but it is the hope of the United Church of Christ that another congregation will use it again some other day and that it will again be a vital part of the community.

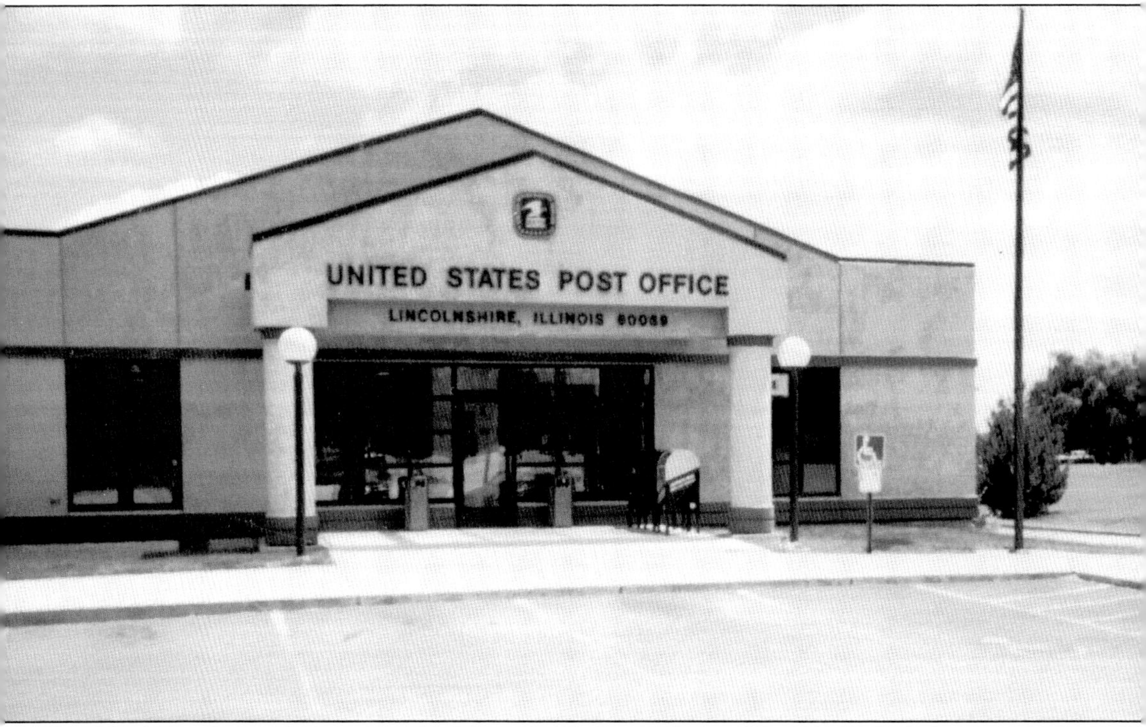

The post office has been in Lincolnshire since February 11, 1989. Before that time, the post office was located in several different locations around Prairie View. There has been a post office in Half Day in the past, but it was relocated to Prairie View to be closer to the incoming mail, which arrived via train. Seth Washburn is reported to have been the first postmaster in Lake County while he lived in Half Day, but unfortunately, many of the old records have been lost over time. Only anecdotal evidence and local histories survive with that information. Having a post office located in Half Day in those early years made sense, as mail would arrive by stagecoach moving north and south on Milwaukee Avenue or by boat on the Des Plaines River. Both methods were officially sanctioned for moving the mail. (Courtesy of the Village of Lincolnshire.)

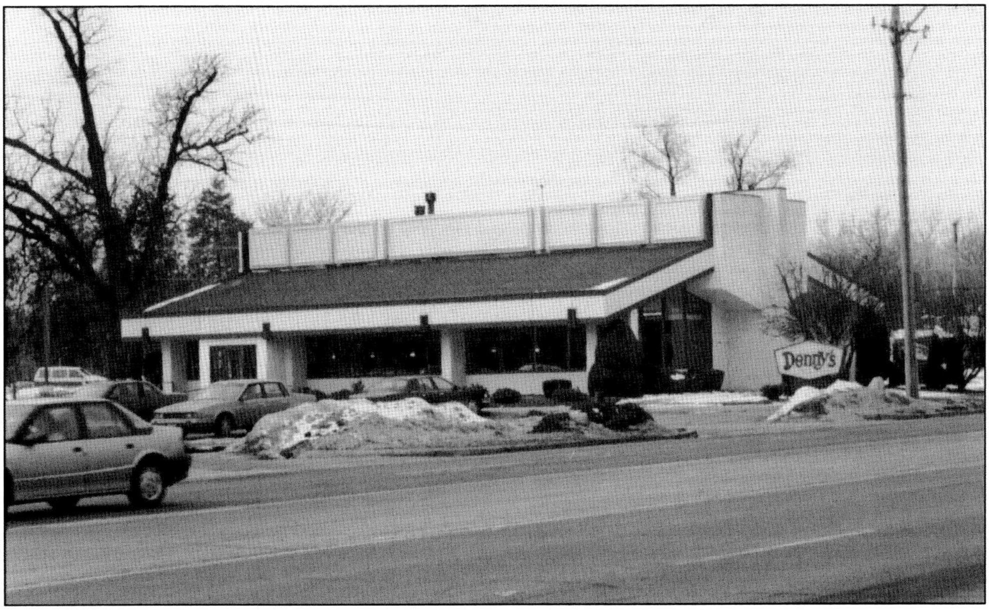

Many businesses have come and gone in the Half Day–Lincolnshire area over the years. The entire look of Milwaukee Avenue between Routes 22 and 45 has transformed time and time again. One example of this is the southwest corner of Milwaukee Avenue at Olde Half Day Road. Over time, that corner has held a house, barn, general store, Coca-Cola stand, automobile garage, and gas station as well as a restaurant. The latest two incarnations are pictured above and below. The Denny's Restaurant built its facility in the 1970s. After the chain closed that location, a different kind of restaurant opened. In 2003, Simon Lin's Asian Fusion Bistro was the next to put its face onto the familiar landscape and bring international cuisine to Lincolnshire. (Both, courtesy of the Village of Lincolnshire.)

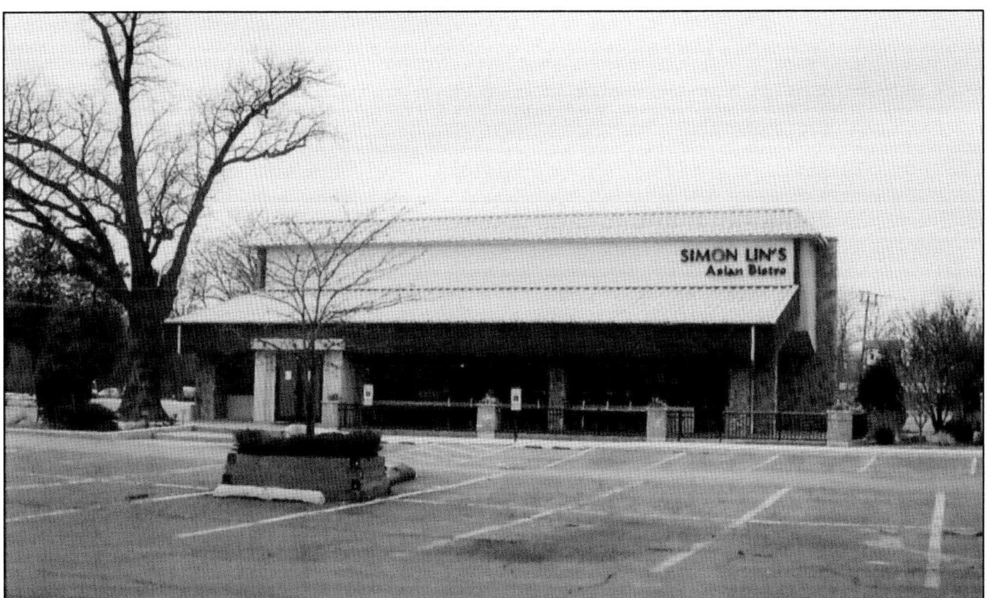

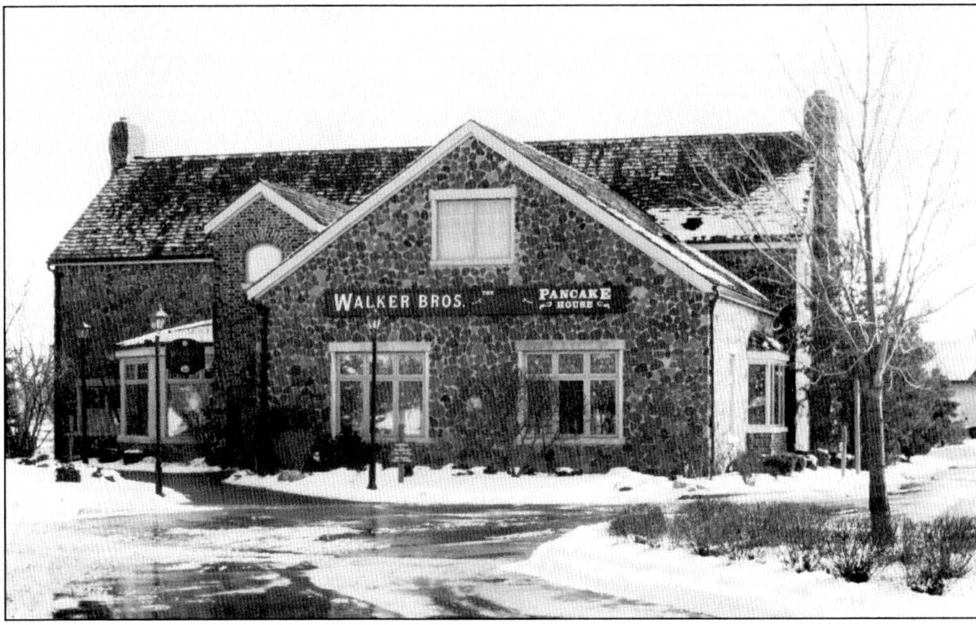

These two businesses from the area, one current and one former, share a strange coincidence. Walker Brother's Pancake House, built on what used to be the Chicagoland Airport facility, was designed to resemble a house. P.J. Willicker's Saloon and Dining, formerly known as Fiddlesticks among other names, is a restaurant that used to be a house. The very top of what used to be the roof of the house, in the photograph below, has a railing and an antenna that is visible. The building has had several additions but started its life as a single-family dwelling. (Both, courtesy of the Village of Lincolnshire.)

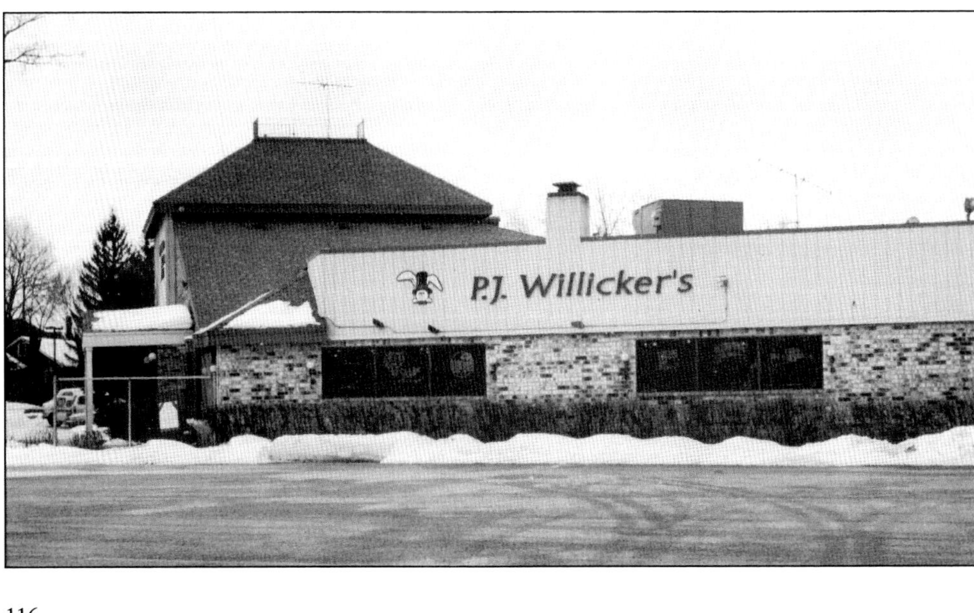

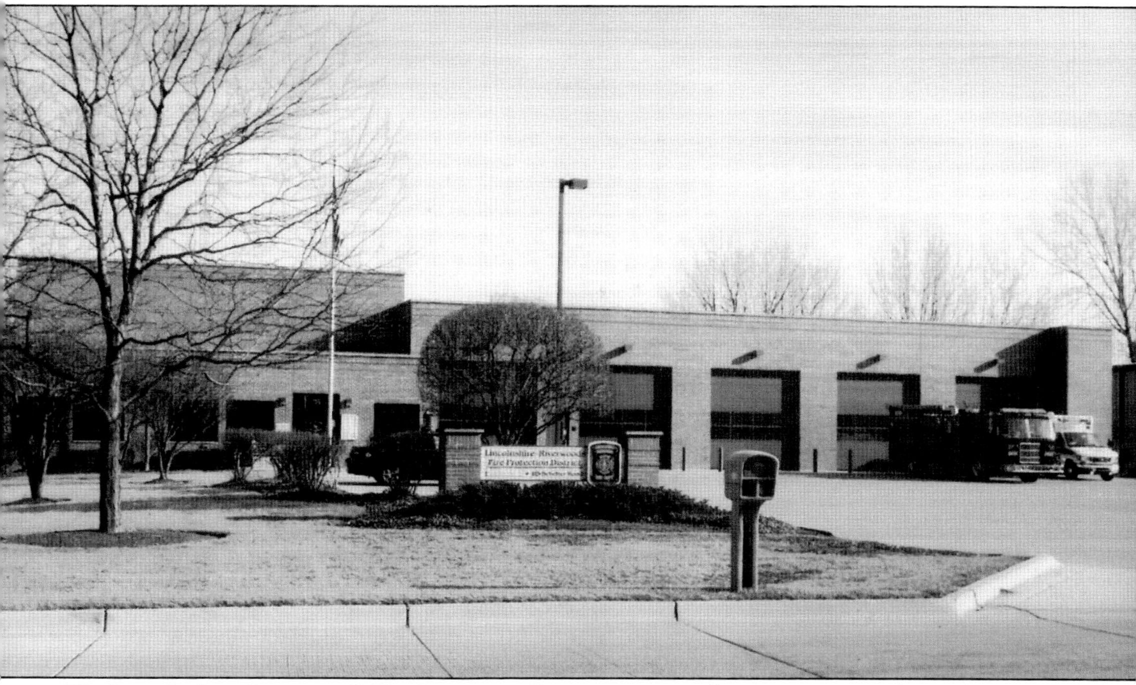

The Lincolnshire-Riverwoods Fire Protection District protects the communities of Lincolnshire, Riverwoods, and portions of Vernon Hiils, Mettawa, Prairie View, and unincorporated Vernon Township. The department has grown and now has three stations—one in Lincolnshire, one in Vernon Hills, and one in Riverwoods—and serves a 16-square-mile area. The department has a staff of 40 full-time firefighters and five civilian employees. They protect a wide variety of structures, such as residential dwellings from single-family to retirement communities, commercial businesses, parking garages, a commuter and freight rail line, and many other varied locations. The main headquarters in Lincolnshire is shown above. (Courtesy of the author.)

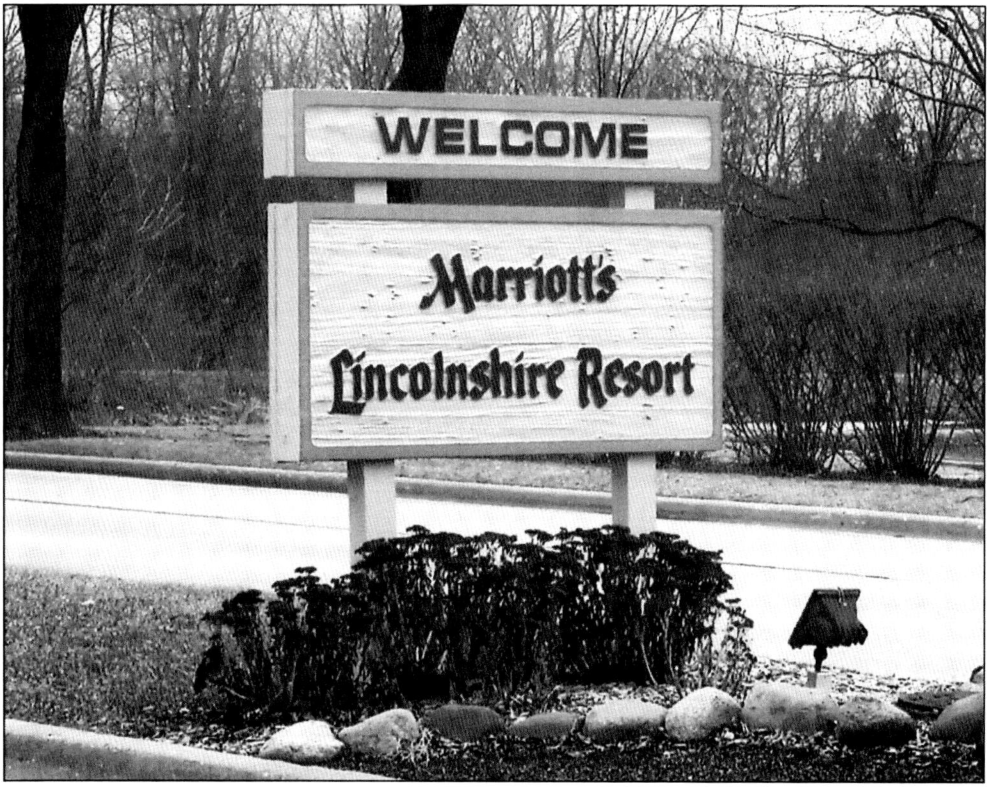

The Marriott Corporation constructed a hotel complex within the village limits and named it Marriott's Lincolnshire Resort. Lincolnshire's first mayor, Fred Balzer, was instrumental in getting the agreement in place. The facility opened in 1975 and consisted of a hotel, restaurants, shops, banquet facilities, and a theater. The acclaimed theater opened that same year, and an astonishing 7,000,000 people have seen its performances during the course of its existence. The company has received a record 370 Joseph Jefferson Award nominations, Chicago's highest theatrical honor for artistic achievement. (Above, courtesy of the Village of Lincolnshire; below, courtesy of the author.)

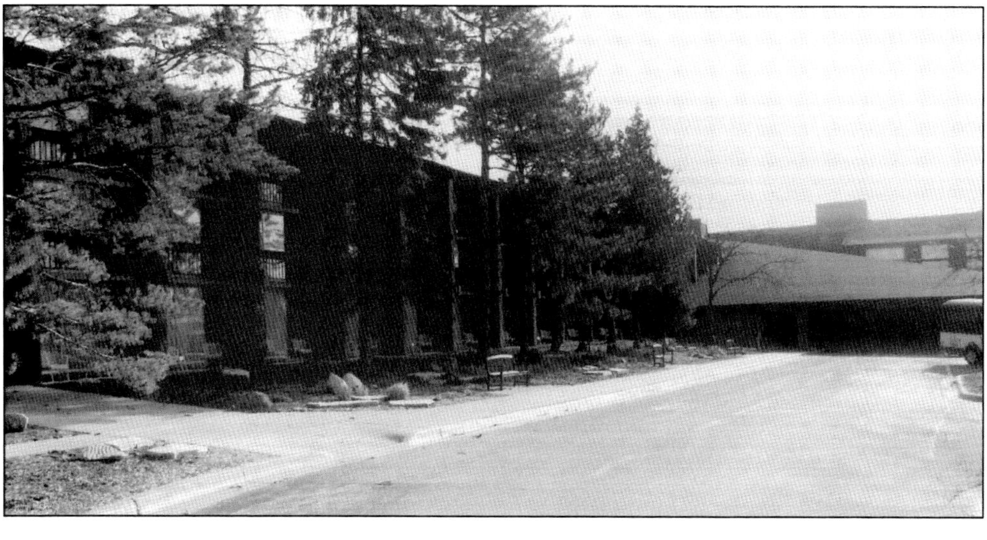

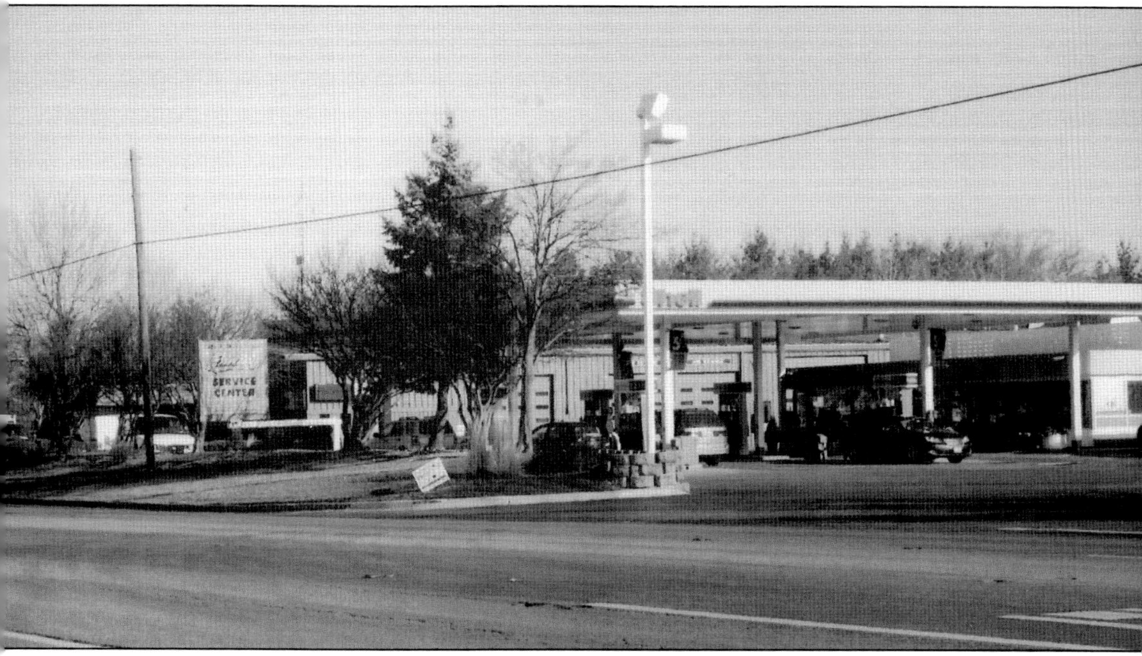

Ernie's Towing has been an institution in the Half Day area since 1956. It was founded by Ernie Vole Sr., who opened the business as Ernie's 24 Hour Towing Service. Vole began the establishment with only a homemade wrecker. The name changed when the business was expanded, since it did more than just towing cars. The fleet has expanded to include more than 20 pieces of specialized equipment and over 30 employees. The area they service has expanded as well and is now not only in the state of Illinois but well into southern Wisconsin. (Courtesy of the author.)

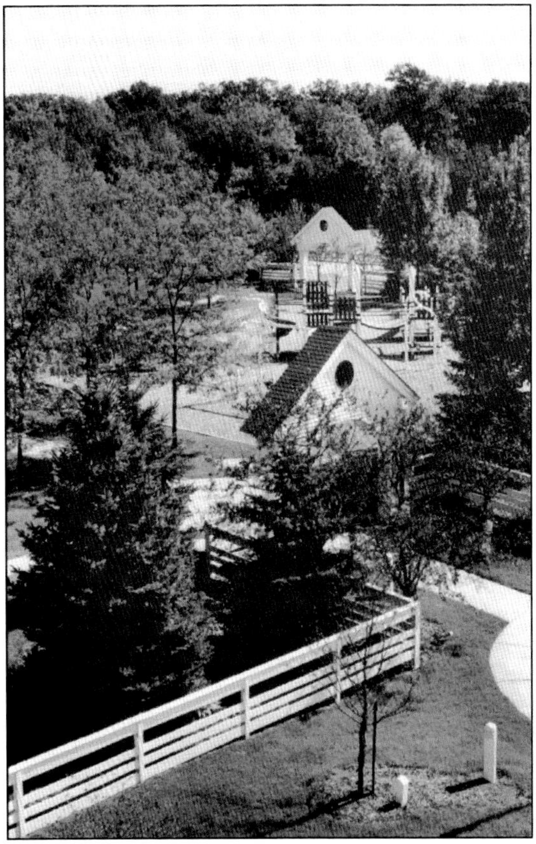

Harham Farm was originally owned by Harold M. Florsheim and built as a weekend house and summer retreat in 1932. Florsheim, of Florsheim Shoe Company fame, trained championship Airedale, Welsh, and Wirehaired Terriers there. He also raised racehorses and turkeys on the property. The Whytegate Park was created in 1985 and has a very genteel equestrian look. It won the president's award from the Illinois Chapter of the American Society of Landscape Architects. The park consists of four acres and has a variety of activities available, including tennis, volleyball, baseball, a picnic area, playground, and fitness course. (Both, courtesy of the Village of Lincolnshire.)

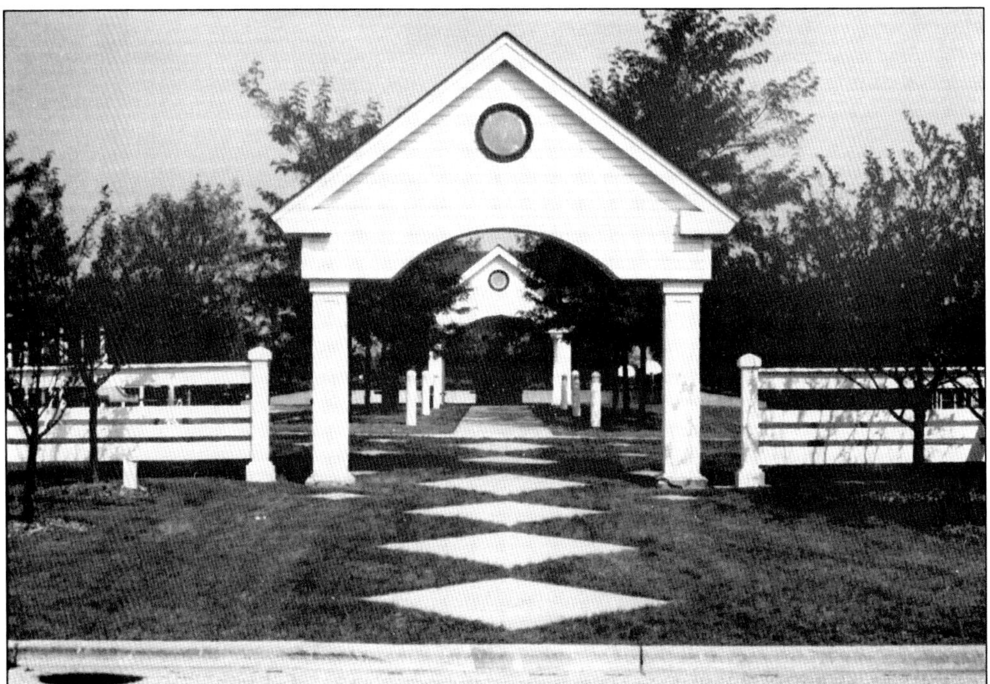

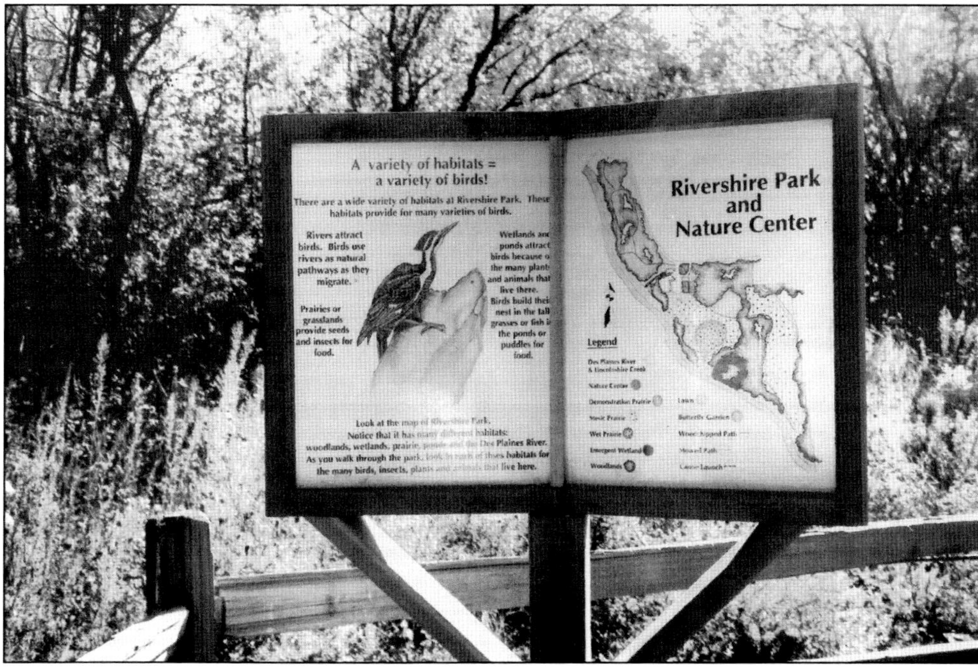

Rivershire Park and Nature Center is a 15-acre nature preserve and outdoor education area. The village began an extensive restoration of the natural habitat along Lincolnshire Creek at Rivershire with a majority volunteer labor force from the community. The nature center was developed cooperatively between the Village and School District 103 in 1998. Since then, not only have Lincolnshire schools used it but neighboring districts have as well. School children visit with their classes to learn about the outdoors, in particular native habitats and species. The facility also has a canoe launch, picnic area, and trails to explore. (Both, courtesy of the Village of Lincolnshire.)

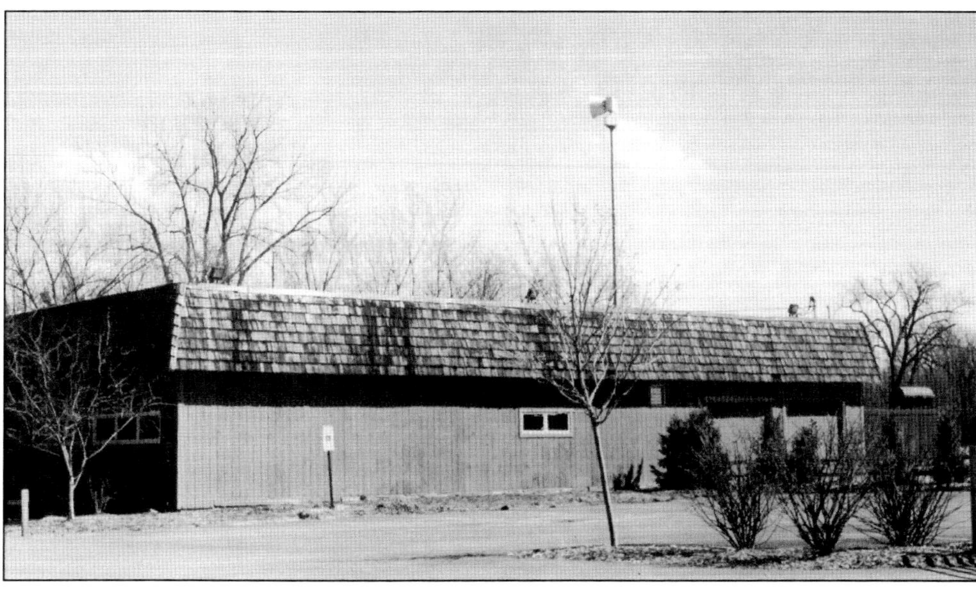

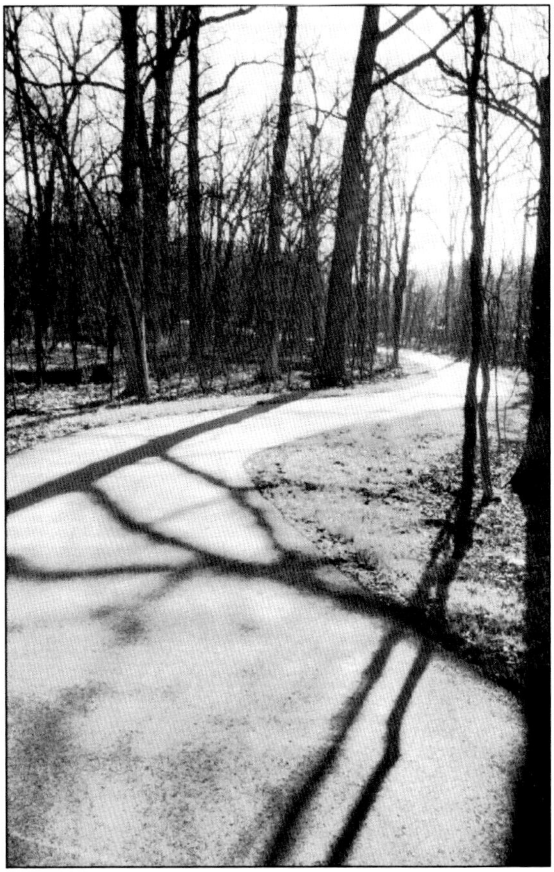

Lincolnshire has a wealth of recreational activities for its residents. It has an unusually high number of parks for a village of its size. There are eight parks, a large bike path (see left), and a nature preserve, all within village limits. The Florsheim Illinois Nature Preserve is a pristine environment that is home to many native species. The original 40-acre parcel was donated in 1985 by Harold and Sarabel Florsheim and has grown to 110 acres. A study of the area was done, and it was determined to have a floristic quality index (FQI) of 82.01, meaning that it has an unusually high percentage of native quality. Areas of a 60 or higher rating are very rare and can only be found in a tiny portion of places. (Both, courtesy of the Village of Lincolnshire.)

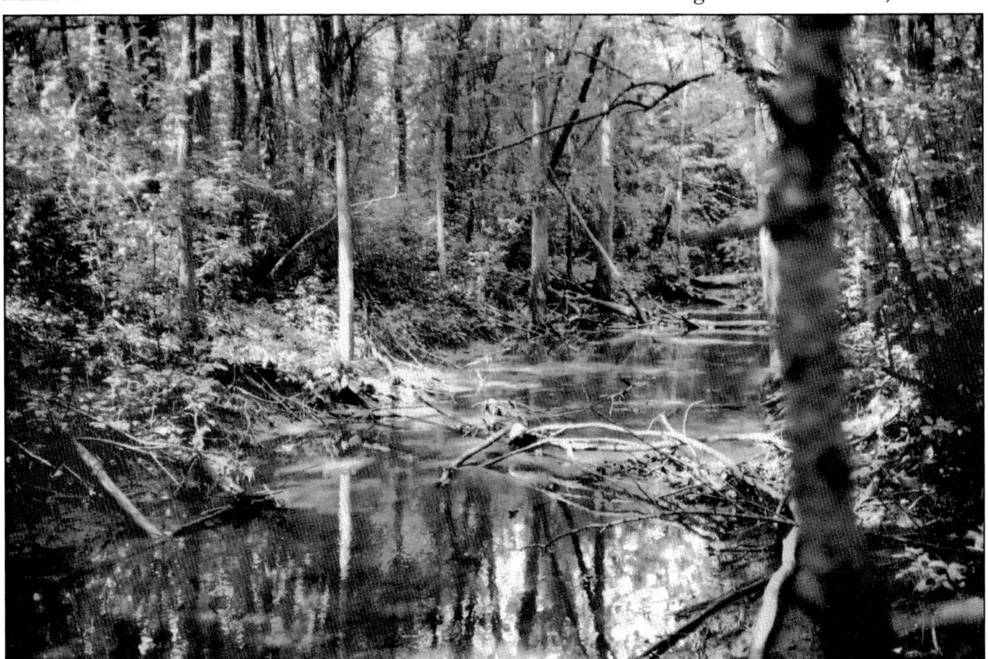

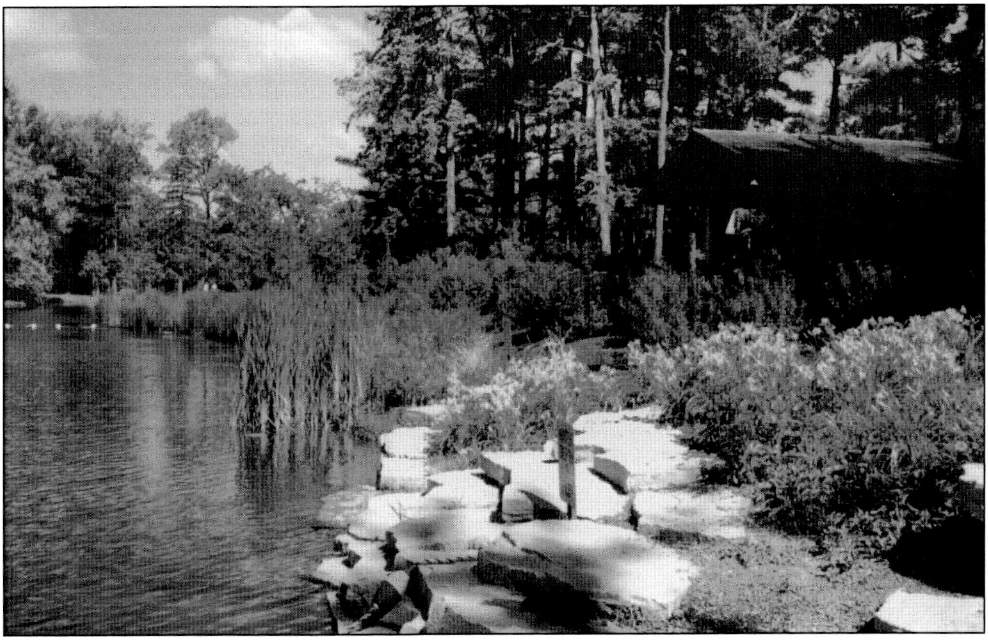

Spring Lake Park was originally created by Louis Leverone as a picnic area for employees of his Canteen Corporation. Roger Ladd gave it to the community after the subdivision was completed. One of the earliest concerns the new residents of Ladd's Lincolnshire had was maintenance of the park as well as the streets in their development. (Courtesy of Village of Lincolnshire.)

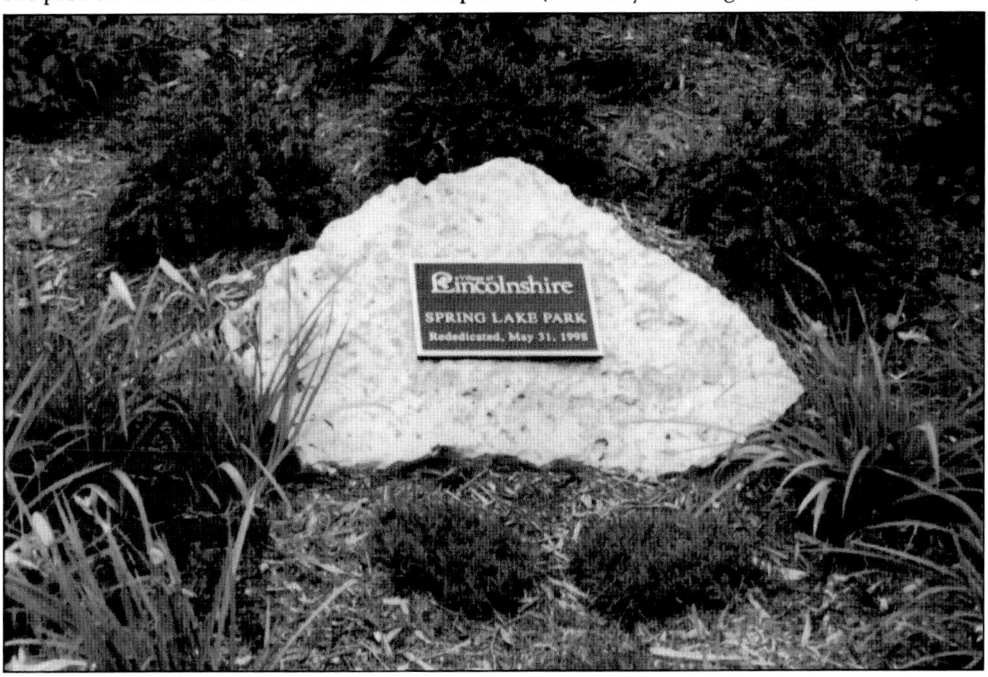

The Village of Lincolnshire rededicated Spring Lake Park on May 31, 1998. There is a plaque commemorating the occasion on the premises. The park is approximately eight acres in size, and the "old swimming hole" and park have been refurbished so that residents may enjoy it for years to come. (Courtesy of the Village of Lincolnshire.)

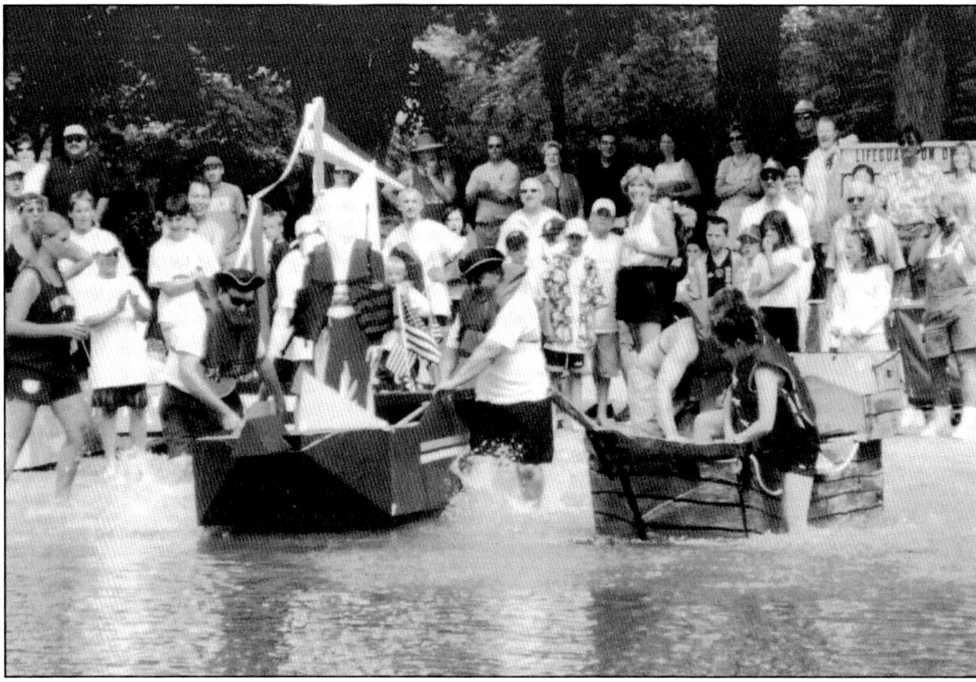

The Cardboard Boat Regatta at Spring Lake has become a tradition in Lincolnshire with many different generations of residents participating. Held on the Fourth of July, competitors build their own boat using paint, duct tape, and cardboard and compete against one another by taking a lap around Spring Lake. Trophies awarded are the Titanic trophy, the patriotic red, white, and blue trophy, and an overall winner is crowned. For those boats that remain floating at the end of the competition, there is a "Last Boat Floating" demolition derby. The day's activities draw huge crowds of cheering spectators. (Both, courtesy of the Village of Lincolnshire.)

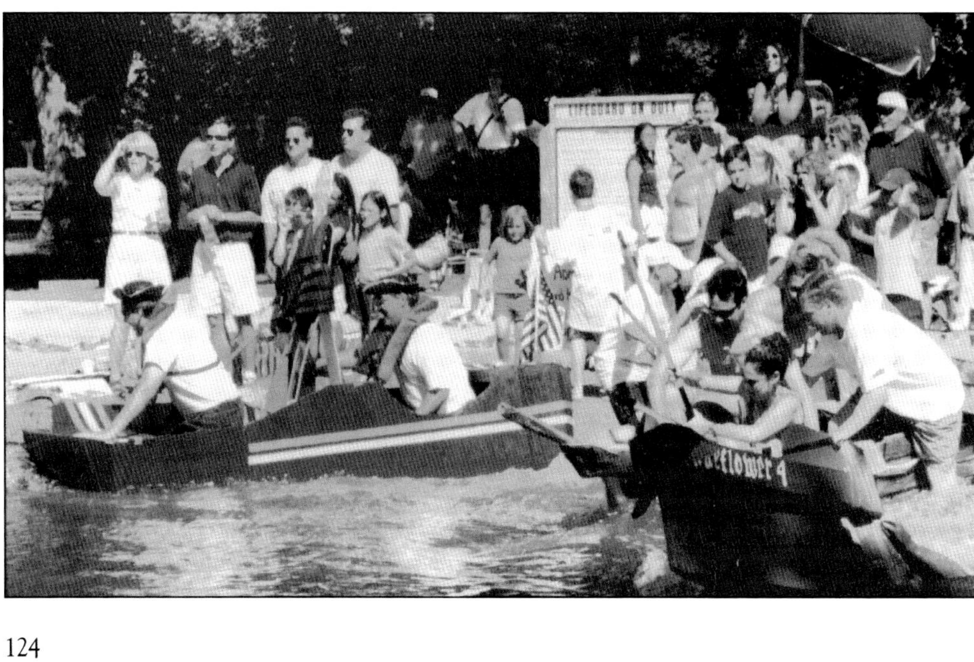

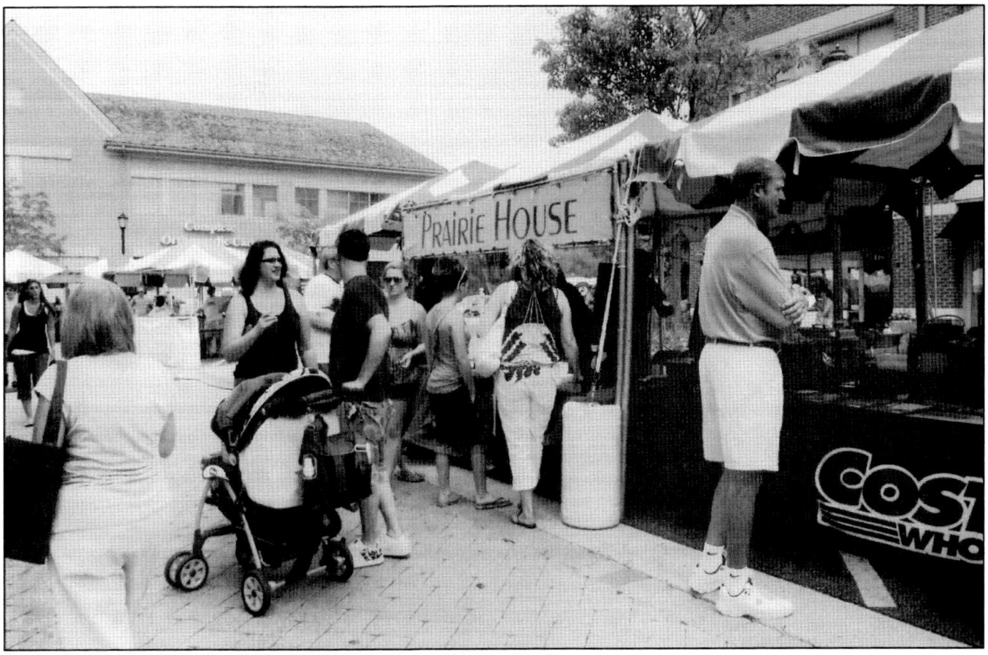

The community offers several special events for families to participate in that have quickly become modern traditions. The Lincolnshire Art Fair showcases some of the very best artists the North Shore has to offer. This two-day festival hosts over 120 juried artists working in the mediums of photography, jewelry, painting, and sculpture. The annual Taste of Lincolnshire is sponsored by the Lincolnshire Chamber of Commerce and promotes local businesses and provides tasty treats from a variety of cuisines at the same time. This three-day party is a beloved event in the community and also offers numerous children's activities and live music for all to enjoy. (Both, courtesy of the author.)

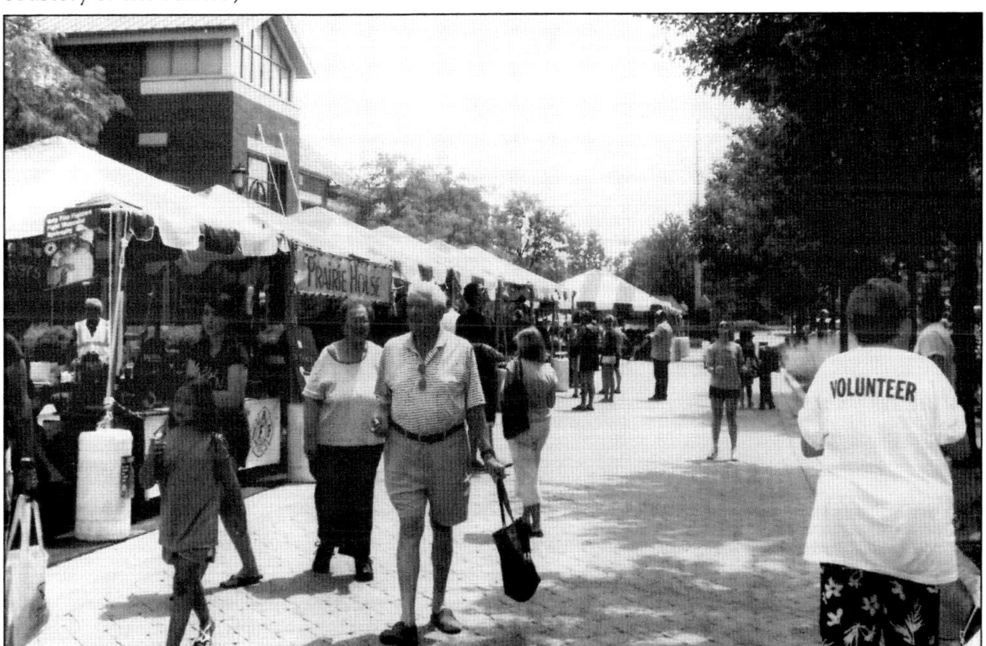

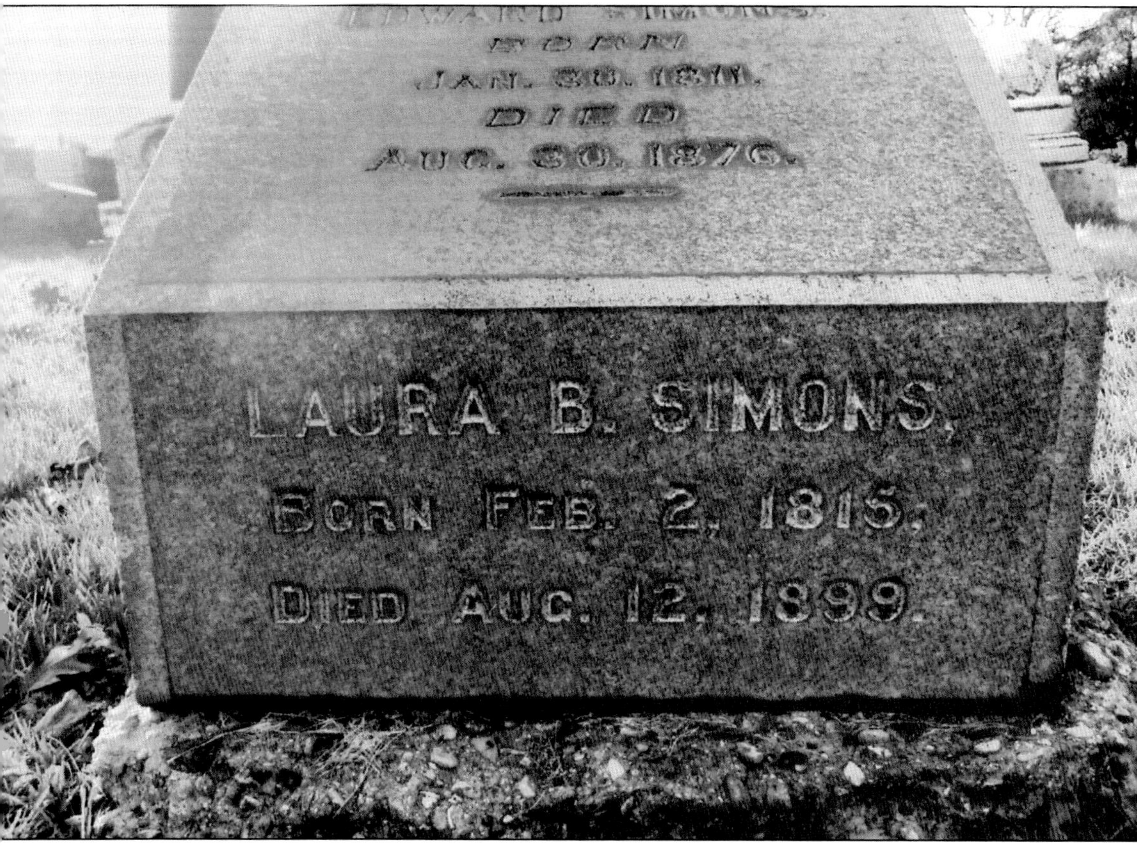

Laura B. Sprague Simons and her husband, Edward, are buried in Chicago's Rosehill Cemetery, a short distance from where they lived and raised their family. The union produced seven children, four of whom survived. Edward, a successful farmer and store owner, died in 1876, leaving Laura a widow for the next 23 years until her death in 1899. Laura lived out the remainder of her life with her daughter Almira Simons Winkelman and her husband, Frederick. The city of Chicago honored Laura, Edward, and their daughter by naming a park after them. Simons Park is located on a small parcel of land that once comprised a portion of their farm. (Courtesy of the author.)

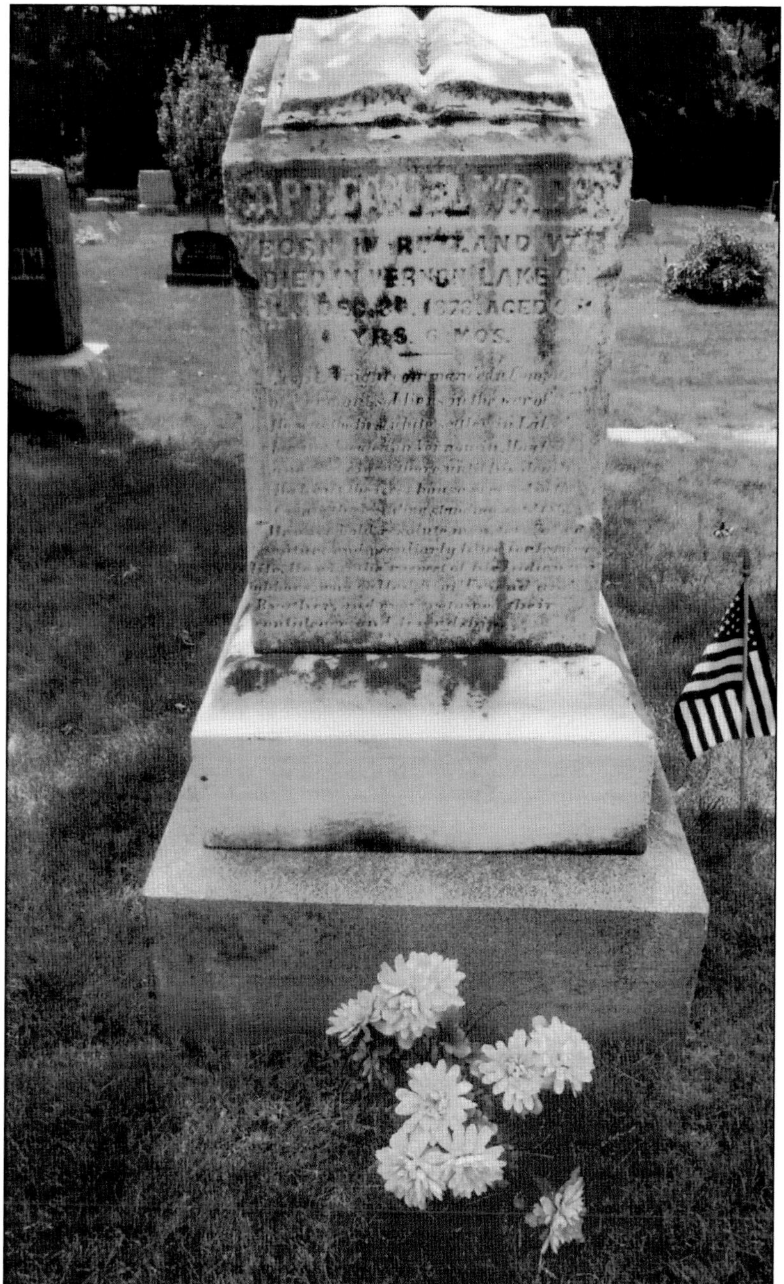

Daniel Wright's final resting place is located in the picturesque Vernon Cemetery and is marked with a stately memorial. The decorative grave is a very elaborate memorial to a man who, by all accounts, led a very simple and homespun existence for all of his 95 years. The marker also serves as a family plot that memorializes his two wives, Ruth Todd Wright (his first wife) and Rachel Millard Wright. The graves of several other family members can also be found adjacent to the spot. Daniel Wright, an ardent Democrat and Mason, was a very highly regarded man with many friends in the county, of which he inadvertently found himself the patriarch. (Courtesy of the author.)